THE WAGES OF WINS

Taking Measure
of the Many Myths
in Modern Sport

DAVID J. BERRI

MARTIN B. SCHMIDT

STACEY L. BROOK

STANFORD BUSINESS BOOKS
An Imprint of Stanford University Press

Stanford University Press
Stanford, California
© 2006 by the Board of Trustees of the
Leland Stanford Junior University
All rights reserved

Library of Congress Cataloging-in-Publication Data

Berri, David J.
   The wages of wins : taking measure of the many myths in modern sport / David J. Berri, Martin B. Schmidt, and Stacey L. Brook.
      p. cm.
   Includes bibliographical references and index.
   ISBN 0-8047-5287-7 (cloth : alk. paper)
   1. Professional sports—Economic aspects—United States.
2. Professional sports—Social aspects—United States. I. Schmidt,
Martin B. II. Brook, Stacey L. I. Title.
GV716.B47   2006
338.4'37960440973—dc22

                                                  2005036651

Printed in the United States of America on acid-free, archival-quality paper

Original Printing 2006
Last figure below indicates year of this printing:
15   14   13   12   11   10   09   08   07   06

Typeset at Stanford University Press in 10/14 Minion

Special discounts for bulk quantities of Stanford Business Books are available to corporations, professional associations, and other organizations. For details and discount information, contact the special sales department of Stanford University Press. Tel: (650) 736-1783, Fax: (650) 736-1784

CONTENTS

LIST OF FIGURES AND TABLES

TABLES

TABLES

PREFACE

Every day sports are played. Teams win and teams lose. Joyous fans celebrate each win while losers dream of better days. With each event, numbers are recorded. These numbers tell us who won, who lost, and more importantly, these numbers tell us why some fans are so happy and others so sad. The question "why?", though, is difficult. To know why, one has to understand the stories the numbers tell.

This is where we step into the picture. As professors of economics, we have been trained in the art and science of statistical analysis. In fact, this is our job. Our job is to use statistics and math to study economics. Of course, no one told us what specifically we should study. So while sports fans go to work each day at a job they may love or hate, we go to work every day applying our skills to the study of professional sports. Yes, we get paid to study sports.

What have we learned from our studies? We have learned that the numbers generated by sports are poorly understood. Much of our research, which employs the standard tools of economic theory and statistical analysis, contradicts what we hear repeated by sports writers and the players and coaches working in professional sports.

Much of this research has appeared previously in such academic journals as the *American Economic Review*, *Economic Inquiry*, *Applied Economics*, and the *Journal of Sports Economics*. Unfortunately, these journals are not generally read by many people. So the stories we have told have not been widely heard. And that is the basic problem. Although there may be "fans" of our work, we think we can count the number of "fans" on one hand—and we probably do not have to use all our fingers. Granted, it is not the size of the audience but its enthusiasm that matters. Nevertheless, we would like to bring our work to a wider audience.

Hence we come to the purpose behind this book. We wish to explain to as general an audience as possible the findings we previously only presented in academic journals and at academic conferences. Given that our work is about sports, and many people find sports to be both fun and interesting, there is some reason to believe such a book will be of interest to people outside of academia.

We do face one problem in telling our story. All of our writings to date have been written for a very tiny audience of fellow academics. We were quite certain that the approach we offered in our academic articles could not be used in a book for a general audience. Hence we faced a dilemma. How can we explain what we have done in economics and sports without using the math and statistics we have grown to love and adore?

Our answer was found in *Freakonomics*, the book by Steven Levitt and Stephen Dubner. Levitt and Dubner collaborated on the story of Levitt's academic research, and in the process, wrote a best-selling book. What lesson did we learn from this work? In economics, math and statistics rule the day. From Levitt and Dubner we learned that one can tell the story of research in economics without relying on any technical details. Although our story is about the numbers sports generate, the math and statistics we employ will be relegated to endnotes and the web site [www.wagesofwins.com] associated with the book. If you are not interested in the technical details, your ability to enjoy our story will not be impaired.

Although we are economists, the stories we tell are first and foremost about sports. So as you turn the pages you will see the names of Ty Cobb and Tony Gwynn, Michael Jordan and Allen Iverson, Brett Favre and Peyton Manning, and many other sports stars from yesterday and today. We will also mention the work of many great writers, like Bob Costas, Allen Barra, Alan Schwartz, and John Hollinger. We need to emphasize, though, that this book is also about economics, so we will be mentioning major names in our disciplines, such as Adam Smith, Alfred Marshall, John Kenneth Galbraith, Ronald Coase, Douglas North, and Herbert Simon. And finally the book is about sports economics, so we will also mention the "stars" of our field. Hence we will discuss the work of Simon Rottenberg, Andrew Zimbalist, Gerald Scully, and Roger Noll, as well as many others.

Much of this work could not have been completed without the help of many, many people. We wish to thank the people who took the time to generously review earlier drafts of this work: Our list of reviewers includes Richard Campbell, Stef Donev, John Emig, Rodney Fort, Michael Leeds, Jim Peach, and Dan Rascher. The suggestions each offered greatly enhanced this work.

Additionally we wish to thank the people who answered various questions we had along the way. This list includes Allen Barra, Richard Burdekin, John-Charles

Bradbury, John Fizel, Jahn Hakes, Brad Humphreys, Anthony Krautmann, Dean Oliver, Darren Rovell, and Stefan Szymanski.

Much of the academic work we based this story upon could not have been completed without the help of several economists we have written with in the past. This list includes: Erick Eschker, Aju Fenn, Bernd Frick, Todd Jewell, Rob Simmons, Roberto Vicente-Mayoral, and Young Hoon Lee. We would also like to thank all of the economists who have participated in sessions on sports economics at the Western Economic Association. These sessions, organized in the past by Larry Hadley and Elizabeth Gustafson, have been a tremendous help in our work.

The people of Stanford Press, specifically Martha Cooley, Jared Smith, John Feneron, and Mary Bearden have been tremendous. This book would not have been possible without Martha, so she certainly deserves a great deal of credit—although none of the blame for any of our mistakes.

Finally, the list of people we have to thank includes our families, whose support is very much appreciated. So Dave Berri would like to thank his wife, Lynn, as well as his daughters Allyson and Jessica. Lynn took the time to read each chapter of this book, and her suggestions went far to overcome the limitations in our writing abilities. Martin Schmidt would also like to thank his wife, Susan, as well as his children Michael, Casey, and a third one to come soon. Finally, last but not least, Stacey Brook would like to thank his wife, Margy, and his sons Joshua, Jonah, and Jeremiah.

January 9, 2006

THE WAGES OF WINS

1 GAMES WITH NUMBERS

Sports are entertainment. Sports do not often change our world; rather they serve as a distraction from our world. Though sports can often lead to heated debates and occasional violence, in the final analysis sports are mostly about having fun.[1]

Beyond the painful losses and possible violence, there is another not-so-fun aspect of sports. Sports come with numbers. And analyzing these numbers involves math. For many, math was not a favorite subject in school. Math can be hard. Math can be confusing. Math can be scary. So why do people in sports introduce something that is not fun into something that gives our life so much joy and pleasure? Why do sports need all these pesky numbers?

Our answer begins with a simple observation. Typically fans follow teams, not players. Jerry Seinfeld has observed that people can hate a player who plays on an opposing team, then love the very same player when he plays for their team. For Seinfeld, this means that people are really just "rooting for clothes."

Although teams are what people follow, the actions of the individual players impact what we see for the team. When a team wins, we praise the players who we think made this happen. When our teams lose, we are just as quick, if not quicker, to blame the players who are responsible for making us feel so bad. How do we evaluate these individual players? Without numbers, this would be difficult. To see this point, consider the question of who is the best. Any fan of a team sport like baseball, basketball, or football can answer this question. Can one answer the question, though, without using any numbers?

Of course, every once in a while a coach or sportswriter will argue that the games are not about the numbers. From their logic, if one really understands the games, then all those numbers are unnecessary. To test the necessity of numbers, let us consider the decisive game of the 2005 NBA Finals. In this game the San Antonio Spurs scored 81 points and the Detroit Pistons scored 74. Quickly, who won the game? For those who believe statistics do not tell us the story, this question is hard to answer.

If we can't refer to numbers in our assessment, we could never know who won any game. In fact, all those numbers on the shiny score board probably just seem like a distraction in our efforts to enjoy watching very tall people run around a basketball court.

As our simple thought experiment illustrates, numbers are important. Numbers do more than tell us who won and lost. Numbers allow us to see what our eyes cannot follow. In baseball, where numbers have been tracked since the 19th century, numbers are obviously crucial. To illustrate, let us imagine that we wished to identify the greatest hitter in baseball history. As long as we are using our imagination, let's say we had access to time travel so that we could actually watch every single player in the history of the game. Finally, let's also say that we think that the best measure of a hitter's ability is batting average, or hits per at bat. Yeah, we know. We lost you on that last bit of imagination. Time travel you could buy. We all know, though, that batting average is not the best measure of a hitter's performance. You would think that if you figured out time travel you would have more sophisticated measures of baseball performance at your disposal.

Still, let's stick with our story. Here we are traveling through time. We come across Ty Cobb. He looks like a very good hitter. Maybe not a nice person, but still, he seems to get hits a bit more frequently then other players. Is Cobb the best? Well, after a bit more travel we see Tony Gwynn. He also seems to get hits a bit more frequently then other players. If all we did was look at these two players, could we see who is better?

Well, let's look at batting average. We see that Cobb's lifetime mark was 0.366. When Gwynn retired his career mark was 0.338. So Cobb hit safely 37% of the time while Gwynn hit safely on 34% of his at bats. If all you did was watch these players, could you say who was a better hitter? Can one really tell the difference between 37% and 34% just staring at the players play? To see the problem with the non-numbers approach to player evaluation, consider that out of every 100 at bats, Cobb got three more hits than Gwynn. That's it, three hits. If you saw every at bat for both players, could you see this difference? Back in the 19th century the answer must have been no, since people started to calculate batting averages.[2] Then, because people began to suspect that there is more to hitting than a batting average, a host of other statistics and measures began to be tracked.

These numbers allow us to master time travel. We do not need to travel through time to compare Cobb and Gwynn. Now we can just look at the numbers, and like magic, we are transported across space and through time.

Of course, historical comparisons are not always possible. There is one small step that must have been taken in the past if we wish to compare players today. Someone in the past had to record the numbers. To see this point, let's think about basketball. One of the best basketball players today is Shaquille O'Neal. How does O'Neal compare to Wilt Chamberlain, one of the best players from the 1960s? Well, now we are out of luck. For us to make this comparison we needed people in the past to keep track of all the numbers. Unfortunately, much of the data we use to evaluate performance in NBA today was not tracked by the NBA for individual players before the mid-1970s. Wilt retired in 1973. So today we really can't say if Wilt was better or worse than Shaq.

Now people who have seen both players might insist Wilt is better. Or they might insist Shaq is better. Without all the numbers, though, how can we tell? To illustrate, let's just think about one of the missing stats, turnovers.

Allen Iverson in 2004–05 led the NBA with 4.6 turnovers per game. So every quarter or so, on average, Iverson turned the ball over. Chauncey Billups that same season only averaged 2.3 turnovers per game, or about one turnover per half. If you were only watching, could you tell the difference? Remember, turnovers are not the only thing happening in a basketball game. Players are making shots, missing shots, blocking shots, collecting rebounds, and creating steals. All ten players on the court are taking these actions. While all this is going on, Iverson is committing two turnovers each half while Billups only loses the ball once. If we just stare at all these players, is it possible to see the difference in turnovers committed between Iverson and Billups?

Obviously we are arguing that without the numbers you really couldn't tell. Basically, numbers are necessary to answer the question, who is best? We would also argue that numbers can be used to tell us so much more. Of course, the analysis of numbers can be difficult. For people who are not accustomed to looking at numbers systematically, the stories they might believe may not be consistent with the stories the numbers offer. In the end, this is the tale we tell. We wish to show that these numbers tell stories that differ from popular perception.

FREAKONOMICS AND ALFRED MARSHALL

The approach we take in our work is quite similar to the approach taken by Steven Levitt. In 2005 economist Steven Levitt co-authored a book with Stephen Dubner entitled *Freakonomics*. A reading of this work reveals that Levitt considers himself a bit of an outsider in the world of economics.

> Despite Levitt's elite credentials (Harvard undergrad, a PhD from MIT, a stack of awards), he approached economics in a notably unorthodox way. He seemed to look at things not so much as an academic but as a very smart and curious explorer. . . . He professed little interest in the sort of monetary issues that come to mind when most people think about economics; he practically blustered with self effacement. "I just don't know very much about the field of economics," he told Dubner at one point. . . . "I'm not good at math, I don't know a lot about econometrics, and I also don't know how to do theory." . . . *As Levitt sees it, economics is a science with excellent tools for gaining answers but a serious shortage of interesting questions.*[3]

His dissatisfaction with economics has led Levitt to invent a field he calls "Freakonomics." Levitt and Dubner define "freakonomics" as a field that "employs the best tools that economics can offer . . . (and) allows us to follow whatever freakish curiosities may occur to us" (p. 14). What Levitt appears to be saying is that he is taking the methodology of economics and applying it to real world problems, problems that are not only interesting to him but also to the vast population of non-economists who live on this planet. Although Levitt's approach is not emphasized today as often as it should be, it is hardly a new approach.

To understand this point you need to understand that economics is a relatively young discipline. Adam Smith, who wrote both the *Theory of Moral Sentiments* (1759) and *The Wealth of Nations* (1776), is considered the founder of classical economics. Smith, though, probably did not consider himself an economist. He was specifically a moral philosopher, interested in history, sociology, psychology, and political science, in addition to having a passing familiarity with economics. Surprising to students of economics today, Smith did not offer mathematics or models in presenting his thoughts. Smith simply used words, enough words in *The Wealth of Nations* to fill over 1,000 pages. These words contained the basic theories Smith was presenting, but also stories and illustrations to support his arguments. In other words, Smith made an effort to connect his work to the world where his readers lived.

More than 100 years after Smith, another great economist defined the methodology he believed economists should follow. Alfred Marshall, the intellectual heir of Smith and the man often credited as the father of neoclassical economics, defined economics as "a study of mankind in the ordinary business of life" (Marshall, 1920, p. 1). For Marshall, economics should not be limited to an abstract model presented on the chalkboard, but should move beyond the math and offer useful insights into the lives people lead.

In a letter to A. L. Bowley in 1906 Marshall laid forth his basic step-by-step approach, which we paraphrase below:[4]

The Marshallian Method

Step One: Math can be used, but only as a "shorthand language."

Step Two: Any math should be translated into words.

Step Three: A theory should be illustrated by examples that are "important in real life."

Step Four: With words and real world illustrations in hand, you can now "*burn the mathematics.*"

Step Five: If you cannot find any real world examples, *burn the theory.*

Marshall was only joking when he said one should burn the math. Marshall, though, did place most of his math in footnotes and appendices and primarily used words and illustrations to present his ideas. In essence, the Marshallian method is Levitt and Dubner's "freakonomics." Marshall argued the research must be illustrated "by examples that are important in real life." As the number of economists grew in the century since Marshall wrote this letter, the discipline moved away from this basic sentiment.

Why did economics change? Again, it is all about the numbers. In Marshall's day, when the number of economists was relatively small, an economist who could not communicate with non-economists would not have much of an audience. Today, though, the population of economists is large enough that one can do very well in our discipline speaking only to fellow economists. In fact, as Levitt may feel, those who try to communicate economics to non-economists could be thought of as freaks in the discipline.

Our work will follow in the footsteps of Levitt and return to the original Marshallian method. We will be utilizing the tools of economics. These tools will allow us to make observations relevant to the real life, or what passes for the real life, of sports fans. We hope that much of what we say will be interesting. Although we will of course reference numbers, we are going to follow the example of Marshall and relegate the math and statistical analysis to the endnotes and the web site associated with the book. If you look quickly through this book you will see tables with numbers, but nothing more complicated than what you might find in a box score in the local paper. As for equations, you will be hard pressed to find any of these. Although we did not burn the math, we did make every effort to get it out of the way of the story we are trying to tell.

THE CONVENTIONAL WISDOM

We begin our story drawing upon an important concept employed by Levitt: Conventional Wisdom. This term was both coined and defined by John Kenneth Galbraith, one of the leading economists of the 20th century. According to Galbraith (1958):

> [A] vested interest in understanding is more preciously guarded than any other treasure. *It is why men react, not infrequently with something akin to religious passion, to the defense of what they have so laboriously learned.* Familiarity may breed contempt in some areas of human behavior, but in the field of social ideas it is the touchstone of acceptability. Because familiarity is such an important test of acceptability, the acceptable ideas have great stability. They are highly predictable. It will be convenient to have a name for the ideas which are esteemed at any time for their acceptability, and it should be a term that emphasizes this predictability. I shall refer to these ideas henceforth as the conventional wisdom. (Galbraith, 1958, pp. 6–7, italics added)

An abundance of "conventional wisdom" can be found in sports. Here is a "Top-Ten" list drawn from our research into the economics of sports.

1. The teams that pay the most, win the most. In other words, sports teams can buy the fans' love.
2. Labor disputes threaten the future of professional sports.
3. Major League Baseball has a competitive balance problem.[5]
4. A league's competitive balance is determined by league policy.
5. National Basketball Association (NBA) teams need "stars" to attract the fans.
6. The best players in basketball score the most.
7. The best players in basketball make their teammates more productive.
8. The best players in basketball play their best in the playoffs.
9. Quarterbacks should be credited with wins and losses in the National Football League (NFL).
10. If we understand a quarterback's past performance we can predict his future productivity.

For sports fans most, if not all, of these ideas should be familiar. Players, coaches, and members of the media recite these lines often in the discussion of professional sports. Beyond being representative of conventional wisdom, what else do these ideas have in common? Those numbers we spoke of previously suggest that all of these ideas are not quite true. Of course, to those raised on the conventional wisdom of sports, this contention simply cannot pass the "laugh test."

Are we suggesting that player strikes don't threaten the survival of professional sports? Or that baseball does not have a competitive balance problem? Or, and for basketball fans this might be the greatest heresy, scorers like Allen Iverson are not the best players in the NBA? For some sports fans the mere suggestion that the conventional wisdom is untrue has led to a bit of laughter and the closing of this book. For everyone else, let's think a bit harder about that "laugh test."

THE LAUGH TEST

What is the "laugh test"? As professors of economics, with a passing familiarity with statistical analysis, we looked long and hard for evidence that this test exists. From what we have seen of formal statistics, there is no such thing as a "laugh test." Still, people often employ this term when they come across analysis that violates conventional wisdom.

Consider the following argument from Dean Oliver, author of *Basketball on Paper*. Oliver is basically the Bill James of basketball,[6] devising a number of clever and useful statistical methods to measure a basketball player's productivity. In addition to presenting a number of excellent statistical tools, Oliver also employed the "laugh test" in a critique of a player evaluation method developed by Wayne Winston and Jeff Sagarin. We will discuss the pluses and minuses of the Winston-Sagarin method in Chapter Six. For now, though, we wish to react to the following quote from Oliver:

> Despite the concept making sense, the results—as we like to say in this business—don't pass the "laugh test." Winston/Sagarin's results suggested that in 2002, Shaquille O'Neal, commonly viewed as the best player in the league, was only the twentieth best player in the NBA. Their results also suggested that rookie Andrei Kirilenko, not commonly viewed as even being in the league's top fifty, ranked second among NBA player in overall contribution. See? Doesn't pass the laugh test. (Oliver, 2004, p. 181)

The essence of Oliver's "laugh test" is that statistical evaluations can't stray very far from the assessment of talent offered by what is "commonly viewed" or, in the terminology of Galbraith, from the conventional wisdom.[7] Often this common perception is driven by the views of people employed by the NBA. After all, the paychecks of these people depend upon their ability to answer the question "who is the best?" So these people must know best. If a player evaluation method contradicts what people in the NBA think, the method must be incorrect.

Do decision makers in professional sports truly know "best"? To answer this question, let's consider the relationship between team payroll and wins. One of our myths was that teams that pay the most, win the most. This makes some sense. Assuming people in sports know who the best are, then the best players should be paid the most. Therefore, whoever has the highest payroll will also have the best players, and the team with the best players should win the most.

Of course the story hinges on the idea that people in sports know who is best. We will spend a fair amount of time on this issue, but for now, let's just spend a few moments on the relationship between payroll and wins. If teams that pay more win more, then there should be a fairly strong correlation between payroll and wins.

What do we mean by correlation? Two variables are correlated if they move together. Variables are not correlated if they do not move together. This is not just an either/or issue. Basically we can employ statistical analysis to measure the strength of the correlation between two variables.

So is payroll strongly correlated with wins? Is it the case that these two variables move together? We can test this idea a couple of ways. First we could look at how adding payroll impacts wins. For example, if NBA general managers and coaches know best, then we would expect teams that add to payroll should see more wins. In fact, we should see a fairly strong correlation between the dollars added to payroll and on-court success.

Of course, wins are not just about adding payroll. For one thing, teams could see payroll increases because players currently employed have received a raise. Giving out raises to already employed players will probably not change outcomes. Beyond pay raises, one would probably need to control for other factors, like the quality of coaching.

So how can one determine the relationship between wins and adding payroll, while controlling for the impact of pay raises and coaching? If a chemist wishes to know the relationship between two chemicals, he or she goes into a lab and runs a controlled experiment. In economics, though, we have no controlled experiments. We cannot go to an NBA team and ask the team to add payroll, while holding constant all other factors that might impact wins. Well, we could ask, but we anticipate that teams would be unwilling to let us conduct experiments with their organizations.

Fortunately, we don't have to ask teams to let us run our experiments. For economists, controlled experimentation can be simulated with regression analysis. What is regression analysis? Regression analysis is a technique that allows us to see how two variables are related, while statistically holding all other factors constant. When properly executed, regression analysis allows us to see if two variables are, or are not, statistically related.

Regression analysis can do more than this. As Deirdre McCloskey notes—over and over again[8]—statistical significance is only part of the story. We also want to know the economic significance of any relationship. In other words, we want to use regression analysis to see the size of the impact one variable has on another. Even more than this, it is also important to look at how much of a variable we can explain with regression analysis. Specifically, we see that some teams win more than others. How much of this variation in wins can we explain when we note factors like adding payroll, the quality of coaching, etc.? And beyond this, actually, we can go on and on. For now, let's just say that regression analysis allows us to see a whole bunch of stuff.

Let's go back to how adding payroll impacts team wins.[9] As we have said, one might expect that adding more expensive players to the payroll should lead to more wins, while just increasing the pay of existing players would not have any impact. This is indeed what we see when we look at the data. Adding payroll in the NBA does have a statistically significant impact on wins. What does this mean? We have evidence that more pay leads to more wins. So teams must know what they are doing? Well, before we jump to that conclusion we need to note that less than 10% of the change in a team's winning percentage from year to year can be explained by adding additional payroll.[10] If we look at this the other way, more than 90% of the change in a team's winning percentage cannot be explained by additions to a team's payroll. Adding payroll may be statistically significant, but our ability to explain wins with additions to payroll seems quite limited.[11]

We would note that NBA teams are not alone. Stefan Szymanski (2003) looked at the relationship between a team's payroll and team wins in the NBA, NFL, the National Hockey League (NHL), and the American League (AL), and National League (NL) of Major League Baseball. Szymanski did not consider the difference between adding pay and increasing the pay of existing players. His approach was a bit simpler. All he considered was how much of a team's wins could be explained by the size of the team's relative payroll.[12] In the NBA, only 16% of team wins could be explained by a team's relative payroll. In the NFL, NHL, AL, and NL the explanatory power varies from 5%, 11%, 26%, and 11% respectively.[13] In other words, across all the major North American sports, payroll and wins do not have a high correlation.[14]

We thought it would be fun to update Szymanski's work—well, maybe fun is not the right word. How about, we thought it might be interesting? So we collected data on relative payroll and team wins in the NBA, starting with the 1990–91 season and concluding with the 2004–05 campaign. For these fifteen seasons, relative payroll only explains 12% of team wins. For the NBA Szymanski looked at 1986 to

2000. The data we used included more recent years, and we find, compared to what Syzmanski reports, an even weaker relationship between wins and payroll.

When we update the analysis of baseball, we again find that payroll and wins are not highly correlated. Specifically we looked at the relationship between relative pay and wins in Major League Baseball from 1988 to 2005. Our research indicates that only 18% of team wins can be explained. A bit better than basketball, but still quite low.[15]

Of course we do not expect a perfect relationship between payroll and wins. Salaries are based upon expected performance, and injuries alone can cause expectations to differ from what we observe. As we will see in Chapter Nine, player performance in football can be very hard to predict. To a lesser extent this is true in baseball. Some of the deviation between payroll and wins in these sports can be explained by the uncertainties associated with player performance. In the NBA, though, player performance is not nearly as random. Yet, despite the greater predictability in performance, we do not see a very strong relationship between payroll and wins in basketball.

So what does all this tell us? By itself the payroll-wins relationship merely suggests that the people who are paid to know may not always know best. As we move forward in our discussion, more evidence will be offered in support of this sentiment. We realize of course that this statement is difficult for people to digest. How can it be that three economists see things that people employed in sports do not see?

An answer can be found in Michael Lewis's (2003) *Moneyball*. In this book Lewis tells the story of the Oakland A's, a team whose on-field success seems out of step with its limited payroll. The answer for Lewis was the ability of Billy Beane, Oakland's general manager, to exploit statistical analysis in the evaluation of playing talent. Because Beane knew more about player stats, he could build a team of cheap yet efficient baseball players.

In essence, *Moneyball* is the story of systematic inquiry told with anecdotal evidence. We wish to tell the same story, but we will offer systematic evidence. Such evidence will suggest that many commonly held beliefs about sports are inconsistent with the data. It is our ability to analyze the numbers that allows us to tell stories that contradict conventional wisdom. Such contradictions, or heresies if you follow the religion of sports, begin with the story of the contentious relationship between players and management in professional sports.

2 | MUCH TALKING, LITTLE WALKING

In 1964 Judge Robert Cannon, a lawyer representing the Major League Baseball Player Association (MLBPA), offered this insight into the plight of the American athlete. Testifying before the U.S. Senate, Cannon observed: "If I might, Senator, preface my remarks by repeating the words of Gene Woodling . . . 'we have it so good we don't know what to ask for next.' I think this sums up the thinking of the average major league ballplayer today."[1]

The person who replaced Cannon at the MLBPA was the legendary Marvin Miller. Miller and his ultimate successor, Donald Fehr, were able to find a few issues for players to quibble about with owners. For the most part such quibbling has been about how much of the revenue baseball creates each year should go to the players on the field and how much should go to the owners in the stands. The specific issues discussed have filled many books, and will be briefly discussed in the next chapter. For now, though, we merely wish to note that contrary to the view expressed by Woodling and Cannon, players have not always been happy with ownership and the feeling is often mutual. We would note that such animosity is not restricted to baseball. Labor disputes have also occurred in basketball, football, and hockey.

These fights are not just between players and owners, but also often involve the fans. As Table 2.1 highlights, from 1981 to 2005 there have been seven disputes in these sports that have led to the cancellation of regular season games. Whether these disputes were officially a player strike or an ownership lockout,[2] fans have been forced to miss games because the players didn't come to play.

Since 1981 the league has averaged a major labor dispute, defined as a dispute that caused games to be cancelled, once every three or four years. The latest event,

TABLE 2.1

25 Years of Labor-Management Strife in Professional Sports

League	Year	Days	Games Lost
Major League Baseball (Strike)	1981	50	712
National Football League (Strike)	1982	57	98
National Football League (Strike)	1987	24	56
National Hockey League (Lockout)	1994	103	442
Major League Baseball (Strike)	1994–95	232	920
National Basketball Association (Lockout)	1998–99	191	424
National Hockey League (Lockout)	2004–05	310	1,230

in the NHL, cancelled the 2004–05 season. This event in hockey allows the NHL to match both MLB and the NFL in the number of labor disputes that have resulted in cancelled games since 1981. All three leagues now have had two such events. So far the NBA is lagging behind. The 1998–99 lockout in basketball remains the only time the NBA has lost games to a labor dispute. In the summer of 2005 the NBA reached an agreement with its players well in advance of the 2005–06 season. The NBA's ability to reach an agreement without placing any games in serious jeopardy, though, has proven to be the exception to the general rule.

To put the frequency of these tragedies in perspective, let's briefly consider how often work stoppages occur in the United States.[3] The United States Department of Labor tells us that between 15 and 16 million workers in the United States belong to unions. There are approximately 4,000 unionized athletes in MLB, the NFL, the NBA, and the NHL. From 1981 these workers were involved in seven labor disputes. So if 4,000 workers are involved in seven stoppages, how many work stoppages should we see if we look at 16 million workers?

We know, who likes word problems? Here is the quick answer. If non-athletes experienced the same number of work stoppages as we see in sports, there would have been approximately 28,000 stoppages from 1981 to 2004. From 1981 to 2004 the same Department of Labor reports only 1,109 work stoppages in non-sports industries. In sum, these numbers tell us that athletes are about 25 times more likely to stop work when compared to workers in other industries in the United States.

Why are athletes so often involved in labor disputes with management? As we noted, these work stoppages occur because the players and owners cannot decide how to divide the billions of dollars in revenue sports generate each year. Given the small number of people involved, the dollars per person are quite substantial. Consider the 1994–95 labor strike in Major League Baseball. The strike led to the cancellation of the 1994 World Series and reduced the regular season in both 1994 and 1995. Roger Noll, an economist at Stanford, explained why the strike was so difficult to resolve.[4] According to Noll, the owners' efforts to limit the growth in player salaries would have cost the players $1.5 billion over the life of the proposed agreement. The strike only cost the players $300 million. Given these numbers, it is easy to see why the players didn't come out and play.

Once we see the dollars involved, it is easier to understand why these disputes occur with such frequency. Still, there is one party that seems ignored at the negotiating table. As the media often notes, isn't it the fan who gives sports the billions of dollars the players and owners squabble about? Shouldn't the fans have a place at the negotiating table?

THE SUMMER OF 2002

These were the questions people were asking during the summer of 2002. At this time negotiations between baseball players and owners were not progressing to the satisfaction of the MLBPA. Consequently, the players set a strike date of August 30. A strike by players would be the third such event in a little over twenty years.

The reaction of both the media and the fans could hardly be described as enthusiastic. A quick review of newspaper articles from August 2002 highlights the displeasure fans and the media had with those managing and playing the game of baseball. Specifically the fans, the media, and even the players and owners argued that if the game was taken away from the fans again, the fans would retaliate in the future. For many, the future of the game itself was in doubt.

To highlight this point, let's consider the work of Chuck Cavalaris (2002) of the *Knoxville News-Sentinel*. A few weeks before the strike deadline Cavalaris asked people from around the country to comment on the potential player strike. Cavalaris introduced the responses he received with the following: "The players, who have set an Aug. 30 strike date, and owners need to realize they are on the verge of ruining a great sport. Scores of people from across the country have joined our pledge to boycott major league baseball, if a strike wipes out the playoffs. We simply will not be held hostage any longer."

In 2001 Major League Baseball sold more than 72 million tickets. So the displeasure of "scores of people" may not have had much impact. Still, despite the disparity in numbers between respondents and ticket sales, we think the following sample from the more than 30 responses posted in the Cavalaris article captures the sentiment of many baseball fans in 2002.

I am possibly the biggest St. Louis Cardinals fan in the South. My father instilled his love for baseball in me when I was very young. To fight over the money they are making is absurd. I never thought I would ever say this, but I will never watch my beloved Cardinals play another game—or spend another dime on any baseball stuff again. Terry Copeland, Knoxville, Tennessee

Baseball, as we used to know it, is apparently dying. Another strike will drive a stake through the heart of baseball. Walt Henry, Sevierville, Tennessee

I gave baseball one chance to right itself after the '94 strike. I won't waste my time on a bunch of overpaid whiners whose jobs aren't important to begin with. Dick Dobins, Hooks, Texas

Go Braves! But Go Away, if you strike! David Gilbert, Oak Ridge, Tennessee

Most of the comments posted by Cavalaris were sent in from fans in Tennessee. We would note that Major League Baseball has never had a team in Tennessee. So whether the players went on strike or not, these people were not going to see Major League Baseball in their hometown. In fact, given the distances these people would need to travel, we are not sure that these fans actually attended very many Major League Baseball games. Despite this observation, polling data from this time seemed to confirm the expressed sentiment.

A Joe Henderson (2002) article posted in the *Tampa Tribune* reported the results of two fan surveys.

Fabrizio, McLaughlin and Associates of Arlington, Va., recently surveyed 1,000 adults and concluded fans would abandon baseball if players strike. . . . The survey found that less than half the adults in this country (49 percent) consider themselves baseball fans, and 36 percent of those are just "casual fans." Nearly half say they're "not really baseball fans." The results mirror surveys being done all over the country, including an exclusive SurveyUSA poll for WFLA-NewsChannel 8 of Tampa Bay area baseball fans. More than half of them, 56 percent, say they wouldn't attend Major League Baseball games after a strike. Thirty-seven percent say they wouldn't even watch games on television.

The voice of the fans was effectively dramatized in the words of Bob Klapisch (2002). The day of the strike deadline Klapisch had the following warning for Baseball Commissioner Bud Selig and MLBPA union chief Donald Fehr: "[I]t will all come to a crashing end if Selig and Fehr can't find common ground. The deadline is here. The apocalypse is at our doorstep. If the commissioner and union chief can't see the Dark Age that awaits, not only should they be fired, they didn't deserve the job in the first place."

We've read the book of Revelation and cannot find any mention of baseball. So we are not sure the end of baseball is the beginning of the apocalypse. Still comments from baseball players, both before the settlement and after the strike was avoided, echo the belief that there would be consequences if the players had failed to come to work. Consider the following player quotes before August 30, 2002.[5]

"My main concern is the fans," first baseman Derrek Lee said. "You don't want to alienate them. Without them there's no game."

"I was a fan and 7 years old when they struck in 1981," third baseman Mike Lowell said. "I thought the world was going to end. The Phillies were my favorite team and they couldn't defend their title."

After the strike was avoided, players again acknowledged the potential reactions fans would have had to a strike.[6]

"I'm just happy we're playing baseball," Red Sox union player representative Johnny Damon said late Friday after owners and players came to terms on a bargaining agreement that prevented the game's ninth work stoppage since 1972. "(A strike) would have been a travesty for the game of baseball and I think both sides realized it."

Left-handed reliever Steve Kline, the Cardinals' player representative, said he thought the union had little choice but to settle. "It came down to us playing baseball or having our reputations and life ripped by the fans," Kline said. "Baseball would have never been the same if we had walked out."

Hence we have the conventional wisdom with respect to labor disputes in sports. From the fans, the media, and the players we see a common theme. If the players walk we can expect the fans to walk.

In the summer of 2002 with the conventional wisdom being shouted from the mountaintops, two lone voices were speaking in the wilderness. On the pages of the *Los Angeles Times*,[7] the *Cincinnati Inquirer*,[8] the *Chicago Sun-Times*,[9] the *Orlando Sentinel*,[10] and the *San Jose Mercury News*[11] two economists were quoted as saying the conventional wisdom was incorrect. According to these professors, although the fans frequently argue that they will walk, in the end it is all just talk. The two economists were named Berri and Schmidt, and the comments we made that summer were based upon research we had published in academic journals.[12] Unfortunately, few people read academic journals. That's why we felt the need to write this book.

CAN THE FANS WALK?

Let's begin with a confession. When we began this research we believed the conventional wisdom. It certainly seemed reasonable to us that fans would become unhappy with sports when the squabbling over money forces fans to find other entertainment options. Given this viewpoint, our purpose in looking at the impact labor disputes have on attendance was not to establish whether there was an impact. Of course there had to be an impact. We only wished to know how long it took fans to return to the game once the players came back. How big a penalty did the fans impose on players and owners when the games were taken away?

The methodology we followed came from the field of macroeconomics, a field where Schmidt has published extensively. To understand our approach to the study of strikes and attendance, we need to discuss, ever so briefly, a particular event in macroeconomic history. Let's return to the 1970s, a time when disco was king and polyester was the fabric of choice. At this time the price of oil rose dramatically. The sudden increase in the price of oil, coupled with the sight of millions of Americans dressed in polyester—okay, we made that part up—led to a decline in the growth rate of the U.S. economy. Eventually the economy recovered from the impact of higher oil prices. What researchers in macroeconomics wondered was how long it took the economy to recover from the external shock of rising oil prices.

Initially, we thought a player strike or ownership lockout had the same impact on fan attendance as higher oil prices have on economic growth. In a year where a strike happens, average fan attendance declines. Over time, though, fan attendance eventually returns. What we wished to measure was the time it took fans to return.

To answer this question we collected data on attendance for the NBA, NHL, NFL, and Major League Baseball.[13] We then calculated how long it took fans of each league to return when labor disputes took away the games the fans love. Although we have talked mainly about baseball thus far, we will begin our discussion with the labor dispute in basketball. Basketball has had the most recent event we can analyze, which also is the one event we did not examine in our previously published research. In other words, for the three or four fans of our published work, the discussion of the NBA will be new stuff. After we discuss the NBA, we will then touch briefly upon hockey and football and conclude our discussion with player strikes in baseball.

The Story in the National Basketball Association

The NBA has historically had relative labor peace. Up until the lockout of 1998 the NBA had prided itself on being the only major team sport in North America that had not lost games to a labor dispute. Why did the peace end? Well, the whole story would take us far from the subject of this chapter. For the most part the problem was typical: How should the revenue the NBA generates be divided between players and owners? Players themselves added a new wrinkle to the story when they ar-

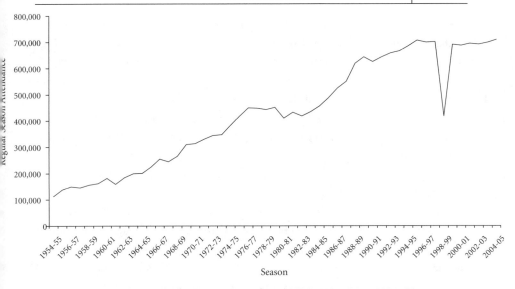

FIGURE 2.1. Average Regular Season Attendance, NBA, 1954–55 to 2004–05

gued about how to divide money between the stars and the non-stars the league employs. Although the reasons for the dispute may be fascinating,[14] at least to the players and owners fighting for the money involved, we wish to focus on one question: How did the fans respond to this squabble?

To answer this question we could ask the typical fan of the NBA. Economists, though, are not by nature very social. One of the reasons people self-select into economics is that our methods allow us to investigate human behavior without actually talking to people. Fortunately our lack of social skills is not a problem. As it often turns out, what people say is not quite the same as the actions people take. And it is the latter that is most important. What we wish to know is the actions people took when the game of basketball was taken away. Did the fans walk?

To answer this question let us consider how NBA attendance responded to this event. Figure 2.1 presents average regular season attendance in the NBA from the 1954–55 season up to the 2004–05 campaign.

Before we discuss that big downward spike in the late 1990s—yes, that's the lockout—let's say a few words about how attendance changed over time in the NBA. Our attendance story begins in 1954. This was the first season of the shot clock, an innovation that many people argue ushered in the modern NBA era. Of course, even with the shot clock, the NBA was not quite what it is today. In 1954 the NBA consisted of eight teams playing a 72-game regular season schedule. Not one team in the league was able to convert 40% of its field goal attempts, which was an improvement over the 1946–47 campaign where no team surpassed a field goal percentage of 30%. The NBA champions in 1954 were the Syracuse Nationals, who managed to defeat the Fort Wayne Pistons in seven games. As time passed the Syracuse Nationals became the Philadelphia 76ers, the Pistons moved to Detroit, and the league managed to find players who could hit an occasional shot.

What did attendance look like in the early days of the NBA? From Figure 2.1 we see this basic story: The average team attracted 112,502 fans over the course of the 1954–55 season, or a little bit more than 3,000 people per contest. Over the next 40 years the NBA attendance picture would improve dramatically. In the mid-1970s per team attendance surpassed the 400,000 mark. In the 1980s average attendance passed 500,000 for the 1986–87 campaign, and then went past 600,000 for the 1988–89 season. Seven years later, the NBA's average attendance went past the 700,000 mark, which works out to more than 17,000 fans per game. All of this indicates that the NBA was an increasingly popular attraction in the latter years of the 20th century. How did the lockout impact the fans' interest in this sport?

In 1997–98 average attendance stood at 701,799 fans per team. The lockout of 1998–99 reduced the schedule by 32 games, and as a result aggregate attendance dropped to an average of 418,445; a total quite similar to what the league achieved over 82 games in 1982–83. In 1999–2000 the NBA returned to a full schedule and average attendance rose to 691,674. So the lockout cost the league about 10,000 fans per team, right?

Actually, this wouldn't be correct. We really can't be sure that drop in 10,000 fans was due to the lockout, or just part of the typical pattern we observe in league attendance. Although attendance generally rises, declines do occasionally happen. In 1990–91 NBA attendance declined 18,000 fans from the previous season. For the 1996–97 season we observe a decline of more than 7,000. Hence, a drop of 10,000 fans is not unusual. Can we argue the observed decline in 1999–2000 was significant in a statistical sense?

To answer this question we have to do more than just stare at the numbers. We need to measure how labor disputes impact attendance. Our specific method is called intervention analysis.[15] Basically, intervention analysis looks at how the average value in a series of numbers changes given a specific intervention. If we study the macroeconomy, an intervention might be a sudden increase in oil prices. In our study of attendance, the intervention is a labor dispute that leads to the cancellation of games.

As we noted in our first chapter, we shall be employing the Marshallian approach. This means the math and statistics will hide out on our web site. So if you are interested, our analysis of the NBA is presented in all its gory details online. If you just wish to know what we found, here is the story. When we employ intervention analysis to assess the impact of the NBA lockout on attendance we find that there wasn't any statistical impact. NBA fans did not walk, in a statistical sense, when the players walked.

The Story in the Other "National" Sports

So maybe basketball fans didn't get the memo that labor disputes should cause fans to walk away. What about the National Hockey League and National Football League? Surely fans in these sports pay enough attention to care when games are taken away.

In Figure 2.2 we present an abbreviated history of attendance in the NHL, beginning with the 1960–61 season and ending with the 2003–04 campaign. We see that attendance in the 1960s was quite volatile, but the NHL did experience substantial growth beginning in the late 1970s. For the 1978–79 season average regular season attendance was 456,356. By 2003–04 attendance per team was 677,872. Over that 26-year period there is one substantial drop. This occurred in 1994–95 when a labor dispute in the NHL caused the schedule to be reduced from 84 games to only 48. As a result, attendance dropped from nearly 620,000 in 1993–94 to less than 360,000 in 1994–95. In 1995–96, though, despite playing a regular season that

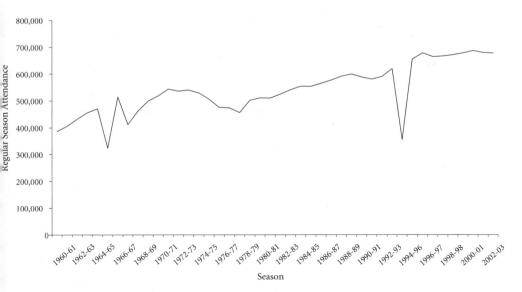

FIGURE 2.2. Average Regular Season Attendance, NHL, 1960–61 to 2003–04

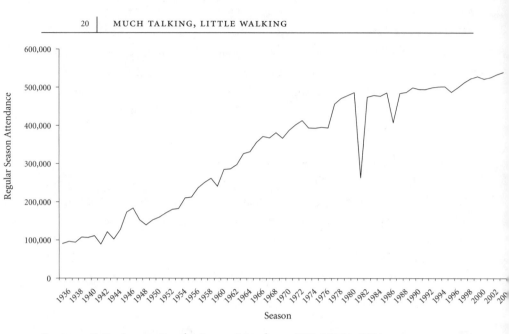

FIGURE 2.3. Average Regular Season Attendance, NFL, 1936 to 2004

was only 82 games, the NHL actually saw attendance rise to more than 650,000 fans per team.

So after the lockout, attendance actually increased. On a per-game basis, the average NHL team after the lockout season drew more than 1,000 additional fans. Not surprisingly, intervention analysis fails to find a negative consequence from the lockout. NHL fans did not seem to respond in quite the way sportswriters predicted. We would add that the early returns from the 2005–06 season show that history for hockey fans does repeat itself. As of January 1, 2006, per-game attendance for the 2005–06 campaign, relative to the season before the 2004–05 lockout, had actually increased.

Of course we are talking about hockey fans. Would we see the same if we look at the NFL? In 1982 a player strike cost the NFL seven regular season games. In 1987, another strike ultimately cost the NFL one regular season contest. With two strikes over such a short period of time, fans should have been enraged. To assess the impact of these strikes, we offer Figure 2.3.

Figure 2.3 shows a clear pattern of growth in NFL attendance. Average team attendance in 1950 was only 152,135. By 2004, the average NFL team was drawing more than 539,000 fans per season. The two strikes stand out in Figure 2.3 as the loss of games leads to a loss of attendance. Was there any permanent impact from either event? In 1981 the average NFL team attracted 485,964 fans in a season. In

1983 this number was reduced to 474,187, for a decline of nearly 12,000 fans. In 1986, the year before the next strike, attendance was 485,305 fans. In 1988 attendance declined less than 2,000 fans from the 1986 total. So in absolute terms, both strikes were followed by a decline in attendance. Was the decline statistically significant? Our intervention analysis indicates that neither event had a statistically significant impact on fan attendance.

So we have looked at four events and the story is the same each time. Players have gone on strike. Owners have locked out the players. In the end, the labor disputes do not seem to matter. Fans of basketball, hockey, and football still come back when the players return.

The Story in Our National Pastime

The statements from the media we cited at the onset of this discussion all talked about baseball. Although fans of the other sports may not care, those who follow our national pastime were clearly angry when baseball players threatened to go on strike. Once again we look at the data to see if this anger ever led to any action.

In Figure 2.4 we present the history of baseball attendance from 1901 to 2004. Although many stories can be told, and we are sure some of these are actually interesting, we wish to draw your attention to baseball attendance in the 1930s and 1940s. Attendance in 1945 was 677,570 per team, a record for baseball up until that time. The previous record of 633,266 per team occurred in 1930, the first year of

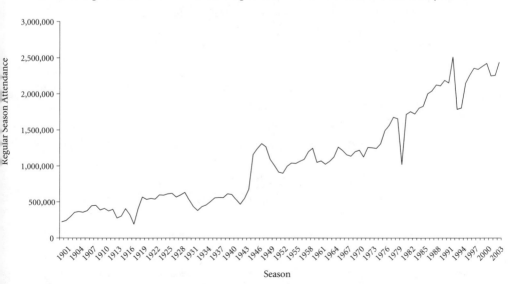

FIGURE 2.4. Average Regular Season Attendance, MLB, 1901 to 2004

the Great Depression. Years of economic malaise coupled with World War II led to a decline in baseball attendance. The low point in this time period was 1933, when teams were only able to average 380,540 fans. Compared to the depths of the Great Depression, attendance in 1945 looked quite good.

Still, although 1945 was record setting, it was nothing compared to 1946. For 1946 average attendance soared to 1.16 million per team, a 71% increase over the previous season. Attendance continued to soar in 1947 and 1948, hitting a high of 1.31 million fans for each franchise in the latter season. After this peak, though, baseball attendance leveled off. The 1948 peak was not matched again until 1977, when a then-record average of 1.49 million fans per team was observed.

Four years after this peak, baseball experienced its first significant labor dispute that clearly involved the fans. On June 10, 1981, negotiations between the players and owners ended and when the sun rose on the next day, the players decided not to play baseball. The owners had prepared for this possibility by purchasing strike insurance from Lloyds of London. After about seven weeks the insurance fund was depleted. With the departure of the insurance fund went the owners' resolve and the strike was soon settled.[16]

The strike cost baseball about one-third of the regular season. How did fans react to this event? In 1980 the average team drew 1.65 million fans over the course of the regular season. In 1981, with a schedule shortened by more than 50 games, attendance was little more than one million per team. When a full season of games was played in 1982 baseball fans came out in force. Attendance per team rose to a new record of 1.71 million per team. One does not need sophisticated analysis to see that the 1981 strike had no lasting impact on demand.

The other significant work stoppage that occurred in Major League Baseball was the 1994–95 players' strike which, at that point, was the longest in professional sports history. When the strike was settled, 912 games had been cancelled. Perhaps more importantly, the strike forced the cancellation of all 1994 playoff games, including the World Series, an occurrence unprecedented in modern baseball. The World Series was played in every year from 1904 to 1993, despite World War I, the Great Depression, and World War II. All of these truly significant events in American history could not accomplish what the owners and players in Major League Baseball wrought in the fall of 1994.

In contrast to the obvious pattern for all other work stoppages, the 1994–95 labor dispute appears to have had an impact on attendance. In 1993 the average team attracted 2.51 million fans. The next complete season was 1996. For that season average attendance was only 2.15 million. In fact, the 2.51 million peak in 1993 is a record that still stands as we write in 2005. Clearly the evidence suggests that the strike of 1994–95 mattered.

Actually this view depends upon how one regards the 1993 peak. Our analysis has not focused on attendance in one or two years, but rather we have considered a substantial portion of attendance history. Such an approach allows one to put attendance in any one year into some perspective.

To illustrate, consider attendance in the early 1990s. In 1991 baseball set a record for attendance when teams averaged 2.19 million fans. In 1992 there was a bit of a decline from this high, but the 2.15 million per team still was the second highest in baseball history. The next season, though, attendance spiked 16.5%. The increase observed for 1993 was the largest increase in baseball since the late 1940s. We saw earlier that the increase observed in the late 1940s was not permanent. It took nearly 30 years for baseball to match the attendance observed for 1948. Is there reason to believe the 1993 peak was the beginning of a new higher trend in baseball attendance history?

Actually, there is reason to believe that the 1993 increase was not likely to be permanent. Let us begin with the Colorado Rockies and Florida Marlins, the two expansion teams from that season. These two teams attracted nearly 7.5 million fans, a total that accounted for more than half of the observed increase in baseball attendance. The Rockies, playing in Mile High Stadium—home of the Denver Broncos—set a major league attendance record in their debut year with more than 4.4 million fans. Was the expansion effect permanent? The answer appears to be no. While the Colorado Rockies became the youngest expansion team to make the playoffs in 1995 and the Florida Marlins became the youngest expansion team to win the World Series in 1997, neither team has come within 600,000 of their 1993 levels.[17] It would seem more likely that the record levels had more to do with the novelty of the new teams and with the Rockies playing in a stadium best suited for football.

The impact of football stadiums was not restricted to the Rockies. The top teams in baseball in 1993, Atlanta, Philadelphia, San Francisco, and Toronto, all shared a stadium with a football team. Toronto by itself topped four million fans in 1993. In essence, 1993 was a perfect storm, in a positive sense, for Major League Baseball attendance: two expansion teams opened in markets starved for baseball along with the best teams playing in very large stadiums.

By 1996 the perfect storm seems to have passed. Attendance in 1996 was 2.15 million. As our intervention analysis indicates, this is similar to what we observe for 1992. Again, 1992 was a very good year in the history of baseball attendance. If you wanted to argue that the 1994–95 strike devastated the game, you would have to argue that baseball was struggling in 1992 when attendance was quite near base-ball's all-time high.

To hammer home this point, consider one last piece of evidence. Population since 1980 in the United States and Canada has grown approximately 30%. In this same time period, average attendance for Major League Baseball teams grew from 1.65 million in 1980 to 2.43 million in 2004. A bit of quick math reveals that this represents a 47% increase. Despite repeated labor disputes people are coming out to the ballpark in much greater numbers.[18] Given these numbers it is hard to believe the conventional wisdom that the repeated fights between owners and players dramatically harm professional sports.

Although we can go back and forth on the 1994–95 experience, we should not lose sight of the larger picture the data are telling. In our study of the NBA, NHL, NFL, and the 1981 strike in baseball, the data speak clearly. Again, we began this research believing that fans did respond negatively to strikes and lockouts. Despite our prior belief, we go where the data take us. And the data clearly take us to a very different answer. Consumers of sport may publicly talk, but the data show no evidence that many fans choose to walk.

A FEW LINGERING QUESTIONS

Our analysis of the impact of strikes and lockouts on attendance leaves a few unanswered questions. We would begin by noting that the data we examine are not entirely obscure. Anyone who sat down and looked would come to similar conclusions. Yet the words of the media and the fans are inconsistent with the observed behavior of fans. We believe such inconsistencies can be explained via the answers to the following questions.

Why do the media tell us that labor disputes threaten the survival of sports in America? We cannot provide a definitive answer, but we can offer a bit of speculation. We would imagine that people choose to write about sports because they are interested in sports. A person who is interested in sports wants to talk about the games and personalities that make sports so fun. When a strike or lockout occurs these games are taken away. To make matters worse, sports writers are then asked to cover the labor dispute. So not only are sports writers not able to talk about the games they love, now they have to talk about the business of sports. When this happens, a person who loves sports must be quite unhappy. From the perspective of these writers, these labor disputes are clearly a tragedy. Labor disputes force writers to stop talking about what they love and start talking about salary caps and revenue sharing, which must be topics that leave much to be desired.

Why do the fans return when the players return? Some have said that fans are but sheep,[19] unable to stand up for the rights to baseball, hot dogs, and Cracker Jacks; rights that have to be spelled out somewhere in the Constitution. As we said, we are only speculating. We suspect, though, that fans come back because *fans like sports.* Yes, we realize this is a novel proposition. Fans keep coming back for the same reason fans were there before the players walked. Fans of sports like sports. If they liked sports before the players walked, we suspect, these same people liked sports when the players returned.

Of course some people will tell us that they personally did not come back. So, for these people, strikes and lockouts matter. One must remember, though, that we are looking at the big picture. Although it is tempting to draw inferences from our own personal experiences, if one truly wishes to understand the world we observe we must move beyond our own lives. In the words of statisticians everywhere, a person can't draw inferences from his or her life, which is just a sample of one.

Why do fans tell us that they will not return when strikes and lockouts occur? We must remember that we are academics. With that in mind, let's get all academic for a moment. We have seen that millions of fans attend sporting events each year. As economists, we generally argue that people take actions when the perceived benefits exceed the perceived costs. Given this basic axiom, we would argue that fans attend games because the benefits the fans get from attending the game exceed the costs in money and time spent. If this were not the case, people would just stay home. So, as economists, we would say that attending a game provides positive net benefits.

Now when labor disputes occur, all these future net benefits are threatened. In other words, we suspect that when these games are taken away, people who were going to attend these games are now worse off. How can fans prevent this loss of happiness? When the fans tell the players and owners that they will not return after a strike or lockout, these fans are now threatening the future benefits players and owners derive from sports. In other words, the threat to stay home threatens the wages and profits players and owners plan to earn in the future. Without resorting to legal action, the threat to walk is the only recourse for fans who wish to continue the flow of games they have grown to know and love.

Okay, so the fans are making a threat. Is this threat credible? Well, actually it's not. The fans are basically saying that if the players and owners do not settle today, in the future fans will forgo the pleasure they derive from sports. Fans are really saying, "if you don't do as I wish today, I will hurt myself tomorrow." This is very much like a child who doesn't get his way promising to hold his breath until he turns blue. Given the obvious love many fans have for sports, the promise of retribution tomorrow can't be believed. This last statement leads to one final question in our discussion.

Why do fans like sports? There are probably many answers to this question. One that we have focused on in our research is uncertainty of outcomes. Sports are perhaps the only entertainment option where the outcome is truly unknown when the event begins. Think about movies for a moment. When you went to see *Star Wars*, did you think Luke Skywalker would lose and the Dark side of the Force would ultimately prevail in the galaxy? Or in the *Lord of the Rings*, did you think the Dark Lord would win and the all the cute little hobbits would be crushed? Basically a character in a movie associated with "darkness" is not looking at a happy ending. And if you go see the same movie twice? Well, the ending is the same both times. And still people enjoy seeing the same movie over and over again. Although we can occasionally be surprised by a new movie, uncertainty of outcome is not the hallmark of these entertainment choices.

Sports are quite different. In 2004 the Yankees once again played the Red Sox in the post-season. People who know the history between these two teams were not surprised to see the Yankees win the first three games of the series. Still, although game four was in a sense a rerun—same teams, mostly the same players—the outcome of game four was in doubt. When the Red Sox won game four, and then five, six, and seven, history was made. At the time, this event captured the attention of baseball fans around the nation.

Why was this story so compelling? Boston's comeback was unexpected and not known before it happened. It is the fact that we do not know the final outcome that attracts us to the event. We can see this most clearly by the dismal ratings ESPN Classic earns from showing reruns of the greatest contests in sports history.[20] If ESPN Classic showed each game of the Yankee–Red Sox series its ratings would be merely a fraction of what we observed when these games were televised live. Although ESPN Classic is showing the greatest sporting events in history, relatively few people tune to this channel because the main attraction sports has for the fan has been taken away.

The subject of uncertain outcomes takes us to our next subject. Many believe that in baseball the lifeblood of the sport is being threatened by the increasing difference between the teams that have and those that have not. If the Yankees simply buy the championship every year, why should anyone want to watch? The answer to this question depends upon the answer to this query: Can a baseball team simply buy the fans' love?

3 | CAN YOU BUY THE FAN'S LOVE?

In 1752 the English philosopher David Hume wrote the following in the midst of an academic discussion of England's foreign trade: "Our jealousy and our hatred of France are without bounds; and the former sentiment, at least, must be acknowledged reasonable and well-grounded."[1] We mention this quote, not because we share Hume's feelings about France. It's also not because we wish to draw a connection between the work of David Hume and the career of Tom Hume, the relief pitcher with the Reds and Phillies from 1977 to 1987. No, we mention this quote because we are about to note that, like David Hume, we are not always dispassionate academics objectively observing the world without emotion. In fact, each of us has felt the pangs of hatred. What is the object of our hatred? Before we answer this question, let's look at Major League Baseball in the years following the 1994–95 player strike.

ARE THE YANKEES GOOD FOR BASEBALL?

In 1996 baseball players came to work every day. After the strike shortened the 1994 and 1995 seasons, happy days were here again. Unfortunately something else returned with the players. In 1996 America once again had to hear "The New York Yankees are World Champions."

To understand the problem many Americans have with this statement, let's briefly review the history of the New York Yankees. Before the arrival of Babe Ruth, the Yankees never appeared in a World Series. Beginning in 1921, though, the Yankees began an era of domination unmatched in Major League Baseball history. Let's take a decade-by-decade view of what the Yankees did from 1921 to 1964.

- In the 1920s the Yankees won the American League pennant six times, resulting in three World Series titles.
- In the 1930s the Yankees moved beyond the era of Ruth, yet still captured the World Series on five different occasions.
- In the 1940s the Yankees were defeated in the World Series once, yet still won the title four other times. The crown in 1949 was the first of five consecutive World Series titles, an accomplishment unmatched in baseball history.
- In the 1950s the Yankees record in World Series play was six wins versus two losses.
- From 1960 to 1964 the Yankees again won five consecutive American League titles, but fortunately for those who had grown to dislike the Yankees, they were only able to capture the World Series title twice.

In sum, from 1921 to 1964 the Yankees won the American League pennant 29 times, while all other American League teams only finished first on 15 occasions. These 29 pennants resulted in 20 World Series titles. If we look at the 40 years beginning in 1923 to 1962, the record in the World Series is Yankees 20, every other team in North America 20. For 40 years you could bet on the World Series champion before the season began, and if you took the Yankees against the rest of baseball you would have an even chance of winning the bet.

After 1964 the domination of the Yankees was stopped briefly. For eleven seasons teams other than the Yankees won the American League pennant. Then in 1976, the Yankees again returned to post-season play. After losing to Cincinnati's Big Red machine in the 1976 classic, the Yankees won the World Series in both 1977 and 1978. Again, though, the Yankees' winning ways were stopped. In 1981 the Yankees appeared in the World Series but lost. It was not until 1996 that they were again crowned champions of baseball. For Donnie Baseball—Don Mattingly—whose stellar career corresponded exactly with this drought, the failure of the Yankees to appear in the World Series from 1982 to 1995 was probably a source of some sadness. For many Americans, though, the Yankees failure to win for two decades was a welcome respite. Unfortunately, all good things must come to an end; and in 1996, the Yankees won once again. And then, to the chagrin of many, it happened again in 1998, 1999, and 2000.

As you may have guessed, like many, many Americans, the object of our hatred that we noted at the onset of this chapter is the New York Yankees. Berri grew up in Detroit and remains to this day a fan of the Tigers. The Tigers last won a title in 1984, after capturing the crown in 1935, 1945, and 1968. Schmidt grew up in Tucson and given no geographic preference chose at the age of six the Boston Red Sox.

The Red Sox won the World Series in 1912, 1915, 1916, 1918, and then under "the curse" failed to win again until 2004. Brook was born near Philadelphia. The Philadelphia Phillies' only title in its history occurred in 1980. In sum, the three franchises we follow have won only ten titles in the past century. The Yankees in their history have won 26 times. Hence, for many Americans, life seems a bit unfair when the Yankees win yet another championship.

When the Yankees began winning again in 1996 we were not alone in our unhappiness. After the Yankees won four of five World Series titles in the late 1990s, the alarm bells were ringing. Writers began to claim that baseball was in trouble. The problem people claimed was not with the Yankees winning, but how it was perceived the Yankees had achieved their success. In 1996, 1999, and 2000 the Yankees had the highest payroll in baseball and won the World Series. In 1998 the Yankees took the on-field title while finishing second in the payroll rankings.

The Yankees were not the only team to exhibit an apparent link between payroll and success. Bob Costas summarized the evidence in *Fair Ball: A Fan's Case for Baseball*. Writing after the 1999 season, Costas made the following observation: "The numbers tell the true story: Since the strike . . . teams in the top half of payrolls won 24 post-season series. Teams in the bottom half won precisely zero. I'm no sabermetrician, but I think I've spotted a trend here" (p. 185).

Costas is an Emmy award-winning broadcaster. Few announcers can match his skill in the booth. Unfortunately, the skills necessary to call games may not be the same as the skill necessary to statistically analyze trends in sport. Costas, though, is not alone in his observation. Andrew Zimbalist, a Harvard trained economist and author of several wonderful books on the economics of sports, made a similar observation in the foreword to the Costas book: "[C]ompetition on the playing field has become acutely imbalanced. Since 1995 only three out of 189 postseason games have been won by teams in the bottom half of payrolls. That is, these teams have less than 1 chance in 50 in qualifying for and then winning a postseason game" (p. xiiii).

The observations of Costas and Zimbalist were also reached by Major League Baseball. In July 2000, MLB published "The Report of the Independent Members of the Commissioner's Blue Ribbon Panel on Baseball Economics." The Commissioner's Blue Ribbon Panel on Baseball Economics was convened by MLB in 1999 to investigate the issues of competitive balance and economic health. Specifically, the panel's stated purpose was to "examine the question of whether Baseball's current economic system has created a problem of competitive imbalance in the game" (Levin et al., 2002, p. 59).

The panel consisted of Yale president Richard C. Levin, former Federal Reserve

TABLE 3.1

Linking Payroll to Post-Season Success in Major League Baseball: 1995–1999

	Percentage of World Series Games Won, 1995–99	Percentage of Division and League Championship Games Won, 1995–99
Payroll Quartile I	100.0	81.7
Payroll Quartile II	0	18.3
Payroll Quartile III	0	0
Payroll Quartile IV	0	0

chairman Paul Volcker, former Senator George Mitchell, and columnist George Will. These four smart and accomplished individuals noted the following:

> [F]rom 1995 through 1999, a total of 158 postseason games were played. For analytical purposes, it is useful to divide the clubs into "quartiles" by ranking them (based on payroll) from high to low and separating the clubs into four equal size groups. For example in 1995, the seven clubs with the highest payrolls would constitute Quartile I. During this five year period, no club from payroll Quartiles III or IV won a DS or LCS game, and no club from payroll Quartiles II, III or IV won a World Series game. (p. i)

Table 3.1 summarizes the observations of Costas, Zimbalist, and the Blue Ribbon Panel. As noted, the teams in the top of the payroll rankings won 100% of the World Series games from 1995 to 1999.[2] Of Division and League Championship Games, teams at the top won 81.7% of these contests.

Such evidence appears fairly compelling. We are clearly led to believe that Major League Baseball teams must pay to play in the post-season. Furthermore, given the success of the Yankees, it looks like those who pay the most get to win the most. Consequently, we don't really need to play baseball anymore. All we need to do is look at each team's payroll and we know who is ultimately going to win.

What does this mean for baseball? Again we turn to the words of Costas, Zimbalist, and the Blue Ribbon Panel. Costas observed the following: "The fact is, the single biggest indicator of a team's opportunity for success from one year to the next is whether that team has a payroll among the top few teams in the league. Period" (p. 58).

Employing some basic regression analysis, Zimbalist appeared to confirm the Costas contention: "the correlation between team win percentage and team payroll has been significant at the highest statistical level every year between 1995 and 2000—and not significant at this level in any year between 1985 and 1994" (p. xv).

The Blue Ribbon panel did not need regression analysis to reach basically the same conclusion. The panel began by noting the significant disparities that existed in MLB team payrolls. For example, for the 2000 season the salary of the highest paid player in MLB exceeded the entire payroll of the Minnesota Twins.[3] According to the panel, such differences in payrolls have allowed a collection of teams to consistently field playoff-contending teams, while other teams, located in what the panel considers smaller markets, are incapable of fielding teams that can challenge for post-season success. Consequently, consistent with the comments of Bob Costas, the panel argued that for a number of MLB teams the outcome of the season is known before the season is started.

Having concluded that a problem existed, the panel proceeded to offer the following solutions to baseball's competitive imbalance.

1. Baseball should increase revenue sharing. Currently each team shares a limited portion of its local revenues, the biggest of these being television and radio broadcast rights. The panel recommended that MLB increase this to between 40 and 50% of these local revenues.

2. Baseball should impose a competitive balance tax. The tax would impose a 50% tax on payrolls above $84 million. In addition, the report suggested that teams should be encouraged to set their payrolls to be at least $40 million. The panel further recommended the creation of a central fund which would be used to redistribute the monies, from revenue sharing and the competitive balance tax, in an unequal fashion so as to assist low-revenue clubs when needed.

3. Baseball should change the rules of the amateur draft. For example, the panel recommended that foreign players be subject to the draft and that teams maintain the rights to draftees beyond the one-year period they currently hold. Many of the players who helped the Yankees regain prominence in the late 1990s were foreign-born players, not subject to baseball's annual amateur draft.

4. Baseball should hold an annual "competitive balance draft" where the eight clubs with the worst records could draft players not on the 40-man roster of the eight playoff teams.

5. Baseball should allow teams to relocate from smaller markets to cities where teams could generate greater revenues.

What do all these ideas have in common? These recommendations would allow teams in smaller markets like Milwaukee, Kansas City, and Minnesota to increase their revenue while causing the fortunes of teams like the New York Yankees to decline. Now, given our feelings for the Yankees we are not necessarily opposed to these ideas. Of course, the punishment is only necessary if a crime has truly been committed.

IS IT REALLY A BLUE RIBBON PANEL?

We were not happy to watch the Yankees win four times in five years. Still, the re-action to the Yankees' success, and the success of other high payroll teams in the late 1990s may not necessarily lead to the conclusions of Costas, Zimbalist, and the Commissioner's Panel. In fact, when we review the analysis offered by the latter, we may want to reassess if this was truly a panel worthy of a blue ribbon.

The Independence of the Blue Ribbon Panel

Our critique of the Blue Ribbon Panel begins with the title of the report: "The Re-port of the Independent Members of the Commissioner's Blue Ribbon Panel on Baseball Economics." Were these members truly independent? Levin drafted the owners' 1989 salary cap proposal, Volcker represented the owners on the last blue-ribbon economic panel (1992), Mitchell has often been mentioned as a possible Commissioner, and Will has sat on the board of both the Orioles and the Padres.' In sum, each of these "independent" voices can be linked to the owners.

Of course, Commissioner Bud Selig is also closely tied to the owners. Although the commissioner of baseball has always been paid by the owners, in the past the commissioner was able to occasionally act independently of owners. In fact, Com-missioner Fay Vincent's unwillingness to follow the dictates of baseball's owners led to the current reign of Selig. In 1992 Bud Selig came to the job of "acting com-missioner" after the resignation of Vincent, a move that was prompted by the own-ers giving Vincent a vote of no confidence. Before becoming commissioner, Selig was owner of the Milwaukee Brewers. Consequently, unlike past commissioners, it is quite difficult for Selig to distance himself from those who own the teams.

Selig's experience as owner also appears to impact his views regarding the level of competitive balance in Major League Baseball. In 1969 Selig purchased the Seat-tle Pilots and promptly moved the team to his home town of Milwaukee. From 1970 to 2004 Selig, or a member of his family, owned the team. Over this time pe-riod the Brewers were not exactly a success on the field. The average winning per-centage for the Brewers for these 35 seasons was 0.473. For 24, or nearly 70% of these seasons, the Brewers had a losing record. Although the Brewers did partici-pate in the post-season in 1981 and 1982, appearing in the World Series in the lat-ter campaign, Milwaukee has not often come close to contention in the American League.

How can Selig explain this lack of success? He could argue that he and the peo-ple who manage the Brewers have made a number of poor decisions regarding player personnel and coaching talent. Due to these decisions, the Brewers have not been as successful as Selig and the Brewers fans would like. Or Selig could argue that the game was rigged against small market teams like Milwaukee. Because Milwaukee plays in a small market its revenues lag behind teams like the New York Yankees. Without sufficient revenues, Milwaukee cannot afford the best talent in baseball. Consequently, Milwaukee cannot put a competitive team on the field.

Given a choice between these arguments, Selig appears to choose the latter. It is not his fault the Brewers have failed to compete. Given the current economics of baseball, a team located in a town like Milwaukee cannot expect to win championships. Of course we would note that Selig chose to place his team in Milwaukee. When he bought the team it was located in Seattle. Previously we saw that the Blue Ribbon Panel defined market size in terms of payroll. Although we will discuss the validity of this definition a bit more below, in terms of payroll Seattle would be thought of as one of baseball's top-ten markets in 1996, 1998, 2002, and 2003. If the Blue Ribbon Panel is correct that market size should be defined in terms of payroll, then Selig's first move as owner of the Brewers was to take his team from a relatively large market—or at least a potentially large market—and place the team in a relatively small market.

After years of little success in a relatively small market, Selig has campaigned as commissioner to alter the structure of baseball so that teams located in smaller markets have greater access to the revenues generated in New York. The arguments Selig has often offered about competitive balance appear to be echoed in the work of the Blue Ribbon Panel. And so we have a commissioner who is motivated to believe small market teams need to receive revenues from teams in larger markets. He then forms a panel that offers a report making the very same arguments. All in all, this seems a bit suspect.

Of course, noting a person's motives does not necessarily refute a person's arguments. Although we believe Selig has an incentive to believe the Yankees are why the Brewers can't seem to win each year and, furthermore, we believe that those working for the commissioner have an incentive to tell him what he wishes to hear, these motives are not relevant in evaluating their arguments. It is entirely possible that Selig is motivated to believe the economics of baseball are rigged against his Brewers and for this to be true.

We mention the issue of motives to a make a point about how arguments are often evaluated. Politicians often cite motives, rather than argument, in refuting the claims of an opposing person or group. An environmental group argues that a policy will damage the environment. Rather than take the time to assess the validity of this argument, proponents of the policy in question attack the motives of the environmentalists. A conservative think tank argues for a policy of less government involvement in the economy. Again, rather than assess the validity of the argument, people note the motivations of conservatives. Such an argument is simple laziness. Noting that a person is motivated to make an argument does not refute the content of the argument.[4] If you wish to refute an argument, you need to work a bit harder.

Different Samples Yield Different Conclusions

Our substantive critique follows and builds upon our work—Schmidt and Berri—in a 2002 article published in the *Review of Industrial Organization*. This critique begins with the sample the Blue Ribbon Panel considered. In Table 3.2 we have replicated the analysis of the panel using data from the five years before the Blue Ribbon years, specifically the 1989–93 seasons. Over this time period, teams in the third payroll quartile won the most World Series games. Such a result suggests that payroll and on-field success are not necessarily linked.

Of course Costas and Zimbalist have already observed that payroll and wins were not linked before the 1994–95 strike. So Table 3.2 does not refute their arguments. What about Table 3.3? In this table we again replicate the Blue Ribbon Panel analysis, but this time we look at the five seasons after the Blue Ribbon years, or the 2000–04 seasons.

From Table 3.3 we see teams toward the bottom of the payroll rankings finding success in the post-season. Thirty teams participate in Major League Baseball today. In 2001, Arizona was ranked eighth in payroll yet won the World Series. In 2002 the Anaheim Angels[5] were ranked fifteenth and won the fall classic. In 2003 the Florida Marlins won the World Series with a payroll that ranked 25th out of 30 teams. The Red Sox did end the curse in 2004 with the second highest payroll in baseball. The next season after our 2000–04 sample ends, though, again offered evidence that the link between payroll and playoff success is not very strong. In 2005 the White Sox took the title with a payroll that only ranked thirteenth in baseball. So the six years following the Blue Ribbon Panel years hardly suggest that payroll dictates ultimate success.

One should note that over the years examined in Table 3.3 payroll disparity actually increased. To see this, for each team we calculated relative payroll, or the team's payroll in a given season divided by the average league payroll that season. For example, in 2004 the average payroll in Major League Baseball was $69 million. The New York Yankees had a payroll of $184 million, so compared to the average team the Yankees had a payroll 2.67 times larger. We examined the years 1988 to 2004, and this was easily the highest relative payroll we observed. The next high-

TABLE 3.2

Linking Payroll to Post-Season Success in Major League Baseball: 1989–1993

	Percentage of World Series Games Won, 1989–93	Percentage of Division and League Championship Games Won, 1989–93
Payroll Quartile I	29.6	22.8
Payroll Quartile II	22.2	38.6
Payroll Quartile III	48.1	38.6
Payroll Quartile IV	0	0

TABLE 3.3

Linking Payroll to Post-Season Success in Major League Baseball: 2000–2004

	Percentage of World Series Games Won, 2000–04	Percentage of Division and League Championship Games Won, 2000–04
Payroll Quartile I	62.1	46.5
Payroll Quartile II	24.1	39.4
Payroll Quartile III	0	3.5
Payroll Quartile IV	13.8	10.6

est figure was 2.15, posted by the 2003 New York Yankees. This exceeded the previous best figure of 1.85, which we observe for the 2002 New York Yankees.

You might be spotting a trend. And this trend continued in 2005. For the 2005 campaign, the Yankees' payroll was 2.85 times the average. From 2002 to 2005 the Yankees kept increasing their payroll relative to the average. Overall in the league, the disparity in relative payroll was increasing in the first decade of the new millennium. Yet the team at the top of the increasingly larger payroll volcano actually achieved less post-season success. According to the Blue Ribbon Panel, though, the spending spree by the Yankees should have rendered baseball's post-season a foregone conclusion. This point needs to be emphasized. From 2002 to 2005 the Yankees spent like never before. And after all this spending, not a single title did they buy.

For Samples, Size Matters

Does Table 3.3 and the very recent history of the New York Yankees adequately refute the Blue Ribbon Panel? Actually, the evidence reported so far does not end the debate. A problem with Tables 3.1, 3.2, and 3.3, and also our brief discussion of the Yankees, is sample size. In analyzing data, size definitely matters. Statistical analysis is all about drawing inferences about a population from a sample. The larger the sample, the better the picture of the population you paint. Costas, Zimbalist, and the Blue Ribbon Panel all reached their conclusions based on only a few years of data.

Costas seemed to recognize this problem in 2003. In 2002 the Angels won the

World Series with a relatively modest payroll. According to Costas, some people took this one observation as evidence that payroll did not ultimately determine success in baseball. Given this argument, Costas asked, "How is it, then, that the selective results of one season *prove* a point, but the overwhelming evidence of the preceding seven years is a mirage?"[6] From this we see that Costas clearly understands that sample size matters. Unfortunately he did not see that seven years' worth of data is also not an adequate sample.

Playoffs Are for Fun, Not for Science

The issue of sample size leads directly to the next critique we offer of the Blue Ribbon Panel's report. The Panel, as well as Costas and Zimbalist, focused exclusively on post-season outcomes. Does post-season success tell us much about differences in team quality?

Before answering the question, consider the 2001 season. In 2001 the Seattle Mariners won 116 regular season games. The Mariners' winning percentage of 0.716 was the best seen in baseball since the Cleveland Indians posted a winning percentage of 0.721 in 1954. After dispatching the 2001 version of the Cleveland Indians in the first round of the playoffs, the Mariners faced the New York Yankees. Now the Yankees only won 95 games in 2001. After five playoff games, though, the Mariners had lost four and were sent home. The Yankees advanced, ultimately losing in a thrilling seven game World Series to the Arizona Diamondbacks.

Who was the better team in 2001, the Mariners or the Yankees? To answer this question we have two samples. Over 162 games the Mariners were clearly better than the Yankees. Over five games, the Yankees were better. Which sample should we believe? If we are the Blue Ribbon Panel, apparently we should take a sample with five observations.

To illustrate the problem with the post-season, consider the success of the Oakland A's from 1999 to 2004. Over this time period the Oakland A's won more regular season games than every franchise except the Yankees and Atlanta Braves. Both the Yankees and Braves consistently placed toward the top of baseball's payroll rankings. Oakland, in contrast, often ranked in the bottom five. Despite this handicap, the A's were consistently successful.

The architect of the A's success was Billy Beane, the general manager profiled by Michael Lewis (2003) in *Moneyball*, a book we mentioned in Chapter One. As Lewis argues, Beane achieved regular season success because he had a better understanding of statistics. Previously we observed that *Moneyball* is a collection of anecdotes detailing how one team can employ statistical analysis to produce more wins than one would suspect given a team's payroll.

The A's ability to produce wins was strictly confined to the regular season. From 2000 to 2003 Oakland reached a deciding fifth game in the first round of the play-offs. All four years Oakland lost this game. Lewis was able to make the following observation of Beane during Oakland's 2002 loss to the Minnesota Twins:

> Billy Beane had been surprisingly calm throughout his team's playoff debacle. Before the second game against the Twins, when I'd asked him why he seemed so detached— why he wasn't walking around the parking lot with his white box—he said, "My s—t doesn't work in the play-offs. My job is to get us to the play-offs. What happens after that is f—king luck. . . . Billy's attitude seemed to be, all that management can produce is a team good enough to triumph in a long season. There are no secret recipes for the postseason, except maybe having three great starting pitchers, and he had that. (pp. 274–75)

What Billy Bean notes is nothing new. In Alan Schwarz's (2004) work, recounting the history of numbers in baseball, he reviews a paper by Harvard statistician Frederick Mosteller, published in 1952 in the *Journal of the American Statistical Association*. As Schwarz summarized: "Mosteller questioned whether a best-of-seven series was an adequate way to decide which team was better—and in fact, through 25 pages of binomial probability theory, he proved it to be quite unreliable" (p. 75).

As Beane suspects, and Mosteller's analysis confirms, the playoffs are designed for fun, not for science. Consequently, we should not look at post-season outcomes and then make inferences about the level of competitive balance in baseball. We will discuss the measurement of competitive balance in Chapter Four. Before we turn to that subject, though, we have additional problems with the Blue Ribbon Panel.

Size of Payrolls Is Not Equal to Size of Markets

The story told by the Blue Ribbon Panel is that teams in larger markets have an advantage in baseball. How did the panel measure market size? The choice of metrics was size of payroll. This seems to be an odd choice. Market size is typically a reference to the number of people in a specific geographic area. New York City is considered a larger market than Milwaukee because more people live in and around New York City. Likewise, Milwaukee is a small market because of a relative lack of people living in and around Milwaukee.

Implicitly the Blue Ribbon Panel appeared to be arguing that market size, defined in terms of population, should be linked to payrolls. Basically the sequence works as follows:

- Teams located in larger markets like New York and Los Angeles have a larger potential fan base.
- Consequently, these teams can both attract more fans, and because stadiums have a finite size, possibly charge higher ticket prices for the relatively scarce tickets the teams sell. Such larger markets can also be used to secure greater broadcast revenues.
- Each of these events leads to more revenue, and these greater revenues allow a team to afford larger payrolls.
- If larger payrolls are used to acquire better players, then there should be a clear link between payrolls and wins.

We will examine the link between wins and payroll momentarily. For now, let's consider the link between market size, measured traditionally with population, and wins. Our analysis requires some context. So before we examine baseball in the post–1994–95 strike era, let's first consider three alternative data sets: The NFL from 1995 to 2004, the NBA from 1995 to 2004, and Major League Baseball from 1985 to 1994.[7]

With data in hand we examined the link between population and wins for each sport. Specifically, we simply regressed each team's average regular season winning percentage across the noted time periods upon the population in each team's host city. The results indicate that population and wins in each data set are not statistically related. Market size, as it is classically defined, does not determine winning percentage in each of these three data sets.

When we examined the post–1994–95 strike era in Major League Baseball, a different result was uncovered. Although the level of significance was relatively low,[8] population could be said to be statistically significant after 1995 in baseball. The model, though, only explained 11% of wins. So population alone does not explain much of the variation of wins.

Beyond the issue of how much, there appears to be one outlier in the post-strike data set. Our finding of a statistically significant link between wins and population appears to depend entirely on the New York Yankees. If the Yankees are dropped from the sample the statistical relationship between wins and population vanishes.[9]

You Can't Buy Love in Major League Baseball

The Blue Ribbon Panel, though, argued that market size was not defined by population but by payroll. Such a definition implies that in 1998 Baltimore, Seattle, Cleveland, and Atlanta were bigger market teams than the Los Angeles Dodgers or Chicago White Sox. Although we think defining market size in terms of payroll is not entirely sensible, let's proceed as if this really made sense and examine the link between payroll and wins.

We will begin with the analysis of Andrew Zimbalist, who looked at this issue by regressing payroll on wins for each season from 1980 to 2001. Zimbalist's analysis shows that wins and payroll were not statistically linked prior to the 1994–95 strike. After the strike, though, wins and payroll became statistically linked. For Zimbalist, this appears to be the smoking gun.

At this point we must return to the issue of "how much." Allow us to get all academic again. For just a moment let's consider the difference between statistical significance and economic significance. This is a point made repeatedly in the work of economist Deirdre McCloskey (1996, 1998, 2002).[10] According to McCloskey, economists tend to worship at the altar of statistical significance. Upon finding two variables linked statistically, the mind of many economists seems to shut down and further thinking just doesn't seem possible.[11]

McCloskey has argued repeatedly that statistical significance is not the only story we should tell when we conduct empirical studies. Statistical significance might tell us if a relationship exists or not, but it cannot tell us whether the relationship is actually important. As McCloskey (2002, pp. 54–55) states:

> My argument is not against statistics in empirical work. . . . It is against certain very particular and peculiar practices of economic science and a few other fields. Economics has fallen for . . . significant/insignificant "results" in "empirical work." [Economists] are looking for on/off findings that do not require any tiresome inquiry into How Much, how big is big, what is an important variable, How Much exactly is its oomph.

So for McCloskey the key is "oomph." Let us go back to the work of Zimbalist and look for a bit of oomph. Again, Zimbalist found that in the post–1994–95 strike era, payroll and wins in baseball were statistically related. So if we know payroll, do we now know wins? Again we repeat the argument of Costas: "The fact is, the single biggest indicator of a team's opportunity for success from one year to the next is whether that team has a payroll among the top few teams in the league. Period" (2000, p. 58).

Unfortunately, the statistical relationship we see between payroll and wins doesn't seem to confirm the argument advanced by Costas. To see this point we followed the methodology employed by Stefan Szymanski (2003), whom we mentioned in Chapter One. Specifically we regressed wins on relative payroll in baseball from 1988 to 2005. We then repeated this regression for 1988 to 1994, 1995 to 1999, and 2000 and 2005. What do we learn from this exercise? Our answer is reported in Table 3.4.

TABLE 3.4

The Relationship Between Wins and Relative Payroll in Major League Baseball: 1988 to 2005

Time Period	Percentage of Wins Explained by Relative Payroll
1988 to 2005	*17.6*
1988 to 1994	6.2
1995 to 1999	32.5
2000 to 2005	17.6

If we look at the entire time period—1988 to 2005—we see that payroll explains about 18% of wins. In other words, more than 80% of wins are not explained by payroll. Of course, Costas and Zimbalist argued that it is in the post-strike era that the relationship between payroll and wins changed. Our analysis confirms that a change did take place. If we examine 1988 to 1994 we see that only 6% of wins are explained by team payroll. When we look at the Blue Ribbon years (1995–99) we see that payroll explains about 33% of wins. In the six years that follow (2000–05), though, the explanatory power declines to 18%.

So although payroll and wins have a stronger relationship during Blue Ribbon years, it is still the case that for these years about two-thirds of wins cannot be explained by payroll. In the years that follow this time period, the explanatory power is back to 18%, which is what we saw for 1988 to 2005.

We can go a bit beyond this point in our search for oomph. Although we will leave the statistical details for our web site, we will note that our analysis indicates that a team adding a $10 million player in 2005 can expect less than two additional wins.[12] That's all the bang a team would get for their buck—or in this case, many, many bucks. A team would have to add several $10 million players before they could expect to see any real progress in the standings.

There is one more point on these results that we can make, and this actually comes from Zimbalist. Even if we had established that wins and payroll have a strong relationship, it is not clear in which direction the relationship flows. Does increasing payroll allow a team to win more games? Or is it the case that as a team wins more games, its revenue increases, and therefore it is able to afford a larger payroll? Zimbalist argues that during the Blue Ribbon Panel years the causality actually ran in both directions.[13]

We see the analysis offered by the Blue Ribbon Panel is far from perfect. Here were the basic problems we uncovered.

- The sample size (1995–99) was too small to reach definitive conclusions. When we examine the next five seasons (2000–04) the strength of the Panel's conclusions was weakened considerably.
- Competitive balance cannot be measured via a review of playoff outcomes because the playoffs are a sample that is inadequate to support strong conclusions.
- The definition of market size was also problematic. We failed to find a statistical relationship between population, the traditional definition of market size, and wins.
- Although we did find a statistical relationship between payroll, the Blue Ribbon Panel's definition of market size, and wins, the strength of the relationship did not support Costas's contention that payroll was the primary determinant of wins in baseball.

A FEW MORE QUESTIONS

Our critique of the Blue Ribbon Panel still leaves a few questions unanswered. First of all, why doesn't payroll explain more of wins? Additional details on this subject will be offered later. For now, though, we will simply note two issues.

The first is about the age of the free agents teams are buying. A player cannot be a free agent until he has played six years in the Major Leagues. According to a recent working paper by Ray Fair (2005), on average a hitter's performance peaks at 28 years of age. Most free agents are older than 28, so teams that buy many free agents will tend to have high payrolls and rosters stacked with players whose performance is likely to decline. Related to this issue is the ability of teams to predict future performance. We will offer more on this in Chapter Nine. For now, though, we will say that predicting performance in baseball is not easy.

Each of these reasons ignore the *Moneyball* critique, that people in baseball simply cannot identify the most productive players in baseball. Putting all this together, though, it is perhaps not surprising that payroll and wins are not strongly linked.

Does all of this mean that the Yankees are good for baseball? Well, we still hate the Yankees. The arguments offered by the Blue Ribbon Panel, though, do not establish that there is clearly a problem in baseball when the team with the highest payroll over a few seasons manages to win the World Series. Does all of this mean that baseball does not have a competitive balance problem? The answer to this question requires a deeper examination into the theory, measurement, and causes of competitive balance in professional sports.

4 BASEBALL'S COMPETITIVE BALANCE PROBLEM?

In 2002 Major League Baseball experienced yet another labor dispute. The owners, echoing the arguments of the Blue Ribbon Panel, argued that the economics of baseball needed to be changed. Specifically, something would need to be done to control escalating player salaries. The players, understandably, were opposed to the owners' efforts to restrict salary growth.

The owners' argument that the economics of baseball needed to be changed rested solely on one contention: Baseball has a problem with competitive balance. As we detailed in our discussion of the Blue Ribbon Panel report, this contention led Commissioner Selig and the Panel to advocate a variety of policies that would transfer money from the players, and large market teams like the New York Yankees, to teams like the Milwaukee Brewers. All of these policies were designed to combat the problem of competitive imbalance. If the league is not really imbalanced, though, all these policies amount to small market teams getting more money for no reason other than their desire to have more money. Although we can see why people want more money, we are not sure many people would want baseball to stop playing just because owners of teams in places like Milwaukee, who are still relatively rich people, are unhappy with how much money they get from their baseball team.

In the previous chapter we went to some lengths to demonstrate that the arguments offered by the Blue Ribbon Panel did not establish that baseball had a competitive balance problem. Now just because the Panel's analysis was flawed does not necessarily establish that the basic premise was incorrect. To see whether or not baseball has a problem, we need to spend just a bit of time discussing the theory and measurement of competitive balance.

COMPETITIVE BALANCE:
THEORY AND MEASUREMENT

Let's begin with a simple question. Why exactly do we care? Why is competitive balance important? Clearly we think this is important. The team of Schmidt and Berri has so far participated in the writing of at least ten papers exploring various aspects of competitive balance. Certainly we would not spend so much time looking at this if it were not important. Well actually, that may not be entirely true. Much of this work was written when we were untenured assistant professors. We could have simply looked at this issue because we thought it would lead to publications, and we needed publications to advance our careers. Of course, we would not be getting this work published if someone did not think this was important. So why do people think competitive balance is important?

The Theory of Competitive Balance

If we go all the way back to the writings of Adam Smith in the 18th century, economists have consistently trumpeted the virtues of competition. Competition spurs firms to innovate, and innovation leads to economic growth. From the perspective of individual firms, though, profits tend to rise when competition is eliminated. The exception to this rule is professional sports. When a professional sports team eliminates competition, the team also effectively eliminates the primary source of revenue. After all, people pay to see a contest, not an exhibition.

Within the field of sports economics, the idea that the level of competition matters has often been taken as an article of faith. To see this, let's go back to the paper that is generally acknowledged as the first in the field. In 1956 Simon Rottenberg wrote a paper entitled "The Baseball Player's Labor Market." We will discuss this work in some detail below, but for now we will note what Rottenberg had to say about competition. In describing the economics of baseball, Rottenberg observed:

> [T]he nature of the industry is such that competitors must be of approximately equal "size" if any are to be successful. . . . [A] more or less equal distribution of talent is necessary if there is to be uncertainty of outcome; and that uncertainty of outcome is necessary if the consumer is willing to pay admission to the game. (pp. 242, 246)

The words of Rottenberg were echoed in the work of Walter Neale (1964). In discussing the importance of competitive balance, Neale introduced the Louis-Schmelling paradox. For those not versed in boxing history, Joe Louis dominated the heavyweight division from 1937 to 1948. Over this time period Louis was often accused of fighting "the bum of the month" or a fighter who really had no hope of defeating Louis. An exception was Max Schmelling, who first defeated a young Joe Louis in 1936. In 1937, after Louis had taken the heavyweight title from "Cinderella Man" James Braddock, Schmelling and Louis met for a rematch. The fight, between African American Joe Louis and German Max Schmelling had significant geopolitical ramifications. When Louis dropped Schmelling in the first round, more fell than just one more boxer to the fists of Louis. A blow was also landed against the argument that German people, and white people in general, were a master race.

So what does Neale mean by the Louis-Schmelling paradox?

> [C]onsider the position of the heavy-weight champion of the world. He wants to earn more money, to maximize his profits. What does he need in order to do so? Obviously, a contender, and the stronger the contender the larger the profits from fighting him. . . . Pure monopoly is disaster: Joe Louis would have had no one to fight and therefore no income. (pp. 1–2)

The analysis of Neale extends beyond the obvious case of the boxing champion to any professional sport. Again we turn to the writing of those who came before. In 1971, seven years after Neale offered a verbal description of the economics of professional sports, Mohamed El-Hodiri and James Quirk provided the math. As we have done so far, we will skip the math. We offer the following quote from this seminal work:

> [T]he essential economic factor concerning professional team sports is that gate receipts depend crucially on the uncertainty of outcome of the games played within the league. As the probability of either team winning approaches 1, gate receipts fall substantially. Consequently, every team has an economic motive for not becoming "too" superior in playing talent compared with other teams in the league. (p. 1306)

We would note that none of these cited works provide any empirical evidence supporting the claim that uncertainty of outcome, or competitive balance, was a crucial determinant of team attendance or revenue. There are no regressions linking attendance to competitive balance. In fact, later work that looks at this—well, we get ahead of ourselves. For now, let's just say the field of sports economics, without an abundance of empirical evidence, has asserted that competitive balance matters to the survival of a sports league.

The Many Measures of Competitive Balance

If we take as given the proposition that competitive balance is crucial to attendance in professional sports, then Commissioner Selig is correct when he expresses concern over the level of competitive balance in baseball. Of course, even if we believe that competitive balance and attendance are linked, the arguments of Selig, Costas, and the Blue Ribbon Panel still depend upon baseball having a competitive balance problem. Do the data support this claim?

To answer this question we must have a measure of competitive balance. We have already argued that looking at the distribution of playoff wins is not a very good measure. Fortunately, the literature in sports economics provides many, many, many alternatives.[1] In looking at competitive balance you can use terms like Gini Coefficient, Herfindahl-Hirschman, Excess Tail Frequency, and Markov Modeling. To economists, these words conjure up some meaning. For most people, though, a good discussion of each would do little more than ensure a good nap. Fortunately, for our purposes in this current discussion, a simple and accurate alternative to these measures exists.

A Simple Measure of Competitive Balance

For most people the word simple means easy. In academic papers, though, words like simple are often quite deceptive. Often it means, simple for the person writing and incomprehensible to all other people living on the planet. We are hoping for the former definition of the word but we could be wrong.

What do we want in a competitive balance measure? Let's first ask what we are trying to measure. We wish to know the level of competition in the games a league presents. If teams are equal in ability, we can expect a competitive game. On the other hand, if the teams are unequal, games will not be competitive; and following what we learned from the economic theory on this subject, fans should lose interest.

Given all this, how do we measure differences in team quality? The Blue Ribbon Panel looked at playoff wins. As we stated, the playoffs are not a very good sample. A better sample can be found in regular season performance. Now what do we want to do with regular season data? We wish to focus on final league standings. If a league is relatively balanced, then we would expect a little variation in the number of wins for each team. In other words, there would be little difference between the good and bad teams. Of course if a league is not balanced, then we would expect much more variation in the number of victories each team achieves.

To measure this variation we turn to a metric developed in two separate works by economists Roger Noll (1988) and Gerald Scully (1989). Following the lead of Quirk and Fort (1992), we will call this metric the Noll-Scully measure. To calculate the Noll-Scully one simply takes the standard deviation of winning percentage and divides by the idealized standard deviation.[2]

Maybe this is not that simple. Let's briefly explain the elements of the Noll-

Scully. We begin with the standard deviation of winning percentage. Standard deviation[3] tells us how close the observations in our sample are to the average. In terms of sports, the average or mean winning percentage is 0.500. Standard deviation allows us to see how close teams are in general to a 0.500 winning percentage. If the teams in the league are not equal, then the better teams will post a winning percentage well above the mean and the worst teams will be well below 0.500. In this instance, standard deviation will be relatively large. In contrast, if teams are basically equal then winning percentages will tend to cluster around the average and the variation in winning percentage will be relatively small.

Okay, the intuition behind standard deviation seems simple enough—at least to us. Unfortunately, we need a bit more than standard deviation to measure competitive balance. At some point in our discussion of baseball we are going to need to compare what we observe in this sport to what we observe elsewhere. Because different sports play schedules of different lengths, a standard deviation observed in baseball cannot be compared directly to what we observe in a sport like football or basketball.

Fortunately, we can overcome this problem. Specifically we turn back to Noll (1988) and Scully (1989). Each of these authors calculated the idealized standard deviation of winning percentage. The idealized standard deviation measures the distribution of wins that would exist if each team were equal in ability. We will save the details for the endnotes,[4] which we hope you are enjoying as we go along. We will note that the idealized standard deviation depends upon schedule length. The more games a league plays, the smaller will be the idealized standard deviation. So in baseball,[5] the idealized standard deviation is 0.039.

What does 0.039 mean? If baseball teams were equal in ability the probability of each team winning would be one-half. If this was the probability of each team winning we would expect the standard deviation of winning percentage to be 0.039. Compare this result in baseball to what we would see in the NFL. In the NFL teams play sixteen games; consequently the idealized standard deviation is much larger. Specifically in the NFL,[6] if all teams were equal in ability, we would expect the standard deviation of winning percentage to be 0.125.

The Need for "Something Else"

Given a measure of competitive balance we can now answer the question: Does baseball have a competitive balance problem? In other words, we wish to know if the level of competitive balance is currently "good" as opposed to "bad." People often throw terms like good and bad about without noting that for these terms to mean anything you need "something else." For example, we hope that you regard this as a "good" book. If you believe this book is better than other books you have seen, then it would be considered, compared to those other books, "good." Just like the terms "large" and "small," for the terms good and bad to mean anything we need "something else." Specifically, we need a reference point.[7]

If we tell you that the Noll-Scully measure of competitive balance in the American League from 1990 to 2004 averaged 1.82, what have you learned? Well, given how the Noll-Scully is calculated, you know that the actual standard deviation was 1.82 times larger than the ideal standard deviation. Is that good? Is that bad? To see the answer to these questions we need to compare 1.82 to "something else."

We wish to consider two reference points. First, we will examine competitive balance in both the American League and National League from 1900 to 2004. Therefore, the first reference point will be historical values of competitive balance in baseball. The second reference point we will consider is competitive balance in other sports. To understand competitive balance in baseball we need to understand what is possible. And so we need to see the level of balance in sports like soccer, American football,[8] basketball, and hockey.

BALANCING BASEBALL

What do we learn when we analyze competitive balance in Major League Baseball via the Noll-Scully measure? Unlike the Blue Ribbon Panel, we are not going to look at just five seasons. To understand what is happening today, we need to consider the entire history of baseball. This history is presented in Table 4.1, where we note the average level of competitive balance in each decade from 1901 to 2005.[9]

TABLE 4.1

*Competitive Balance in the American and
National League: Decade Averages, 1901–2005*

Decade	American League	National League
1901–09	2.35	3.02
1910–19	2.51	2.18
1920–29	2.24	2.16
1930–39	2.61	2.21
1940–49	2.15	2.34
1950–59	2.35	1.93
1960–69	1.91	2.06
1970–79	1.87	1.76
1980–89	1.66	1.58
1990–05	1.83	1.72

TABLE 4.2

The Recent History of Competitive Balance in
Major League Baseball

Year	American League	National League
1991	1.49	1.49
1992	1.55	1.61
1993	1.34	2.29
1994	1.40	1.49
1995	1.93	1.51
1996	1.70	1.37
1997	1.53	1.42
1998	1.97	2.17
1999	1.88	1.94
2000	1.31	1.72
2001	2.48	1.66
2002	2.70	2.05
2003	2.51	1.77
2004	2.11	2.20
2005	2.04	1.40

Looking at Table 4.1 we see that for the first half of the 20th century, in both the American League and National League, the actual standard deviation was generally twice the ideal. Is this good? Again, we need a reference point. If we look at the second half of the 20th century in both leagues we see that ratio of actual to ideal was generally less than two. In simple words, competitive balance in the latter half of the 20th century improved.[10]

What if we look at the very recent history? From 1990 to 2005, the ratio of actual to ideal was less than two. In other words, these years do not look much different than the 1970s, although not quite as good as the 1980s. What if we look at this on a year-by-year basis since 1990? If we look at Table 4.2 we see how competitive balance looked before, during, and after the Blue Ribbon years (1995–99).

From Table 4.2 we see that right before the 1994–95 strike, competitive balance compared to baseball's history looked quite good in both leagues. Well, it was good in each year except for the National League in 1993. During the Blue Ribbon years (1995–99) the ratio between actual and ideal was still less than two, again, except for the National League in 1998. The average across the Blue Ribbon years in the American League was 1.80, while in the National League the average for these five seasons was 1.68. If we compare these results to the historical values we observe for baseball, it is hard to see how anyone would conclude that baseball had a competitive balance problem during the years examined by the Blue Ribbon Panel.

The argument that baseball had a competitive balance problem during the Blue Ribbon years played a key role in the 2002 labor dispute. The agreement reached between owners and players included provisions to solve what Selig and others perceived to be the growing imbalance in competition. The agreement included both increased revenue sharing and a substantial luxury tax. The latter has been referred to as a competitive balance tax or, more cynically, a "Yankee tax."[11] After reaching a settlement with the players' union, Selig offered the following observation: "the issue here was competitive balance and I feel this deal clearly deals with that."[12]

Was the Yankee tax effective? We have already noted that the payroll of the New York Yankees reached record highs each season after 2002. In 2002 the Yankees had a payroll 1.86 times larger than the average payroll in baseball. In 2003, the Yankees' payroll was 2.15 times higher. The next season the Yankees kept spending, with a payroll 2.67 times the average in the league. The year 2005 brought another record, with the Yankees' payroll now 2.85 times the average payroll. Thus the early returns on the "Yankee tax" are not encouraging. If the 2002 agreement with the players was intended to limit the spending of the Yankees, so far it has failed.

What about competitive balance? We have noted that competitive balance did not appear to be a problem during the Blue Ribbon years. In the next five years (2000–05), though, a different story could be told. Okay, it could be told, but not by anyone who has listened to our discussion of sample size. We are only talking about six seasons, so again we do not have enough observations to reach any conclusions. Nevertheless, it does look like competitive balance has worsened in the first few years of the 21st century.

One should note that despite the Yankees' spending, the worsening of competitive balance does not appear to be driven entirely by New York. Teams like Seattle, which won 116 games in 2001, and the A's, which won more than 100 games in 2001 and 2002, also contributed to the worsening of competitive balance. Both of these teams achieved success without a Yankee-sized payroll.

The story of competitive balance is not entirely driven by those at the top. We also have to look at the bottom of the standings. A problem at the bottom in baseball is Berri's beloved Detroit Tigers. The Tigers managed to lose 106 games in 2002, an accomplishment matched by both the American League's Tampa Bay Devil Rays and the National League's Milwaukee Brewers. In all, 2002 was a year of extremes with six teams either winning or losing more than 100 games.

Apparently the Tigers, though, were unhappy to share the title of worst team in baseball. In 2003 Detroit managed to lose an amazing 119 games. Why did this happen? The Tigers basically made a few personnel decisions, both in the front office and on the field, that did not work out as well as they might like. Such ineptitude cannot be blamed on market size. Detroit, according to the 2000 Census, is the ninth-largest market in baseball. Again we return to the point we made in the previous chapter. One can change the "economics of baseball" but one cannot prevent owners and managers from making bad personnel decisions.

We can go on and on about the last few years, but we must return again to the issue of sample size. In talking about 21st-century baseball our sample is too small to reach definitive conclusions. One could argue that relative to the 1990s, baseball in the 21st century is less balanced. Then again, from 2002 to 2005, despite the Yankees setting payroll records every year, competitive balance improved each season in the American League. What does all this mean? Well, not much. No matter how you slice a small sample, it is never going to allow you to make a point.

When we look at the entire history of baseball we do have a point. With more than a century of observations we can clearly see that competitive balance has improved across time in both the American and the National League. Our next task is to understand why this improvement occurred.

Baseball's Reserve Rule

Before the 1974 season Andy Messersmith of the Los Angeles Dodgers and Dave McNally of the Expos signed one-year contracts with their respective teams.[13] At the end of the 1974 campaign, these players were offered another one-year contract and this time each player refused to sign. Today, given that each player had logged at least six years of service in the majors, Messersmith and McNally would be free to sign with another team. In 1974, though, this was not an option. The one-year contract each player signed contained a clause, quite similar to the following:

> If, prior to March 1, . . . the player and the club have not agreed upon the terms of such contract, then on or before ten days after said March 1, the club shall have the right to renew this contract for the period of one year on the same terms, except that the amount payable to the player shall be such as the club shall fix in said notice. (reprinted in Quirk and Fort, 1992, p. 185)[14]

This is an example of baseball's infamous reserve clause. The key phrase in this clause is "the club shall have the right to renew this contract for the period of one year on the same terms." The owners argued that the renewed contract included this reserve clause. When the renewed contract expired the team would have the right to renew again. This new contract also contained a reserve clause, and therefore the team could renew this contract as well. What did this mean for Messersmith and McNally? Whether these players signed their contracts or not, the

Dodgers and Expos maintained that these players could either play for them or not play baseball at all. In essence, once a player signed with a Major League Baseball team under the reserve clause, he was owned by that team until his abilities were no longer desired.

Why did baseball ever adopt such a clause? The story begins with the following quote: "The financial results of the past season prove that salaries must come down. We believe that players insisting on exorbitant prices are injuring their own interests by forcing out of existence clubs which cannot be run and pay large salaries except at a personal loss" (Sullivan, 1995, reprinted in Eckard, 2001, p. 118).

Such a quote sounds similar to what Bud Selig might have said sometime during the 1990s. The actual quote, though, comes from a statement issued by the National League, September 19, 1879. Yes, more than a century ago, owners of baseball teams were complaining about the high salaries commanded by players.

The statement proceeds with the following: "In view of these facts, measures have been taken by this League to remedy the evil to some extent for 1880" (Sullivan, 1995, pp. 113–14, reprinted in Eckard, 2001, p. 118). What measures were taken to remedy the "evil" of higher salaries? The answer appeared in a Buffalo newspaper about two weeks after the release of the National League statement.

> The principal cause of heavy losses to [NL clubs] is attributed to high salaries, the result of competition. . . . it was proposed that each [club's] delegate be allowed to name five desirable players from his own club . . . and that these chosen men should not be allowed to sign with any other club without permission. . . . The aim of the league is to reduce expenses so that clubs can live. (*The Buffalo Commercial Advertiser*, October 3, 1879, reprinted in Sullivan, 1995, pp. 114–15, and Eckard, 2001, p. 118)

And so the reserve clause was born. As detailed by E. Woodrow Eckard (2001), justification for the reserve rule was extended in later years. In 1889 the National League argued that when the reserve clause was enacted a decade earlier "weaker clubs in the League demanded the privilege of reserving five players" (quoted in Spalding, 1991, p. 174 reprinted in Eckard, 2001, p. 119). The same statement from the National League in 1889 also was the first mention by the league to link the reserve rule to competitive balance. As Eckard notes, with the passage of time competitive balance became a popular defense for the rule. "The favorite argument of the proponents of the reserve [rule] is that in an open players' market the wealthiest clubs would soon corral the best talent, consequently destroying the necessary balance of playing strength among the teams" (Seymour and Mills, 1960, p. 111 reprinted in Eckard, 2001, p. 119).

Eckard's analysis of baseball at the time the reserve rule was adopted suggests that the competitive balance argument was not justified. According to Eckard "small-market clubs fared slightly better on average than large market clubs from 1876 to 1879" (Eckard, 2001, p. 127).

Despite the weakness of the owners' argument, the reserve clause remained in place for nearly a century. As time passed it was eventually extended to all the players a team had under contract. Although the clause was challenged in court, it was upheld by the Supreme Court in 1922, 1953, and again in 1971.[15]

The Messersmith-McNally case, though, finally ended the owners' absolute control over baseball's labor market. Both players argued that the reserve clause only gave their employers the right to retain their services for one additional year. On December 23, 1975, 96 years after the initial reserve clause was enacted, independent arbitrator Peter Seitz ruled in favor of Messersmith and McNally and the reserve system was ended.

The Messersmith-McNally case led to the current system of free agency, which was officially established in the collective bargaining agreement signed between the players and owners in 1976. Players with less than six years' experience were still bound by the reserve system, although salary disputes could be submitted to independent arbitrators if the player had more than two years of service.[16] Players with more than six years' experience, though, were free to sell their services to the highest bidder. So ended baseball's primary policy designed—according to the owners—to promote competitive balance.

The reserve clause is not the only policy baseball has adopted with the expressed purpose of promoting balance. In 1965 baseball instituted the reverse order draft, where the worst teams from the previous season are granted the rights to the best available amateur talent. One should note baseball teams are often selecting players whose future prospects are very difficult to forecast. Many first-round draft picks never appear with the Major League team selecting the player. Draft picks routinely begin in the minor leagues, where progress can be slowed by injuries or a lack of talent. So although the draft can help the less fortunate gain access to the better amateur talent, there is no guarantee that these players will ever make any contribution to the selecting franchise.

Our brief comments on the draft complete our review of league policy in baseball designed to alter competitive balance.[17] With the reserve system and draft noted, we can now explain why these policies are—or were in the case of the reserve system—not likely to accomplish their stated purpose.

A Nobel Prize for Sports Economics

Contrary to almost a century of claims from Major League Baseball, the data indicate that ending the reserve clause was not associated with a worsening of competitive balance. If we return to the work of Simon Rottenberg, we see that this result was not a surprise. Twenty years before the reserve clause ended, Rottenberg predicted that the distribution of playing talent in baseball would not be impacted by baseball continuing with the reserve clause or replacing this system with free agency.

Such brilliance in economics is uncommon. Economists are often asked to make predictions about the future. More often than not, though, we have trouble predicting what will happen next Tuesday. Rottenberg was forecasting the impact of an event that occurred nearly two decades after he put pen to paper. Such an accomplishment surely should be worthy of some sort of prize.

Actually a prize was awarded. Oddly, though, it did not go to Rottenberg. In 1991 the highest prize in economics, the Nobel, was awarded to Ronald Coase. Coase received this award primarily for two works, "The Nature of the Firm" published in 1937, and "The Problem of Social Cost" published in 1960. It is the argument advanced in the latter work that appears quite similar to what Rottenberg said in 1956, which a bit of math reveals, is four years before Coase's discussion of social costs.

Coase has argued that his 1960 work "is probably the most widely cited article in the whole of the modern economic literature."[18] In his article Coase presents what later became known as the Coase Theorem. Actually this story has a bit of an unusual twist. As Nobel Laureate Paul Samuelson observes, the Coase Theorem was not clearly stated in 1960. Although Coase is credited with developing the Coase Theorem, in the words of Samuelson: "Ronald Coase never wrote IT down" (Samuelson, 1995, p. 1, capitalized words in the original).

What became known as the Coase Theorem was actually articulated by George Stigler, a point Coase made in his lecture accepting the Nobel Prize.[19] Stigler, who was awarded the Nobel Prize in 1982—although not for articulating the Coase Theorem—offered the following definition of the Coase Theorem:[20] "When there are no transaction costs the assignment of legal rights has no effect upon the allocation of resources among economic enterprises."[21]

For non-economists, Stigler's statement of the Coase Theorem may not be clear. In fact, this entire story may be a bit confusing. Coase receives a Nobel Prize for not quite saying something clearly articulated by Stigler years after Rottenberg originally made a similar observation. Certainly a puzzle, but what exactly does all this have to do with baseball? To further clarify the Coase Theorem, let's return to the wisdom of Rottenberg. This is the statement he made in 1956: "It seems, indeed, to be true that a market in which freedom is limited by a reserve rule such as that which now governs the baseball labor market distributes players among teams about as a free market would" (p. 255).

The argument that the reserve system and free agency would distribute talent in the same fashion has been called Rottenberg's Invariance Principle. This has been restated by Rodney Fort (2003) as follows: "The distribution of talent in a league is invariant to who gets the revenues generated by the players; talent moves to its highest valued use in the league whether player or owners receive (the revenues the player generates)" (p. 242).

When we look at the Coase Theorem, as stated by Stigler, and the Rottenberg Invariance Principle, as stated by Fort, we fail to see a significant difference. It looks like Rottenberg—or Fort—is making the same observation that Coase—or Stigler—made. Rottenberg is arguing that whether there is a reserve clause or complete free agency, the distribution of players in the league would still be the same, which we think is the same as saying the assignment of legal rights has no impact on resource allocation. Rottenberg, though, did not receive a Nobel Prize for his work. Perhaps this is because the example Coase gave to illustrate his work involved a simple farmer and rancher. Rottenberg, on the other hand, was talking about the game of baseball. So maybe many economists don't like baseball. Or maybe many economists just dream about someday being a farmer or a cowboy. When all is said and done, we are not really sure why Rottenberg's work has not received wider acclaim from economists.

For sports economists, though, Rottenberg's work clearly is important. Specifically, the Rottenberg Invariance Principle is a crucial part of the story we tell about competitive balance. In 1956 Rottenberg argued that the reserve clause would not impact the distribution of talent in baseball. To see his point, consider the career of Reggie Jackson. Jackson began his career with the Athletics or A's. In the early 1970s he helped the Oakland A's win three titles. After a trade to Baltimore, Jackson spent the 1976 season with the Orioles. At the conclusion of the 1976 season free agency was enacted and Jackson sold his services to the highest bidder, the dreaded New York Yankees. With the Yankees, Jackson became Mr. October, leading New York to two additional titles in 1977 and 1978—and putting his name on a candy bar that we remember from our youth to be quite delicious. Today Jackson is linked in the minds of fans with the Yankees, although one could argue he achieved at least as much success in Oakland.

As economists we understand why the Yankees would pay more than Oakland for the services of Jackson. New York is a larger market than Oakland. This was true in the 1970s just as it is true today. In a larger market Jackson is capable of generating more revenues, thus New York is willing to pay Jackson more than Oakland.

What Rottenberg argued in 1956 is that the outcome we observe in the 1970s, superstars like Jackson playing in New York, is the same outcome we would have observed in the 1950s before the institution of free agency. If Jackson generates less revenue with the A's, who played in Kansas City in the 1950s, the A's would have an incentive to sell his services to New York. Or, put another way, in the 1950s the Yankees would have had an incentive to buy the better talent from Kansas City, which indeed they did.

The classic example, here, is the December 11, 1959, Roger Maris trade. Maris was traded from the Kansas City A's to the New York Yankees for a trio of former stars who were at the end of their careers. In return the Yankees got a player who would set the single season home run record and win the AL MVP award in 1960 and 1961. David Fleitz (n.d.) notes that the Maris trade was not the only unequal trade consummated by the Yankees and A's at the time.

> In all, from 1953 to 1961 the two teams made 18 deals in which the Athletics sent 34 players and four hunks of cash to the Yankees and received 42 players and two hunks of cash in return. However, the Yankees got a whole raft of good players—(Roger) Maris, (Clete) Boyer, (Ralph) Terry, (Bob) Cerv, etc.—while the A's got the Yankees' problem children [(Billy) Martin], old guys at the end of the line [(Hank) Bauer, (Johnny) Sain, (Ewell) Blackwell], and players who couldn't get out of Casey Stengel's doghouse [(Norm) Siebern, (Andy) Carey]. It seemed that any time the Yankees needed to fill a hole, they'd find someone in KC to fill it, and the A's would be satisfied with peanuts in return. The real outcome of this series of trades can be measured by the standings. From 1955 to 1960, the Yankees won five pennants and finished third the other time, while the A's never finished higher than sixth in an eight-team league. The A's 73–81 record in 1958 was their best record in the six-year period, but after they traded Cerv, Maris, and Terry they dropped to last place again in 1960.

The story of the Yankees and A's in the 1950s suggests that the reserve clause did not dramatically restrict player movement. Tom Ruane (1998) offered a more systematic study, examining the frequency of player movement both before and after the institution of free agency.[22] His analysis suggested that, contrary to popular perception, players did not move more often after free agency commenced in 1976. The theoretical work of Rottenberg, coupled with the empirical study of Ruane, suggests that the reserve clause did not impact where players ultimately play. Specifically, it makes no difference whether the players own the right to sell their services, as is the case under free agency; or the teams own the right to sell the players, which is the case under the reserve clause.

Now the owners prior to the enactment of free agency in 1976 would not have accepted this argument. Since the late 19th century the reserve clause was justified because it prevented teams like the Yankees from buying *all* the best talent. Rottenberg also had a response to this argument. He began with the following observation: "The wealthy teams will usually prefer winning to losing. If they do, they will prefer winning by close margins to winning by wide ones" (Rottenberg, 1956, p. 256).

When Rottenberg notes the importance of close margins, he is echoing the owners' argument that competitive balance is important to maintain attendance. If this is true, then it must also be the case that the Yankees do not hire every "star" player. Rottenberg explains this argument as follows:

> Beyond some point—say, when a team already has three .350 hitters—it will not pay to employ another .350 hitter. If a team goes on increasing the quantity of the factor, players, by hiring additional stars, it will find that total output—that is, admission receipts . . . will rise at a less rapid rate and finally will fall absolutely. At some point, therefore, a first star player is worth more to poor Team B than, say, a third star to rich Team A. (1956, p. 255)

Assuming that rich owners are interested in competitive balance, then these very same rich owners will not hire every star free agent. As Rottenberg argues, whether we have a reserve clause or free agency, competitive balance would be the same. Of course, when we look at the data, competitive balance did improve in the latter half of the 20th century. This result suggests that free agency might have improved competitive balance. Was Rottenberg wrong?

You Say You Want Some Evolution?

To answer this question, we go outside the field of economics to the work of evolutionary biologist Stephen Jay Gould (1983, 1986, 1996). What does the theory of evolution have to do with competitive balance? In an effort to explain the workings of evolution, Gould, a lifetime baseball fan—he rooted for the Yankees, which we think is wrong but does not invalidate his story—wished to explain the disappearance of the .400 hitter. In 1941 Ted Williams finished the season with a batting average of .406. A batting average this high has not been observed since. People have argued that the reason why such an accomplishment has not been repeated is that baseball players over time have actually become worse. Gould, though, argued exactly the opposite.

Gould's hypothesis starts with a statistical observation. If we measured and plotted the distribution of athletic talent in a population we would see a normal distribution, or a bell-shaped curve. Most people would have talent close to the average. A few people, such as those picked last in elementary school—we suspect many of these became the economists who liked to talk about farming instead of baseball—would be in the far left of the bell curve. Another small group of athletes, though, would be in the far right of the bell. This group of athletes would be the very best in the population.

Gould argued that these very best athletes would be relatively equal. Why? According to Gould there is a biomechanical limit to athletic ability. To see this, consider world record times in the 100 meter dash.[23] On June 14, 2005, Asafa Powell ran 100 meters in 9.77 seconds, breaking the previous world record in the 100 meter dash by 0.01 seconds. Over the past century times in the 100 meters have fallen, but in recent years, progress has been quite slow. When Jesse Owens set the record in 1936 with a time of 10.2 seconds, he broke the previous record of 10.3 seconds set five years earlier. Powell broke the record of Tim Montgomery. Montgomery ran the race in 9.78 seconds. This time broke the record of Maurice Green, who recorded a time of 9.79 seconds. If we round to the nearest tenth, we see that Powell, Montgomery, and Green all ran the race in 9.8 seconds. Nearly 70 years after Owens, times have only improved 0.4 seconds. Owens was 0.1 second better than a record set just five years before his race in 1936.

Why has progress slowed? Following Gould's argument, sprinters are approaching the biomechanical limit. Although world-class sprinters can routinely best a mark of 10 seconds, the biomechanics of the human body prevent a runner from making much progress beyond that mark. In other words, 100 years from now we are not likely to see human beings running this race in 7 seconds.

The idea that there is a limit to athletic ability is important to our story of competitive balance. Consider how many athletes we can expect to see close to the biomechanical limit. This number depends upon the size of the population. If you have a very small population, few athletes will approach this limit. Consequently, teams will have to fill out their rosters with players who are not among the best possible. Or it will be possible that one team will have a number of players close to the limit while other teams will be forced to employ players much further away. What happens if a team with very good athletes plays against a team of not so good athletes?

To answer this question, let us note that Berri's family left Detroit when he was eleven years old. His family moved to Nebraska, where he was introduced to the wonders of Cornhusker football. Although Big Red football has not been so wonderful recently, it used to be the case that the Cornhuskers would routinely demonstrate the outcome of a contest between the talented and the not so talented. Consider the 1997 season, the last time Nebraska finished a season undefeated. The 1997 season began with the University of Akron sending its football team to Lincoln. For those not versed in college football history, Akron is not a school that generally has players who will eventually make an NFL roster. It is likely that many of the players for Akron would not have been able to make Nebraska's roster. Given the quality of players each team employed, the outcome of this game was a foregone conclusion. When the play clock finally expired, Nebraska had won 59 to 14.

Now as the athletic population expands, more and more people will have talent closer to the biomechanical limit. Consequently, more and more teams will have access to talented players. When this is the case, the contests look more like Nebraska playing the University of Colorado. Each of these programs routinely sends players to the NFL, and when they played in 1997, Nebraska won a close contest, 27–24.

What does all this have to do with baseball? Prior to 1947 Major League Baseball players were white and tended to be born in the eastern United States. When Jackie Robinson took the field for the Brooklyn Dodgers, all this began to change. The racial integration of baseball expanded the population of players baseball drew upon. In addition to integration, teams began to look outside the United States for playing talent. Today professional baseball players come from the Dominican Republic, Puerto Rico, Venezuela, Cuba, Mexico, Australia, Japan, Korea, Spain, Belgium, the Philippines, Singapore, Vietnam, Great Britain, Brazil, and the Virgin Islands. Moreover, according to the Blue Ribbon Panel (p. 45), in the year 2000, more than 40% of the players under contract to Major or Minor League clubs were foreign-born.

So here is the basic story. Over the latter half of the 20th century baseball increasingly employed both African Americans and players born in other nations. Following the arguments of Gould we would expect this expansion in baseball's talent pool would improve competitive balance. We do see that competitive balance improved, but can you tie these improvements to changes in the talent pool?

It turns out that you can and we did. In "On the Evolution of Competitive Balance" (Schmidt and Berri, 2003) we examined the relationship between the pace of integration,[24] the number of foreign-born players employed,[25] and the level of competitive balance. Our analysis reveals that the measures of baseball's talent pool and competitive balance were cointegrated.

Okay, that probably doesn't help. What does it mean for variables to be "cointe-grated"? To understand this term, we need to discuss the difference between a "sta-tionary" and "non-stationary" variable. Stationary simply means that over time a variable returns to its average value. Player performance over the course of a sea-son tends to be stationary. Consider the performance of Shaquille O'Neal at the free throw line. Shaq is an extremely talented player, but he consistently hits less than 55% of his free throws. What if you observe Shaq hitting 70% of his free throws in one game? Given O'Neal's historical performance we expect that he will soon revert to form. In other words, we expect a movement back to the mean, or back to the "natural" value of the variable. One can compare a stationary variable to salmon, which must return to a specific place to spawn. Like salmon, stationary variables return to their natural state over time.

One might say a non-stationary variable is just a bit more free-spirited. Unlike stationary variables or salmon, a non-stationary variable does not return to its av-erage value or its natural state. When we look at our measures of competitive bal-ance and population we do not observe these variables reverting back to their means. The Noll-Scully measure for baseball has a clear downward trend. Over time it has not returned to its average value. Our measures of racial integration and foreign-born participation also do not return to their statistical average.

When variables have this characteristic, you can't use standard regression tech-niques. To see if variables such as these are related, researchers today look to see if these variables are cointegrated.[26] When we found that competitive balance and our measures of population had this property, we had some confidence that changes in the underlying population of talent were indeed connected to what we were observing with respect to competitive balance. Furthermore, after controlling for our measures of population, we found that competitive balance was not strongly influenced by the institution of the reverse order draft or by ending the reserve clause. In essence, the key to the competitive balance story is not league policy, but simply changes in the population of athletes the league draws upon.[27]

What does this mean for baseball? If baseball is truly concerned with competi-tive balance, as the owners of the game have asserted for more than a century, then efforts must be made to ensure the size of the talent pool. In other words, the pow-ers that be in baseball must make sure the game continues to be played by as many people as possible. When athletes choose other sports like football over baseball, the talent pool is thinned, and competitive balance in the future will worsen.[28]

For those concerned about competitive balance in baseball, perhaps they should look to Cal Ripken.[29] People argued that Ripken's pursuit of Lou Gehrig's record for consecutive games played saved baseball in the 1990s. In Chapter Two we argued that baseball did not need to be saved after the 1994–95 player strike. In the future, though, if the population of people playing baseball declines, problems might eventually appear. Since Ripken retired from the game he has been making an effort to combat this potential problem. Cal Ripken, with his brother Bill, operates Ripken Baseball. This company owns two minor league teams and, more importantly, designs youth baseball complexes, operates several youth baseball camps, and manages the Cal Ripken World Series for 11- and 12-year-old players. All of these efforts promote the game of baseball among young people. Promoting the game among young people will increase baseball's talent pool and should therefore enhance the level of competition we observe in the future.

Declining interest in baseball could be an issue in the future, but for now, the data we have collected tell a fairly clear story. Competitive balance in baseball has improved across time. Does this mean that baseball does not have a competitive balance problem? Well, not exactly. It could be that balance has improved but that it still is a problem. To see whether or not this is the case, we need an additional reference point.

BALANCING MANY SPORTS

The other reference point we will employ is the level of competitive balance in sports other than baseball. To see this, let us turn to an article written by Berri and Brook, as well as Aju Fenn, Bernd Frick, and Roberto Vicente-Mayoral (2005).[30] The paper is entitled "The Short Supply of Tall People: Explaining Competitive Imbalance in the National Basketball Association." In addition to a clever title, this paper provides further evidence behind the theoretical work of Gould.

Before we start, here is the history of the paper. Vicente-Mayoral was a student of Berri's when he toiled as an assistant professor at Coe College. For Vicente-Mayoral's honors thesis he decided to examine the level of competitive balance in a variety of sports leagues. The basic question he was asking was whether competitive balance was a factor in leagues that had ceased to exist, like the American Basketball Association (ABA), the American Football League (AFL), and the North American Soccer League (NASL). After measuring competitive balance in a variety of sports leagues, he brought his results to Berri. A quick scan revealed a surprise. Competitive balance for leagues that survived and failed did not look much different. What was surprising was the level of competitive balance observed in different leagues within the same sport.[31]

To see this point, we expanded upon Vicente-Mayoral's original work by measuring the level of competitive balance in fifteen sports leagues from five different

TABLE 4.3

*The Average Level of Competitive Balance for a Variety of
Professional Team Sports Leagues*

League	Label	Sport	Years	Number of Observations	Average Level of Noll-Scully
Major League Soccer	MLS	Soccer	1996–2005	10	1.28
North American Soccer League	NASL	Soccer	1967–1984	18	1.34
French Ligue 1	FL1	Soccer	1976–2005	30	1.40
Spanish Primera Division	SPD	Soccer	1976–2005	30	1.42
German Bundesliga 1	GB1	Soccer	1976–2005	30	1.45
Italian Serie A	ISA	Soccer	1976–2005	30	1.58
English Premier League	EPL	Soccer	1976–2005	30	1.61
National Football League	NFL	American Football	1922–2005	84	1.56
American Football League	AFL	American Football	1960–1969	10	1.58
National Hockey League	NHL	Hockey	1917–18 to 2003–04	87	1.85
World Hockey Association	WHA	Hockey	1972–73 to 1978–79	7	1.89
National League	NL	Baseball	1901–2005	105	2.07
American League	AL	Baseball	1901–2005	105	2.13
National Basketball Association	NBA	Basketball	1946–47 to 2004–05	59	2.55
American Basketball Association	ABA	Basketball	1967–68 to 1975–76	9	2.60

sports. These leagues, as well as the average Noll-Scully measure across the sample collected, are reported in Table 4.3.

What do we learn from this work? Basically, within each sport the average level of competitive balance is quite similar. Between sports, though, there are clear differences. Over all these sports we collected 644 league observations. The average Noll-Scully measure across this entire sample was 1.86. All of the soccer and American football leagues have an average Noll-Scully that is less than this average. In other words, these leagues are all more competitive than the average league in our sample. In contrast, baseball and basketball tend to be less competitive than average.

Given the work of Gould, this should not be a surprise. Consider our findings with respect to soccer. This is a sport played by the largest population of athletes in the world. So although there are several top soccer leagues, the population of athletes is sufficient for each league to field fairly competitive teams. Such a result appears to support the contention that competitive balance is primarily dictated by the underlying population of playing talent.[32]

At the other end of the extreme lies the NBA and the ABA. Each of these leagues is less competitive than any other league considered. At first this seems odd, since basketball is possibly the second most popular sport in the world. The problem with basketball, though, is not the population of people who are interested in playing. To play basketball you can't just be interested. To play basketball at the highest level you generally have to be tall.[33]

The average player in the NBA is 6'7". The average American male stands about 5'10". If we look at player rosters from ten consecutive NBA seasons beginning with the 1994–95 campaign, we find fewer than ten players logging significant playing time and standing 5'10" or smaller.[34] At the other extreme we would note that only about 2% of adult males in America are taller than 6'3", and a miniscule number are 6'10" or taller. Yet nearly 30% of the players employed by the NBA over the ten years we examined were at least 6'10". So although basketball may be popular, to play at the NBA level you first must be tall. Unfortunately, as people in the NBA often note, "you can't teach height." As a result, the players the NBA requires are in short supply.

In the "Short Supply of Tall People" we compared competitive balance both before and after 1990. In the AL, NL, NFL, and NHL, competitive balance in the post-1990 era had improved. In the NBA, though, the 1990s was the least competitive decade in its history. Why? The NBA keeps adding teams but the short supply of tall people—yes, we love saying this—persists. There is only one Shaquille O'Neal. No matter what policies the NBA adopts, they cannot manufacture quality big men for every team. This rule doesn't just apply to players like Shaq, but to smaller players like Michael Jordan. There is not an abundance of 6'6" people in the world either, and when you ask for a person of this height with Jordan's skills, you are not going to unearth many candidates.[35]

Given the supply of talent the NBA employs, there is very little the league can do to achieve the levels of competitive balance we see in soccer or American football. When your league depends upon a small population, the number of athletes close to the biomechanical limit will also be small. Consequently, games will often be between the good and the not so good.

DOES BASEBALL HAVE A COMPETITIVE BALANCE PROBLEM?

In the next chapter we will explore how the NBA's lack of competitive balance impacts attendance and revenue. Before we turn to this issue, though, we need to address the question posed in this chapter: Does baseball have a competitive balance problem?

From our measurement of competitive balance we saw that baseball has clearly become more balanced across time. So if we are comparing baseball today to what we observed historically, we would argue that baseball does not have a competitive balance problem.[36]

Now all economists have two hands—even those who don't. So on the other hand, if we compare baseball to some other sports, then baseball might have a problem. The average level of competitive balance in our sample was 1.86. From 1991 to 2005, the Noll-Scully has been less than this average seven times in the American League and ten times in the National League. Still, baseball is not often achieving the levels we observe in football, whether it be the American or international version. Hence you could argue that relative to these sports, baseball has a problem. Given what we learned from Gould, though, it seems unlikely that baseball will ever have the level of competitive balance we observe in soccer. Therefore, if baseball needs to be consistently as balanced as soccer to eradicate any perception people have of a competitive balance problem, then we expect baseball fans will be persistently disappointed.

Such fans can take heart in knowing that baseball will likely remain more balanced than the NBA. The imbalance in the NBA leads one to wonder: How can a league that is so imbalanced survive? The answer to this question surprised us, and will provide further hope to those who still believe that baseball has a problem with competitive balance.

THE NBA'S COMPETITIVE BALANCE PROBLEM?

The Yankees won the World Series four times in five seasons from 1996 to 2000. As we have stated, this made us unhappy. We were not alone. The Yankees' dominance on both the field and the payroll rankings led people to wonder about the future of baseball. As the Blue Ribbon Panel argued, why would anyone watch a sport where only a few teams ever get to compete for a title? Of course, if we look past the baseball diamond to life on the basketball court, one might wonder what all the fuss is about.

BLUE RIBBON ANALYSIS FOR THE NBA

The NBA currently consists of 30 franchises. Of these, sixteen have never won a title. If one looks at the past 50 years, one wonders how the NBA has survived. In this time, the Boston Celtics have won the title sixteen times. The Los Angeles Lakers have been champions nine times. The Chicago Bulls have six championships. A bit of math reveals that three franchises have won 31 titles, or 62% of the championships played over five decades. If we throw in the Detroit Pistons and the San Antonio Spurs—three titles for each franchise—five cities have hosted the NBA champion nearly three-quarters of the time.

The disparity in titles has not improved in recent years. In the past twenty years, only six teams have won the title. Perhaps the good news is that Boston, who has won the most titles in NBA history, has only won once in the last two decades. The other nineteen championships, though, have been captured by five franchises: Chicago Bulls (six titles), Los Angeles Lakers (five titles), Detroit Pistons (three titles), San Antonio Spurs (three titles), and Houston Rockets (two titles). All five franchises won multiple titles across this time frame. Furthermore, on nine different occasions across the past twenty years the NBA champion was a repeat offender. In other words, nearly half the time, if you bet that the past champion would repeat, you would win the bet.[1] So we have a league where the majority of teams have never won a title, and the team that won last year seems to have a decent chance of winning this year. Given such inequity in the distribution of titles, the fans of many NBA teams probably suspect that their team is not likely to win an NBA championship any time soon.

If we look at other sports, championships are distributed a bit more equally. If we look at the past twenty years, spanning the 1985 to 2004 seasons, ten different franchises have taken the Stanley Cup in hockey. Football does a bit better, with eleven teams winning the Super Bowl in the NFL over this time frame. In baseball, the sport that supposedly suffers from a competitive balance problem, fourteen different teams won a World Series from 1984 to 2004. Of these fourteen, only four won multiple titles: the New York Yankees, Florida Marlins, Toronto Blue Jays, and the Minnesota Twins.[2]

Of course, as we noted, playoff results, or the Blue Ribbon approach, will not tell us much about competitive balance. Let's look at the recent history of the Noll-Scully measure. In Table 5.1 we present twenty years of the Noll-Scully in each of the major North American sports leagues. On average, with the glaring exception of the NBA, each league has an actual standard deviation that is less than two times the ideal measure. Remember from the last chapter, the average Noll-Scully across all leagues we examined was 1.86. So every North American league not playing with an orange ball bested the average.

The NBA, though, has an actual standard deviation that is nearly three times the ideal. From these measures we would have to conclude that the NBA is in serious trouble. Baseball, the sport that is supposed to have a problem, looks like a socialist paradise compared to the NBA. So if anyone still believes baseball has a competitive balance crisis, when these people look at the NBA they must expect professional basketball in North America to be in its final days.

If we go back to what we said in Chapter Two, though, we can see this is not the case. For the 1985–86 season the average NBA team attracted 487,604 fans, at that point an all-time attendance record for the league. The NBA has set nine additional attendance records since then, the most recent in 2004–05 when the average team attracted 710,095 people. From 1986 to 2005, when only six teams were able to win NBA titles, per-team attendance rose 46%. We should note that a similar

TABLE 5.1

Twenty Years of Competitive Balance in North America

North American Sports League	Years	Average Noll-Scully Measure of Competitive Balance
National Basketball Association	1985–86 to 2004–05	2.86
American League	1986–2005	1.78
National League	1986–2005	1.76
National Hockey League	1984–85 to 2003–04	1.70
National Football League	1986–2005	1.49

story could be told in baseball. During the Blue Ribbon years (1995–99) when baseball was supposed to be dying at the hand of the dreaded Yankees, per game attendance in Major League Baseball rose 15%.

For those who have invested time in the study of competitive balance, this result is troubling. The NBA, relative to any other league we have examined, is not competitively balanced. Yet fans keep coming to the games. What is attracting the fans in the NBA? Our answer to this question was offered in two articles, entitled "Stars at the Gate" (Berri, Schmidt, and Brook, 2004) and "On the Road with the NBA's Superstar Externality" (Berri and Schmidt, forthcoming in 2006). Again we suspect many people have not taken the time to read these articles. So in this chapter we review and extend the story we have told.

THE STAR ATTRACTION IN THE NBA

The story we tell in sports economics is that the outcome of games must be uncertain for fans to appear in the stands. And outcomes can only be uncertain if there is some balance between the competitors. The NBA, as the data tell us, is lagging behind in the competitive balance department. So how is the NBA attracting all those fans?

Here is a list of possible attractions: Dr. J., The Iceman, The Mailman, Wilt the Stilt, Pistol Pete, Sir Charles, Vinsanity, Starbury, The Answer, The Dream, Hondo, The Glove, Diesel, Magic, Stevie Franchise, The Admiral, C-Webb, The Human Highlight Film, Mr. Clutch, Big O, T-Mac. For a fan of the NBA, each of these names instantly corresponds to a current or past star of professional basketball. Unlike football or baseball, where roster size minimizes the impact of any one player, the fortunes of NBA teams are often attributed to specific stars. Given the league's relatively low levels of competitive balance, perhaps the sport uses its many stars to attract the fans. This led us to wonder, what is the value of the "star attraction" in the NBA?

His Airness

Perhaps the greatest of these stars was MJ. Also known as Air Jordan, or His Airness, Michael Jordan is often labeled the greatest player in the history of the NBA. The Jordan story is well known to all fans of the NBA. Like all great stories, it begins with hardship. Jordan was cut from his high school team. In college he played for the legendary North Carolina coach, Dean Smith, who became known as the one man who could hold His Airness under 20 points per game. After averaging only 17.7 points per game in college, Jordan was passed over in the draft by the Houston Rockets and Portland Trail Blazers.

The Chicago Bulls, the beneficiaries of these decisions, drafted Jordan and installed him as the team's starting shooting guard. Jordan proceeded to average 28.2 points per game and was subsequently named Rookie of the Year. Over the next two decades Jordan played fourteen additional seasons, setting numerous records in the process. When Jordan retired in 2003, he held the official NBA record for points scored per regular season game (31.1), points scored per playoff game (33.4), most scoring titles won during a career (10), most consecutive seasons leading the league in scoring (7), and retirements (3). Well, the last record is actually unofficial.

Jordan, of course, was more than just a scorer. For nine seasons he was named to the All-Defensive First Team by NBA coaches and was selected the NBA Defensive Player of the Year for 1988. In 1988, 1990, and 1993 he also led the NBA in steals per game. Jordan won the Most Valuable Player award in 1988, 1991, 1992, 1996, 1998 and was Slam Dunk champion in 1987 and 1988. Except when injured or retired, Jordan played in every All-Star game from 1985 to 2003. He was also named to the All-NBA first team in every season from 1988 to 1998. Finally, his team won the NBA championship six times. Given all this, we would conclude that Jordan was a pretty good basketball player. In Chapter Eight we will go beyond this statement and demonstrate that the data make it quite clear: Jordan was one of the best players to ever play the game.

The Value of Jordan

Jordan's value as an endorser for products such as Nike, McDonald's, and Gatorade has been well documented. Due strictly to his endorsements, Forbes still listed Jordan as the highest paid basketball player in 2004, the year after his third retirement.[3] Although this record is of interest, we wish to understand MJ's impact upon the NBA.

When Michael Jordan began his career in 1984 the NBA had two national television contracts.[4] On network television the league was shown on CBS, under a contract that began with the 1982–83 season and paid the league $91.9 million over four seasons. The league also had a contract with TBS to appear on cable television. That contract began with the 1984–85 campaign and paid the league $20 million over two seasons. Given these contracts, for the 1984–85 season each NBA team earned, in 2004 dollars, a bit more than $2.5 million.

Over the next twenty years the revenue the NBA earned from national television would increase dramatically. For the 2002–03 season the NBA began a new television contract with ABC, ESPN, and TNT. The contract called for the NBA to receive $4.6 billion over six seasons. For the 2003–04 season each NBA team earned from these contracts a bit more than $26 million. So over the course of twenty years, the money the NBA would earn from television increased more than ten times.

The revenue generated from national television is distributed equally to each member of the league. One should note, though, that each team, and specifically each player, doesn't have an equal impact on the generation of this revenue. To illustrate this point, we turn to the work of Jerry Hausman and Gregory Leonard (1997). These authors published a wonderful study where the term "superstar externality" (p. 588) was introduced. A superstar externality exists when a star player generates revenues for teams that do not employ the athlete. To illustrate this phenomenon, Hausman and Leonard looked at Michael Jordan. In an extensive study of television ratings, these authors offered evidence that ratings were significantly higher when Jordan appeared.[5] Beyond his impact on television ratings, Jordan was also found to have a sizable impact on both attendance[6] and the sale of NBA merchandise.[7] In sum, for the 1991–92 season, Hausman and Leonard estimated that Jordan generated $53.2 million in revenue for teams other than the Chicago Bulls. Given a league of 27 teams, Jordan generated a bit more than $2 million in revenue for each team *not* signing his paycheck. We would note that the Bulls did pay Jordan, although his salary of $3.25 million for the 1991–92 campaign made him only the fifth highest paid player in the league.[8] And given the analysis of Hausman and Leonard, his wage was about $50 million less than the revenue MJ was creating for the NBA. So with respect to His Airness, we have evidence of a substantial "superstar externality."

STARS AT THE GATE

After reading the work of Hausman and Leonard, we were inspired to also hunt down further evidence of the superstar externality. Specifically, we decided to look a bit harder at how NBA teams perform at the gate, both at home and on the road. Let's begin our story at home.

Typically, when one talks about a team's performance at the gate one talks about attendance. Attracting fans, though, should be seen as a means to an end. What teams really want is dollars. More fans can lead to more money, but there is more to the tale. To see this, let's look at the 2004 NBA Champion Detroit Pistons.

The NBA Champions at the Gate?

In 2004 the Detroit Pistons defeated the Los Angeles Lakers in the NBA Finals. The Pistons were not just champions on the court, but also appeared to be champions at the gate. For that season the Pistons led the league in home attendance. This seems to make sense. The best team should attract the most fans.

Well, it was not entirely clear that the Pistons were considered the best team that season. The Pistons did win 54 games. Five other teams,[9] though, managed to accumulate more wins. At the onset of the 2004 NBA Finals between the Lakers and the Pistons, the former were clearly the favorite. The Lakers not only played before a bevy of Hollywood stars in the stands, but also employed a number of NBA stars on the court. Led by Shaquille O'Neal, Kobe Bryant, Karl Malone, and Gary Payton, the Lakers fully expected to return the NBA title to La-La Land in 2004. Before the finals commenced, the media appeared to share this sentiment. So, without completing a comprehensive fan survey, we do not think we are venturing too far out on a limb when we say that Detroit was clearly the underdog before the finals started, and furthermore, was not considered the best team in the NBA during the 2003–04 regular season.

If the Pistons weren't considered the best, why did they draw so well? If we look a bit deeper at the data, though, we can see one reason. The average NBA team charged $44.68 per ticket.[10] The Pistons, though, were a relative bargain. A Pistons fan was only charged, on average, $33.60. So Pistons fans got the NBA, but with about a 33% discount.

For just a moment, let's play the role of economic professors. When we talk about the economics of a business, we begin with the simple Law of Demand.[11] The Law of Demand simply states that if a firm lowers its price people will buy more of what it sells. Sounds pretty radical, huh? Okay, it is pretty obvious that lower prices lead to more sales. At least, we don't often hear people say: "I like this, but the price is just way too low." So it is not surprising that when the Pistons field a good team and charge the fourth lowest price in the league, attendance will be fairly high. Unfortunately for the Pistons, the low price led to less money. Although Detroit led the league in attendance, their gate revenue, which we find by multiplying average price by attendance, was only seventeenth in the NBA.[12]

"The Answer" in Philadelphia

To put this in perspective, the Philadelphia 76ers, which only won 33 games, placed ninth in the NBA in gate revenue. Why was Philadelphia, with a relatively bad team, able to perform better than the Pistons at the gate? One possible answer is "The Answer." For those unfamiliar with the NBA, that would be "AI." Okay, for those who are really unfamiliar, we are referring to Allen Iverson.

"The Answer" has an impressive resume. He was selected by Philadelphia with the first pick in the 1996 draft. After his first season he was selected by the media as Rookie of the Year and was nearly a unanimous selection by the coaches to the All-Rookie team.[13] Iverson was named league MVP in 2001. Three times he has been placed on the All-NBA first team (1999, 2001, 2005), and on three other occasions he was voted to the All-NBA second team (2000, 2002, 2003). Four times he has led the league in scoring (1998–99, 2000–01, 2001–02, 2004–05) and he set an NBA record by leading the league in steals three consecutive seasons (2000–01, 2001–02, 2002–03).

Iverson, though, is not without his flaws. He led the league in turnovers per game his rookie season, and also in 2001–02, 2003–04, and 2004–05.[14] Beyond turnovers, Iverson also has a problem with shot selection. For his career he has attempted more than 2,500 three-point field goal attempts. This works out to nearly 300 per season or four such shots per game. Given such a propensity to take such shots, one would think this was a facet of the game where Iverson excelled. The data tell a different story. Iverson's lifetime conversion rate from beyond the arc is only 31%, well below the NBA average from this range. His shooting ability from inside the arc is also low. From two-point range Iverson only successfully scores on 44% of his shots.[15] In essence, Iverson does score, but he does not score very efficiently.

This is an important point we will return to again and again. Baseball fans are accustomed to thinking about players in terms of efficiency measures. The batting champ each year is not the player with the most hits, but the player with the highest batting average. Although batting average is no longer considered the best measure of hitting prowess, the alternative metrics—which we discuss in some detail in Chapter Nine—are still measures of efficiency. In evaluating baseball players it is clearly efficiency that matters. Imagine if we could take the batting order out of baseball and instead allow teams to bat whoever they like as often as the team likes. How would the team choose who gets to bat most often? We suspect people in baseball would look at and evaluate various efficiency measures. If a player batted fifteen times in a game and only got three hits, baseball fans would not be heard trumpeting how so-and-so's three-hit game really helped the team. Rather, fans would be asking why the team is paying so many millions to a guy who only hits 0.200.

This is not the logic employed by many basketball fans. In Philadelphia's 2004–05 home opener, the 76ers lost to the Phoenix Suns by 10 points. Iverson again led Philadelphia in scoring. Although Iverson scored 25 points, he only made six of the twenty field goals he attempted. The Associated Press story of the game[16] noted that Iverson led the 76ers in scoring, but failed to emphasize his 30% field goal percentage. Such an oversight is not uncommon. Leading scorers are often trumpeted. Inefficient scoring, though, is not as often highlighted.

We would emphasize that the flaws in Iverson's game do not seem to impact his popularity with fans. Iverson has been voted by the fans as a starter in the mid-season All-Star game every season from 2000 to 2005. Although his game has problems, Iverson is clearly considered a star by many. Such star appeal, we suspect, is an important reason why Philadelphia is a top-ten performer in gate revenue with a below average team on the court.

Back to New York

Star power is not the only issue when we look at a team's performance at the gate. Let's head back to New York and once again consider market size. We spent so much time in this book discussing the Yankees, we would be remiss not saying a few words about their counterpart in the NBA, the Knicks. For the record, we don't hate the Knicks. Actually it is hard to have any feelings for a team that has only won two titles in its history, and none since 1973.

Let's say a few words about the relative lack of success enjoyed by the Knicks. Often the success of the Yankees is attributed to the fact that they play in New York, and teams like Milwaukee, well, don't. The Yankees, though, appear to be the anomaly in the Big Apple. The Yankees have won baseball's ultimate prize 26 times. The New York Mets, playing in the same market, have only won twice—1969 and 1986—in their entire history. In football, the New York Giants have won six NFL titles, but only two titles in the past 45 years. Behind Joe Namath the Jets won Super Bowl III in 1968, but this is the team's only title. If we turn to hockey, the story is the same. The New York Rangers won the Stanley Cup three times from 1928 to 1940, and then were unable to win again until 1994. The New York Islanders did win the Stanley Cup four consecutive times from 1980 to 1983, but these are the only times this team has hoisted the cup. All in all, the Knicks appear to be as successful as other teams hailing from New York. Again, we return to the point we have made previously. Despite the historical success of the Yankees, there is little evidence that market size dictates on-field success in professional sports.

Market size, though, does appear to impact team revenues and team payrolls. In ten seasons, beginning in 1992–93 and ending with the 2001–02 campaign, the Knicks led the NBA in gate revenue eight times. In five recent seasons—1995–96, 1998–99, 2001–02, 2003–04, and 2004–05, the Knicks emulated the Yankees by leading their league in payroll. The Knicks' spending, though, did not have much impact on their on-court results. The most wins the Knicks posted in a season where it took the spending crown was 47, which over an 82-game season, is a winning percentage of 57%. In each of the three most recent seasons where the Knicks managed to outspend every NBA team, New York failed to win half their games. In fact, from 1992–93 to 2004–05, the Knicks were the only team to take the spending title in a season and still lose more often than they won. As we detail below, despite such performances, the Knicks do well at the gate.

Understanding NBA Performance at the Gate

We are beginning to see a pattern. Having a star like Iverson seems to be related to higher revenues. Teams located in places like Los Angeles and New York are also quite successful. We also suspect that fans like winning. Which of these factors, if any, is most important? How can we untangle the impact of all these factors on gate revenue?

Of course the answer begins with regression analysis. Before we begin, we have to return to a discussion we offered in Chapter Three. In discussing the impact payroll has on wins, we referenced the work of Deirdre McCloskey. As we noted, McCloskey has documented the tendency economists have to focus on whether the relationship between two variables is statistically significant. In other words, economists tend to look at the data to see whether a relationship exists between two variables or a relationship does not exist.

McCloskey has urged our profession to look beyond the "on-off" question of statistical significance and focus instead on economic significance. What is economic significance? Statistical significance is all about whether a relationship is there or not. Economic significance begins with a relationship existing, and then asks, "How important is this relationship?" Or in McCloskey's terminology, is there any "oomph" to the story?

With the words of McCloskey in our heads, let's look at what regression analysis tells us about gate revenue. Now if this were an academic article we would de-

TABLE 5.2

Leaders at the Gate: 1992–93 to 2003–04

Season	Team	Real Gate Revenue	Regular Season Wins	All-Star Votes Received	Star?
2003–04	LA Lakers	$58,642,878	56	4,420,673	Kobe Bryant
2002–03	LA Lakers	$56,759,114	50	2,708,438	Shaquille O'Neal
2001–02	New York	$76,425,017	30	375,661	Marcus Camby
2000–01	New York	$78,789,689	48	1,936,326	Latrell Sprewell
1999–00	New York	$77,171,542	50	2,162,835	Latrell Sprewell
1997–98	New York	$74,495,822	43	441,347	Patrick Ewing
1996–97	Chicago	$49,473,921	69	5,597,842	Michael Jordan
1995–96	Portland	$43,351,778	44	330,277	Cliff Robinson
1994–95	New York	$44,093,703	55	2,166,957	Patrick Ewing
1993–94	New York	$40,952,534	57	740,895	Patrick Ewing
1992–93	New York	$38,029,253	60	578,368	Patrick Ewing

tail the data we collected, lay forth our model, discuss an array of statistical issues, present our empirical results, yada, yada, yada. If you like that approach, then you can read the 2004 article the three of us published in the *Journal of Sports Economics*. For here, let's take a simpler approach.

We begin with what we want to explain. Specifically we are seeking to explain the differences—or variation—we observe in regular season gate revenue. Our specific data set includes every NBA season,[17] except the lockout season of 1998–99, beginning in 1992–93 and concluding with 2003–04. Over this time period the average team earned per season, in 2004 dollars, nearly $31 million at the gate.[18] There is quite a bit of variation, though, around the average. Some teams collect revenue far in excess of this average. Others are quite a bit below. Regression analysis will help us see why this variation exists.

In Table 5.2 we consider one extreme of the sample. Specifically we list the leaders in gate revenue for each season from 1992–93 to 2003–04. We entered this study believing that both wins and star power played a role in a team's gate performance. Reviewing the leaders, though, we cannot be so sure of this story. In seven of the eleven seasons we examine, the leader in gate revenue was the New York Knicks. Were the Knicks a successful team on the court? Well, in these seven years the Knicks never led the NBA in regular season wins.

Do the Knicks employ a major star? We define a team's star as the player who led the team in All-Star votes received. Of the Knicks stars listed above, the one Knick who might be considered an NBA star was Patrick Ewing. Although Ewing consistently received votes for the All-Star game, in none of the years listed above was Ewing voted by the fans to start the mid-season classic. So why did the Knicks consistently lead the NBA in gate revenue? Table 5.2 suggests that for gate revenue, market size matters.

If we travel to the other end of the gate revenue spectrum, we see that size isn't everything. The lowest mark for gate revenue in our sample was posted by the LA Clippers in 1996–97, when this team only earned $11.7 million at the gate. The Clippers played in the second largest market. The team, though, only won 36 games. Furthermore, with no Clipper placing in the top ten at any position in the fan voting for the All-Star game, its roster seemed to be completely devoid of any star talent.

For those who pay attention to the NBA, the Clippers fielding a poor team is hardly news. The first season the Clippers played in Los Angeles was the 1984–85 campaign. Over the past 21 seasons the Clippers have never won more than 45 games in a regular season. In a league where more than half the teams make the playoffs, the Clippers have made the playoffs exactly three times. These three appearances resulted in four post-season victories. Not surprisingly the team has never advanced beyond the first round of the playoffs. Given all of this, it is not surprising that the Clippers have struggled at the gate. From 1993–94 to 1997–98 they finished last in gate revenue every season.

So we see the two extremes. What we wish to understand are the factors that place a team on a particular spot on the gate revenue spectrum. Part of our list we have already noted. Winning, star power, market size, and past success are all factors that might help us explain gate performance. Is there anything else to the story?

We answered this question by regressing regular season gate revenue on each of the factors listed in Table 5.3.[19] As we note, we found the following factors had a positive and statistically significant impact on gate revenue: various measures of past and present on-court performance,[20] the star power playing for the team,[21] market size,[22] and various characteristics of a team's stadium.[23] In other words, a relationship exists between gate revenue and these factors. We suspected that roster stability,[24] the racial composition of the team,[25] and competitive balance would also impact gate revenue. The data, though, told us otherwise.

As we stated, regression analysis begins with uncovering where statistical relationships exists and where they do not exist. We then move to the subject of economic significance, or the discussion of what looks to be important. Before we get to what looks to be important, let's draw attention to one factor that the data tell us is clearly unimportant. As with our article in the *Journal of Sports Economics*, competitive balance was not found to be statistically related in the larger study of

TABLE 5.3

What Explains Regular Season Gate Revenue?

Factors we found to be statistically related to gate revenue	How factor is measured (more details in endnotes)
Performance this season	Wins in the regular season
Performance last season	Wins in the regular season last year
Historical performance	Past championships won
The star power employed by the team	All-Star votes received by a team's players
The size of a team's market	Population in a team's host city
Age of stadium and stadium capacity	The stadium capacity of a team's home arena and two additional measures for teams that sell out every game and teams that play in a relatively new stadium
Factors we did not find to be statistically related to gate revenue	
Stability of a team's roster	Percentage of minutes played by returning players
Racial composition of a team's roster	Percentage of white players on team, relative to whites in the city population
League competitive balance	Noll-Scully measure of competitive balance for each conference

gate revenue we offer here. Perhaps in a league where competitive balance is always relatively poor, fans are not as concerned with this dimension of the product. Then again, perhaps sports economists—that would be us—have exaggerated the importance of competitive balance.

We will say a bit more on competitive balance in a moment. For now, let's briefly discuss what is important to a team's gate performance. Recall our starting position. The NBA does not have competitive balance so perhaps the league relies upon its stars to attract fans. If this is the case, then we should see that the more star power a team employs the more revenue the team earns.

It is certainly true that we find star power leads to more revenue. How much revenue, though, are we talking about? If you do the math—which we did—an additional All-Star vote received was estimated to be worth 16 cents in gate revenue. In other words, one more vote gets you three nickels and a penny—or one dime, one nickel, and a penny.

We would note that 16 cents is the league average. Given a team's level of revenue and number of votes received, this value can vary. For example, an additional All-Star vote received by a Knick player in 2004 was worth 74 cents. In San Antonio, though, one more vote for a Spur in 2004 was only worth 6 cents. Now we must remember that, on average, players on each team received more than one million votes. Still, the gate revenue generated by all the All-Star votes received by each team was relatively small. The Los Angeles Lakers had the most star power in 2003–04. Remember this was the team with Shaq, Kobe, Karl Malone, and Gary Payton. What was the value of all this star power? Our analysis indicates that the star attraction of these four players was worth about $330,000. Given that the average team in the league received less than $200,000 from the star power it employed, it is hard to argue that it is star power that drives a team's performance at the gate.

Let's contrast this result with the impact wins have on gate revenue. A portion of any team's demand this season is comprised of those who hold season tickets. These people base their decision on their expectation of a team's performance, an expectation based partially on what the team has done recently. As a result the total value of a win includes the revenue it generates this season as well as the next.

When we take into account the total impact of a win, we see that on average one win generated nearly $238,000 in gate revenue during the 2003–04 season. Again, the value varies depending on a team's level of gate revenue and the number of wins the team achieved. For the Los Angeles Lakers in 2003–04, one additional win added more than $325,000 to gate revenue. Given that the Lakers won 56 games, all of its wins were worth more than $18 million. In contrast, the Minnesota Timberwolves won 58 games. Because each win only generated about $143,000 for Minnesota, its earnings at the gate were less than $9 million.

What does this tell us about the value of a team's star attraction(s)? The value of wins is in the millions, while the value of star power is quite a bit less. But doesn't a team need star power to win? We will offer evidence in Chapter Ten that suggests that this is also just a myth. For now, we will simply say we do not believe that star power and winning are the same,[26] and of the two, it is wins that attract fans to the arena. Given a team's market and stadium, if a team wants to see improvements at the gate it must offer real improvements on the court.[27]

STARS ON THE ROAD

We now have evidence that star power doesn't matter much to the team employing the star. Interestingly, on the road we find that a team's star power does matter. Unfortunately, it only matters to all the teams not employing the star.

The Basic Road Story

We begin with two data points. In 2003–04 the LA Lakers drew an average of 19,380 fans for each game the team played on the road. In contrast, the Golden

TABLE 5.4

The Attendance Leaders on the Road: 1992–93 to 2003–04

Season	Team	Road Attendance per Game	Regular Season Wins	All Star Votes Received	Star
2003–04	LA Lakers	19,380	56	4,420,673	Kobe Bryant
2002–03	Washington	19,311	37	1,287,208	Michael Jordan
2001–02	LA Lakers	20,103	58	2,369,191	Shaquille O'Neal
2000–01	LA Lakers	19,628	56	3,343,423	Shaquille O'Neal
1999–00	LA Lakers	19,461	67	3,141,003	Shaquille O'Neal
1997–98	Chicago	21,970	62	2,125,872	Michael Jordan
1996–97	Chicago	20,060	69	5,597,842	Michael Jordan
1995–96	Chicago	19,920	72	3,127,364	Michael Jordan
1994–95	Orlando	18,679	57	2,661,299	Shaquille O'Neal
1993–94	Orlando	18,355	50	964,546	Shaquille O'Neal
1992–93	Chicago	18,433	57	2,480,603	Michael Jordan

State Warriors drew only 15,885 per road game. What explains the difference between these two teams?

In 2003–04, the Lakers had two important qualities. The team was successful on the court and they employed star players. The Golden State Warriors had all but two of these characteristics. Not one player employed by Golden State finished in the top ten at their position in voting for the mid-season classic. Furthermore, the team only won 37 games. Consequently, accountants employed by the Warriors' opponents were not thrilled when Golden State came to town.

Of course one year does not make a story. Table 5.4 reports the leaders in road attendance per game for each season from 1992–93 through the 2003–04 campaign. In our examination of the gate revenue leaders we noted that star power did not seem that important. Our statistical analysis confirmed this conclusion. Although we did find that star power and gate revenue were statistically related, the dollars star power actually generated were relatively small.

On the road we have the makings of a different story. Unlike our study of the gate leaders, the leaders on the road tend to be winners. The average road attendance leader won 59 games, with only the Washington Wizards posting a losing record while leading the league in road attendance. The Wizards, though, were led by Michael Jordan, who at the age of 40 was playing what is still his last season in the league.

This was not the only time a team employing Jordan led on the road. In four other seasons, Jordan and the Bulls were the NBA's main traveling attraction. Matching Jordan in our sample was Shaquille O'Neal, whose employer also led the league five times. The lone exception to the rule of Jordan and Shaq was the 2003–04 Lakers, who were led in All-Star votes by Kobe Bryant. Of course Kobe's teammate that season was Shaq, so teams that employed either MJ or O'Neal led the league in road attendance every season we considered.

Our review of the leaders in road attendance reveals some clues into what drives a team's ability to draw away from home. Our sample includes teams that are both successful on the court and who employ players named Jordan or O'Neal. Is there anything more to this story?

Understanding NBA Performance on the Road

To answer this question we again turn to regression analysis. Specifically we regressed road attendance on each of the factors listed in Table 5.5.[28] These variables are measured exactly as they were for our study of gate revenue, so this information is not repeated.

We found that road attendance is statistically related to present on-court performance, a team's historical success, the star power playing for the team, market size, and competitive balance. Each of these factors had a positive impact on road attendance. Actually let's clarify that statement. Improvements in competitive balance, which would be observed when the Noll-Scully declines, were found to positively impact attendance on the road.

The competitive balance result is certainly a puzzler. Competitive balance statistically impacts road attendance. For us sports economists, this result fits our conventional wisdom. Still, it is hard to reconcile this finding with what we learned about gate revenue. Competitive balance was not found to impact a team's financial performance at home. Well, if improvements in balance lead to more road at-

TABLE 5.5

What Explains Road Attendance?

Factors we found to be statistically related to road attendance
Performance this season
Historical performance
The star power employed by the team
The size of a team's market
League competitive balance

Factors we did not find to be statistically related to road attendance
Performance last season
Racial composition of a team's roster

TABLE 5.6

Stars on the Road in 2004

2004 "Star"	Team	All-Star Votes Received	Wins Produced	Value of Votes	Value of Wins
Vince Carter	Toronto	2,127,183	6.0	$1,588,791	$240,977
Ben Wallace	Detroit	1,982,251	20.4	$1,480,542	$818,517
Kevin Garnett	Minnesota	1,780,918	30.5	$1,330,166	$1,223,509
Kobe Bryant	LA Lakers	1,759,717	12.2	$1,314,331	$487,925
Allen Iverson	Philadelphia	1,731,648	0.9	$1,293,367	$34,920
Tim Duncan	San Antonio	1,681,435	19.7	$1,255,863	$789,495
Jermaine O'Neal	Indiana	1,629,054	8.8	$1,216,739	$351,860
Yao Ming	Houston	1,484,531	11.8	$1,108,795	$474,137
Shaquille O'Neal	LA Lakers	1,453,286	15.4	$1,085,458	$618,452
Tracy McGrady	Orlando	1,231,825	11.8	$920,049	$472,487
AVERAGE		1,686,185	13.7	$1,259,410	$551,228

tendance, we would then expect to see an increase in someone's home attendance. So these results are clearly inconsistent.

Assuming our road attendance results are valid, let's look a bit more closely at the actual impact competitive balance has on road attendance. We measured the Noll-Scully for both the Western and Eastern conferences[29] from 1992–93 to 2003–04. The lowest value we observed was 1.96 (Eastern conference, 2002–03). The highest value was 4.47 (Western conference, 1997–98). What if a conference moved from the most balanced position we observed (1.96) to the least balanced (4.47)? Our results indicate that a move from the highest level of balance to the least in our sample would cause road attendance to decline by about 750 fans. Now the average team draws approximately 16,800 fans per road game, so a severe worsening in competitive balance only lowers attendance by 4.4%. What have we learned? Competitive balance might be statistically related to attendance, but it is hard to argue that it plays a major role in determining how many fans fill the seats each night.

We want to say a bit more on this before we conclude this chapter. Before we get to this, though, let's talk about the value of star power on the road. Our analysis shows that a team that wins one more game can expect to draw nearly 900 additional fans during the course of a season on the road. One more All-Star vote for the team's players is worth 0.017 additional fans.

What does it mean to admit 0.017 fans? Is that even legal? Well, these results don't mean much by themselves. To illustrate the impact stars have on the road, let's consider the ten players who led the league in All-Star votes in 2004. These players are listed in Table 5.6.

The ten stars we list are familiar to most fans of the NBA. We rank these players in terms of All-Star votes received in 2004. Additionally, we list how many wins each player produced during the 2003–04 regular season. We promise to explain how we calculate "Wins Produced" in the next two chapters. For now, we wish to note that although these players may be stars, their on-court productivity varies quite a bit. We estimate that Kevin Garnett was worth more than 30 wins to Minnesota while Allen Iverson's performance was worth less than one victory.

Let's say a few more words about Iverson. One of our friends is Peter von Allmen, co-author of one of the very best textbooks on *The Economics of Sports* (Leeds and Von Allmen, 2005).[30] Although we are happy to plug Peter's book, we bring him into our story because he lives near Philadelphia and he really likes Allen Iverson. Whenever we point out the flaws in "The Answer's" game, he is quick to voice his disagreement. In an effort to make Peter and the other fans of Iverson a bit happier, we would add that Iverson was hurt in 2003–04, and it was easily his worst season. Furthermore, his performance in 2004–05 was above average, despite leading the league in turnovers again. We should also repeat what we said in the first chapter. Payroll does not explain much of the variation in wins in the NBA. So perhaps some of what people think about player performance and wins in basketball is incorrect.

For now, that is enough about Iverson. We will return to "The Answer" in Chapter Seven. What do our results say about star power on the road? To answer this question we determined how many additional fans these players drew on the road via their star appeal and their on-court productivity. We then multiplied the number of additional fans by $44.68, or the average ticket price in the NBA in 2003–04. From this calculation we were able to see how much revenue a player created on the road.

It is important to note a curious feature about the NBA. The home team keeps all of the gate revenue generated by the game. Although there would be no game without the visiting team, the visiting team receives no income. So the nearly $1.6 million generated by Vinsanity's (Vince Carter) star appeal did not go to the team paying his salary. This money was pocketed by the teams hosting Carter.

A perusal of our list reveals that the revenue generated by a player's star appeal on the road always exceeded the revenue generated by his wins production. In fact, for these ten players, star appeal was more than twice as valuable to the player's opponent than his on-court production.

What does all this mean for the NBA? Players can generate revenue via their star appeal and their ability to generate wins. For the team paying the player, wins are what matter the most. AI's star appeal does not matter nearly as much to

Philadelphia as his ability to win games. On the road, though, "The Answer" generates substantial revenue for his opponent. Hence, it appears that there is a substantial superstar externality in the NBA. Star power seems to matter to everyone in the NBA, except the team that has to pay the star's salary.

BACK TO COMPETITIVE BALANCE

With that statement we should end this chapter. We have made a fairly interesting statement about the value of star appeal and on that high note, let's move on. Unfortunately, we can't. The competitive balance story calls to us once more.

Here is the competitive balance story thus far. Sports economists—that would include us—believe that competitive balance is crucial to the survival of a sports league. We talk about this in our research. We teach this in our classes—yes, there is a class called the Economics of Sports. Our competitive balance story goes back to the original work of Rottenberg, and after writing several papers on the topic, we would seem to be the last people to question the validity of this tale.

To demonstrate our blindness in this particular area, let's review what we said about competitive balance and consumer demand in the academic papers we have written on this subject. In both "Stars at the Gate" and "Stars on the Road" we looked at the relationship between competitive balance and demand in professional basketball. Now we reexamined these papers in this chapter using a much larger data set. So although we did report a link between balance and road attendance in this chapter, in our academic articles a different story was told. Specifically, in our academic articles we failed to find a relationship between competitive balance and consumer demand at home or on the road in the NBA. We would emphasize that although this finding contradicted decades of established theory in the sports economics literature, we did not spend much time discussing our results. In fact, in our paper "Stars on the Road" we barely offered any discussion of this finding at all.[31]

The measure of competitive balance we employed in these two basketball articles was the Gini Coefficient.[32] In using the Gini Coefficient we were following our own lead, since this was the measure we employed in two studies of attendance and competitive balance in baseball (Schmidt, 2001; Schmidt and Berri, 2001). We are not going to detail the math involved in calculating the Gini Coefficient here, but we will note that with respect to consumer demand in baseball we did find that competitive balance was statistically significant.

Economic significance is still the key idea. We found the impact competitive balance has on demand in baseball depended upon the time period one considered. If one looks at changes in competitive balance from year to year, the impact was quite small.[33] In fact, for one data set we examined, improvements in baseball's competitive balance actually were found to decrease attendance. Again, though, the impact was not very large.

We also measured balance in baseball across three seasons and again across five seasons.[34] In other words, we looked at how balanced baseball was across time. For the longer time periods we found that improvements in balance had a positive impact on attendance. We summarized these results by noting: "These results suggest that fans may not prefer competitive balance in a given season, but over time, the slogan 'wait till next year' must remain valid for the teams located toward the bottom of the standings" (Schmidt and Berri, 2001, p. 162).

What about the size of the impact? The largest impact was seen when we looked at improvements in our five-year measure. A movement from the least competitive five-year measure to the highest level of balance would result in about 3,500 additional fans per game for each team. This works out to a 14% increase in attendance. Again, this was the largest impact we found. So a very large change in competitive balance across the longest time period we considered, and 14% is all the "oomph" we uncover.

Let's try and clarify our new thinking on this subject by briefly going beyond our work on the subject. Brad Humphreys (2002) examined attendance in Major League Baseball from 1901 to 1999. Specifically he looked at how well alternative measures of competitive balance could explain league attendance, once one controlled for a list of other factors that impact consumer demand.[35] His results indicated that whether balance is measured with the Noll-Scully metric or the Herfindahl-Hirschman Index,[36] the level of competitive balance did not have a statistically significant impact on attendance. In contrast, when balance was measured with Humphrey's Competitive Balance Ratio,[37] competitive balance was found to be statistically significant. Again we come back to the issue of economic significance. Although Humphreys does not address this issue, his results suggest that a movement from the lowest observed level of balance to the highest would increase league attendance by 8,400 fans. This works out to 280 fans per team, or less than four fans per game. Cleary this is not much of an impact.

Where does all this leave us? The process of telling our stories in this book has led us to question one of our core beliefs. Does competitive balance truly matter? We think more work needs to be done in this area—and we plan on doing some more. In closing this chapter we wish to make two observations.

There is a disconnect between the theoretical and empirical treatment of competitive balance. We do not believe the empirical work necessarily contradicts the theoretical perspective on balance offered by Rottenberg, Neale, etc. It seems plausible that if uncertainty of outcome was completely taken away, as is the case when ESPN Classic rebroadcasts a game, then demand would suffer. After all, rebroadcasts of the greatest games in history don't seem to attract much of an audience.

The problem with empirical studies of competitive balance is that we are not looking at a world where uncertainty of outcome doesn't exist. Even when a team dominates a sport for a period of time, like the Yankees in baseball or the Bulls in basketball, there is still uncertainty of outcome. Although looking back we may now tell ourselves that we knew Jordan and the Bulls would prevail in the NBA Finals, each year the Bulls won we could not have been sure of the outcome until it happened. So does competitive balance matter? We still think if people were completely certain of outcomes, stands would be mostly empty. The sports we have examined, even when the level of balance is quite low, still present games with uncertain outcomes.

Do professional sports leagues truly want competitive balance? Although we think completely removing uncertainty of outcome would hurt attendance for professional sports, we are fairly certain the other extreme is not ideal. Our analysis of gate revenue suggests that perfect balance would lower league revenues. For the 2003–04 season an additional win had a greater value for the Chicago Bulls, New York Knicks, and Los Angeles Lakers than one more win had for the Minnesota Timberwolves, Indiana Pacers, and San Antonio Spurs. In a study of Major League Baseball, John Burger and Stephan Walters (2003) reached a similar conclusion. For the Yankees one more win creates more revenue than this win would create in Milwaukee. These results are perfectly consistent with Rottenberg, who suggested that wins in larger markets would be more valuable relative to wins in smaller markets.[38] If a league is interested in maximizing profits, such analysis suggests that wins should not be equally distributed. The league is better off with winning teams located where wins generate more revenue.

With all this said, let's take a step back and see what lessons we have learned about competitive balance.

1. The measurement of competitive balance should focus on outcome in the regular season, not the post-season.

2. Relative to its history, baseball is more balanced today.

3. Relative to sports like football and soccer, baseball is not as balanced. Compared to basketball, though, baseball does not have a competitive balance problem.

4. Competitive balance appears to be dictated primarily by the underlying population of talent, not league policy.

5. Although we can find a statistical relationship between competitive balance and attendance, the estimated economic significance seems quite small. Consequently, it is not clear whether the fans truly care about the level of balance in a league.

6. The relationship between team revenue and wins suggests that perfect competitive balance would actually lower league revenues.

Given our last point, let's imagine a league that wished to institute a policy to maximize profits. To pursue this policy the league needs the best teams to be located where wins have the highest value. As we will note in the next chapter, the best teams employ the most productive players. So if the league is focused on profits, what the league needs to do is be sure the most productive players are in the largest market. Unfortunately there is one problem. Exactly who are the most productive players? It is the answer to this question we turn to next.

6 | SHAQ AND KOBE

Why study sports? The obvious answer—sports are interesting. Of course we are not saying that other topics examined in economics are not interesting. Well . . . maybe we should say this. Someone should at some point say that a few topics examined by economists—mind you, we are not naming names and we are just saying a few—are really not interesting. The topics are not interesting to us, our students, or probably most non-economists. We are not even sure these topics are interesting to most other economists.

So we are drawn to sports because we find this subject to be interesting. There is more to the story. As we noted at the onset, with sports you have numbers. Oodles and oodles and oodles—that is a scientific term which means "a whole bunch" or "lots and lots"—of numbers are generated in the world of sports. Each and every day a game is played somewhere. In that game people record the actions of each individual player. This record, or the data, can be used by economists to address an assortment of interesting and entertaining questions.[1]

What is the purpose of tracking all the data collected in sports? We talked about this in Chapter One. Still, we wanted to mention another great answer to this question which was provided by Allen Barra:

"Stat Nerds" they snort contemptuously at me, and probably at you, too, if you're smart enough to have picked up this book—but the truth is that they depend as much on numbers as anyone else when it comes to making decisions. What else, after all, are you going to rely on? *What, in the final analysis, are statistics but a record of what a player does when you're not watching him?* And we don't have time to watch 99 percent of the players 99 percent of the time. (2002, p. 139, italics added)

Barra summarizes nicely the purpose behind statistics. Statistics tell us what a player is doing when we are not looking, which, as Barra notes, is most of the time. Furthermore, and more importantly, statistics help people make decisions.

SHAQ AND KOBE, THE SAGA BEGINS

What decisions are we talking about? To answer this query, we will discuss in detail two NBA stars we first mentioned in Chapter Five, Shaquille O'Neal (a.k.a. Shaq or Diesel) and Kobe Bryant. Both players came to the Los Angeles Lakers in 1996. Led by these stars, the Lakers captured titles in 2000, 2001, and 2002. In 2004 the team came close to a fourth title, losing in the NBA Finals to the Detroit Pistons.

The 2003–04 season, though, was not a happy time for the Lakers. Through the course of the season an apparent rift appeared in the Shaq-Kobe relationship. When the 2004 playoffs concluded the Lakers appeared to have a choice. The team could go forward with either Kobe or Shaq, but because the two players did not appear to be happy in each other's company, the team could not employ both. During the summer of 2004 the Lakers made their choice. Kobe was signed to a lucrative new contract and Shaq was traded to Miami. Looking back, though, who should the Lakers have chosen?

We should note that Kobe is six years younger than Shaq. So if both players were equally productive, the younger player would look like the better choice. However, if Shaq was significantly more productive than Kobe, perhaps the team would have been better off with the Diesel.

A bit of thought reveals that the team needed to assess the productivity of each player. Both are considered stars, but did each have the same impact on team wins? Is one player more important to the team than the other?

An answer can be found in the statistics tabulated for each player. The NBA tracks a host of player statistics that might help one decide between Kobe and Shaq. The difficulty with the abundance of data tracked, though, is determining the relative importance of each piece of information. To illustrate this point, consider each player's statistical production. Of these two players, Kobe scored more points, recorded more steals, and committed fewer turnovers. Shaq accumulated more rebounds and if we consider points scored per field goal attempt, appeared to be a more efficient scorer.[2] Given this information, who is better?

A FEW DIFFERENT ANSWERS

The answer to the question "Who is the best?" depends upon how you define "best." Best can be defined in terms of popularity, salary, height, shoe size, etc. For our purposes, we are going to focus on a player's contribution to team wins.[3] Consequently, when we say "Who is the best?" what we are actually saying is "Who is the most productive?"

We believe the statistics the NBA tracks can help us answer this question. It is important to note that we are not alone in this belief. Many people have developed measures[4] that are designed to tell us the answer to our query: Who is better, Kobe or Shaq?

The NBA Efficiency Measure

Let us start with the approach advocated by the NBA. A visitor to the NBA's official web site (NBA.com) will come across the following measure of an NBA player's efficiency:

$$\text{Points} + \text{Rebounds} + \text{Assists} + \text{Steals} + \text{Blocks} - \text{Missed Field Goals}$$
$$- \text{Missed Free Throws} - \text{Turnovers}$$

If we use this measure we learn that in 2003–04 Shaq's value equaled 1,670 while Kobe's was 1,474. So from this, Shaq is worth almost 200 more than Kobe. One might ask, 200 more of what? Basically the NBA measure adds together the positive statistics a player accumulates and subtracts the negative. When you take this approach, you learn how many statistics each player has amassed.

We need to note that this approach is quite similar to Dave Heeran's (1994) TENDEX model and Bob Bellotti's (1992) Points Created measure.[5] Heeran notes that his TENDEX method was invented around 1960, so this basic metric has been around a while.[6] Still despite this history, is it true that the most valuable players produce the most statistics? Is it simply the objective of the players to accumulate stats?

We would think that players are trying to win, so we need to value these statistics in terms of that objective. Now if it is the case that all these statistics have the same impact on wins, then the NBA approach will serve us well. Unfortunately, it is not clear that this is the case. For starters, would one expect a missed field goal to have the same value as a missed free throw? Each free throw made is only worth one point, while made field goals can be worth two or three points. So missed field goals and missed free throws probably do not reduce a team's chances to win by the same amount.

What of the other stats? Are an assist and a point of equal value? How about a blocked shot and a rebound? As we will show, the answer is that these statistics are not all equal. In the end, metrics like the NBA Efficiency measure are very easy to calculate. Still, it is not clear that such a measure provides a very accurate evaluation of each player's performance.

Plus-Minus Moves from the Ice to the Hardwood

The statistics in basketball seem quite difficult to interpret. To see this point, consider baseball. One does not need an advanced degree in statistics to know that a home run in baseball is worth more than a single. Basketball, though, is a bit more difficult. How does one compare rebounding to scoring or steals to assists? The NBA data seem to contain a few "apples and oranges" that make constructing a single metric difficult. The difficulty in using the data the NBA tracks has led to the development of a plus-minus metric for the NBA.

We mentioned in Chapter One the performance measure developed by Wayne Winston and Jeff Sagarin.[7] In our discussion we argued that one cannot evaluate a performance metric by simply looking at how it ranks players relative to conventional wisdom. If one wishes to be critical, one has to work a bit harder. So here is our brief critique of this approach, which as you shall see, is completely free of any mention of the words "laugh test."

Okay, we have a confession. We do not have access to the specific Winston-Sagarin ratings. As far as we can tell, Winston and Sagarin skipped the journal publication route we generally follow and sold their method directly to Mark Cuban, owner of the Dallas Mavericks. And it is not surprising that Cuban does not want to share information he had to buy. What we do have is the Roland Ratings, a plus-minus measurement presented by Roland Beech.[8] We have reason to believe that what Winston and Sagarin did is similar to the work of Beech, but then again we cannot be sure. Still, paraphrasing Donald Rumsfeld, you critique the rating you have, not the rating you would like to have.

So what are the Roland Ratings? Beech looked at each player during the 2003–04 campaign, examining how the player's team did per 48 minutes the player was on the court versus the team's performance, again per 48 minutes, when the player was on the bench. For example, the 2003–04 Lakers scored 8.5 more points than their opponent when Shaq was on the court. When O'Neal was on the bench, the team scored 3.6 fewer points than its opponent. In other words, the team was winning with Shaq and losing when he sat. Given this analysis, Shaq's Roland Rating, or the difference between the team's performance with Shaq and without, was a net 12.1 points per 48 minutes played. The same analysis for Kobe reveals that the Lakers scored 6.1 more points than their opponent when Bryant was on the floor. The Lakers also outscored their opponent without Kobe, but the margin was only 0.3. So the net contribution of Kobe was 5.8. From this analysis, Shaq is better than Kobe.

For fans of hockey, a plus-minus statistic is quite familiar. Why would such a measure be used in hockey? The answer is that much of what happens in hockey is not tracked by any statistics. The lack of statistics has led people to a system that appears to link goals scored and goals allowed to individual players. Basically, if your team scores while you are on the ice, you get a plus. If the other team scores when you are playing you get a minus.[9]

Although we acknowledged that NBA statistics may be difficult to interpret, unlike hockey, basketball does have an abundance of statistics. And we will show that with a bit of work one can untangle the "apples and oranges" problem. So we are not sure whether the justification for plus-minus that exists in hockey also applies to basketball. Still, this measurement is quite interesting, and as noted by John Hollinger (2005), a columnist for ESPN.com and author of the *Pro Basketball Prospectus*, this is a wonderful instrument if interpreted correctly. Unfortunately, for our purposes, the plus-minus measure has one basic shortcoming which derails our efforts to answer the question: "Who is the best?"

This specific problem is identified by Roland Beech. On the specific web page listing the leaders in Roland Ratings is the following disclaimer: "These ratings represent a player's value to a particular team and are not intended to be an accurate gauge of the ability and talent of the player away from the specific team." Why is this disclaimer necessary? According to Hollinger, one would have trouble comparing the net plus-minus of two players on two different teams. He argues that how well a team performs with and without a specific player depends upon the team that employs the player, the specific teammates the player plays with, and the specific back-ups who take the player's place on the court when he is on the bench. Players on better teams tend to have higher plus-minus ratings. Players who play with better teammates also will have higher ratings. Finally, if a player has a quality back-up, his rating will tend to be lower.

If we want to compare players on different teams net plus-minus may not be that helpful.[10] And comparing players on different teams is ultimately what we need to do if we wish to know "Who is the best?" We would also add that ultimately, as we have noted, the plus-minus system for the NBA may not be necessary if we simply take the time to learn how the individual player statistics connect to team wins.

The Labor Theory of Value

Before we try to connect player statistics to team wins, let's spend a bit of time discussing . . . well, Marxism. We know that this is clearly an obvious direction to go in this story. Many readers were probably wondering when we were finally going to connect the writings of Karl Marx to the study of basketball. Although Marx died before the game of basketball was invented, clearly what Marx wrote in the 19th century provides many keen insights into player productivity in the NBA.

We are of course approximating humor. We don't really think Marx had any keen insights into basketball. Dean Oliver, though, has many. In *Basketball on Paper* (2004) Oliver introduces a number of ideas and tools that deepen our understanding of the game. A list of his contributions would include offensive score sheets,[11] a variety of measures of team offense and defense,[12] and an entertaining analysis of winning streaks.[13] All of this is just in the first 20% of his book.

Who does Oliver say is better, Kobe or Shaq? Via an extensive mathematical exercise that we will not even begin to describe, Oliver concluded that Kobe was the seventh "best" player in 2003–04 while Shaq was ranked fifteenth. From this, Kobe is the best.[14]

Oliver's methodology for evaluating players centers on what he calls "my personal Difficulty Theory for Distributing Credit in Basketball: The more difficult the contribution, the more credit it gets" (2004, p. 145). Again, the mathematics behind Oliver's methodology is more than a bit difficult. We would, though, like to address the underlying rationale.

How will Marx help us in this endeavor? One of the tenets of Marxian thought is the labor theory of value, which argues that the price of a good is determined by the amount of labor used to produce the good. To be fair, Marx took this concept from the work of David Ricardo, and Ricardo was influenced by Adam Smith. In other words, this is not strictly a Marxist idea. Still, it was Marx who used this concept to argue that the system of capitalism leads to the exploitation of labor, which is the fundamental idea underlying the economics of Marxism.

The problem with the labor theory of value is that it ignores the impact the wants and needs of consumers have on prices. Just because a good requires more labor, it does not follow that its price will necessarily be higher. For example, we have spent a fair amount of our labor writing this book. Hey, just reading the stuff on Marx was difficult. Given Marx's labor theory of value, we think the price of our book should be in the thousands. Yet this is not what our readers have been asked to pay for our work.

Soon after Marx published *Das Kapital*—yes, that is spelled correctly—economists like Alfred Marshall—we mentioned him in Chapter One—began to question the labor theory of value. Today, following the work of Marshall and others, we use the supply and demand model to explain prices. The supply of a good depends upon the resources, including but not limited to labor, that were used in making the good. Demand, though, depends upon how much people want the product. It is possible that as people learn about our musings on Marx, the demand people have for this book will decline, and eventually our work will find its way into the bargain bin.

The point we are making—and we do have a point—is that Oliver appears to be making the same mistake made by proponents of the labor theory of value. Now we are not saying that Oliver is advocating the overthrow of capitalism. Oliver, though, is arguing that the value of a rebound, point, etc. depends upon the difficulty of taking the action, which strikes us as a return to the labor theory of value. Although difficulty may be important, ultimately the game is about winning. Oliver's difficulty measurement does not connect player action to wins. And because we think players and teams are trying to win, it makes sense to value the actions the players take in terms of this objective.

The Market Approach

We now have seen three approaches based upon what we see the players do on the court, and we have problems with all three. Maybe the answer is not what happens on the court, but what happens in the marketplace.

As economists we tend to think markets work. We have good reason to come to this conclusion. The living standards enjoyed today in industrialized countries around the world can at least partially be attributed to societies using markets to allocate resources. The standard of living in industrialized countries, by virtually any measure, exceeds what we observe through much of human history. In essence, because markets encourage innovation and the efficient allocation of resources, people in industrialized countries live much better than people in the past could have ever dreamed was possible.

What does the market tell us about Kobe and Shaq? In 2003–04 Shaq was paid $26,517,858 while Kobe was paid $14,175,000. What do we learn from this? Perhaps all three of us should have spent a whole lot more time playing basketball as children. Forty million dollars for two people playing a game is simply amazing.

Once again, we digress. We see that in the marketplace, Shaq is considered the best. Are salaries, though, the best measure of a player's productivity? Let's go back to the point we have made repeatedly. Wages and wins are not highly correlated. In our view, the lack of a strong relationship between payroll and wins casts serious doubt on the proposition that a player's salary accurately captures the impact a player has on team wins. As we have argued before, and will again and again later in this book, it is entirely possible that mistakes are made when people in sports evaluate player value.

MODELING TEAM WINS IN THE NBA

The weak link between payroll and wins in basketball suggests that player evaluation is not perfect. Can we do better? We would like to think so, but then again, our view is no different from many sports fans. Sports fans in general believe that they can evaluate talent better than the professionals. Spend a few minutes listening to sports talk radio, or hanging out in a sports bar, and what will you hear? Endless debates about the relative merits of this and that player. Many fans of sports may not know where they left their car keys, but they "know" which players are the best and which are the worst.

Unfortunately one cannot create a statistical measure that will match perfectly every person's ranking of NBA players. So our research into the value of NBA players will offer answers that must contradict what fans already "know." Is Shaq better than Kobe? The NBA Efficiency measure, Roland's ratings, and the marketplace all say Shaq is the best. Dean Oliver says it is Kobe. Ask many fans of the NBA and you will hear an impassioned defense for Shaq or Kobe that could easily steal hours from your life. People may not know the size of the national debt, the rate of crime in their city, or the details behind the troubles in the Middle East, but on the topic of which player is best, all the statistical analysis anyone can offer is unnecessary. The answer is already "known."

As we move forward in our discussion of player productivity we wish to be clear about where we are coming from and what we hope to achieve. Sports provide an abundance of data on worker productivity. Such data can be used to address a host of interesting questions. Before the questions can be addressed, though, one has to make sense of the data. We wish to develop a measure of productivity that accurately captures the value of a player's performance. Beyond accuracy, it would also be nice to have a measure that is both simple and complete. Once we have a measure that is accurate, simple, and complete, this will be employed in our study of various questions that we find to be interesting. "Who is the best?" is one of these questions.

The Simple, and Occasionally Misleading, Correlation Coefficients

Before we explain our approach, let's begin with a simple statistical exercise. In Table 6.1 is listed the simple correlation coefficient between team winning percentage and ten different statistics that are tracked for NBA players.[15] What is a correlation coefficient? The correlation coefficient tells us how strong a relationship exists between two variables. The coefficient can be negative or positive, and ranges—in terms of absolute value—between 0 and 1. If the correlation coefficient is 1, then a perfect relationship exists between two variables. If it is 0, then there is no statistical relationship between two variables. One last note before we discuss Table 6.1. A positive correlation coefficient means that two variables move together. When one rises, the other tends to rise also. A negative coefficient means that two variables move in opposite directions. When one rises, the other tends to fall.

Now that we know the basics of the correlation coefficient, what do we learn from Table 6.1? The first lesson is the lack of a really strong correlation between any one factor and team wins. None of the reported correlation coefficients exceed, in absolute terms, one-half. This suggests that you cannot look at any one factor and say, "See, that is why the team won."

The second lesson we learn is that just looking at the correlation between any two factors can be very misleading. Consider the relationship between offensive rebounds and team wins. The correlation coefficient between offensive rebounds and wins is –0.20, which implies an increase in offensive rebounds actually leads to a decline in wins.

TABLE 6.1

*Correlation Coefficients for Various NBA Statistics
and Winning Percentage*

Variable	Correlation Coefficient
Defensive rebounds	0.46
Missed field goals	−0.46
Assists	0.43
Points scored	0.41
Turnovers	−0.39
Personal fouls	−0.22
Offensive rebounds	−0.20
Steals	0.14
Blocked shots	0.11
Missed free throws	0.05

NOTE: Ranking based on the absolute value of the correlation coefficient.

Bob Bellotti, creator of the aforementioned Points Created measure, examined the relationship between where a team ranks in wins and where each team ranked in a variety of statistical categories.[16] He found that offensive rebound differential, or the difference between how many offensive rebounds a team and its opponent accumulates, was the statistic with the lowest correlation with team wins. Dean Oliver came to the same conclusion when he looked at how often teams both won a specific statistical battle and also won the game.[17] As Oliver notes, 80% of the teams with the highest field goal percentage in a game also won the game. In contrast, only 46% of teams with the most offensive rebounds in a game were victorious. From this analysis, both Bellotti and Oliver conclude that offensive rebounds must not be as important as other factors in determining wins.

If we examine the simple correlation coefficients reported in Table 6.1, the analysis of Bellotti and Oliver is confirmed. Our analysis shows that the correlation coefficient between wins and offensive rebounds is –0.20. Just as Oliver noted, teams that lead in offensive rebounds are more likely to lose.

What lesson do we learn from this analysis? If we were to interpret the correlation coefficient literally, a step we would emphasize was not taken by Oliver and Bellotti, we could imagine a revolutionary change in coaching in the NBA. If more offensive rebounds lead to fewer wins we should observe coaches in the future telling players to avoid rebounding their teammates' missed shots. Future coaches might be observed telling their players, "When your teammate takes a shot you should get back on defense very quickly. This way, even if there is a long rebound, there is less of a chance it might end up in your hands. Remember, offensive rebounds do not help us win, so avoid these at all costs." Of course, before we see an NBA coach screaming at his players for rebounding their teammates' missed shots, we might wish to consider an alternative explanation for this negative relationship.

For a team to collect an offensive rebound someone must first miss a shot. As teams miss more shots, offensive rebounds likely increase. When we examine the relationship between wins and offensive rebounds, without holding missed shots constant, what we are likely observing is the relationship between team wins and missed field goals. Because missed shots lead to fewer wins, and more missed shots lead to more offensive rebounds, we end up seeing more offensive rebounds result in fewer victories.

This story highlights the importance of regression analysis. If we wish to understand the value of any one factor in terms of wins, we must hold constant the impact of all other factors.[18] If we do not do this, the lessons we teach might lead coaches to tell their players, "Leave your teammates' missed shots alone!"

Building a Better Model

We have seen that there is no one statistic that can tell us why teams win or lose. We have also seen that our analysis of the relationship between wins and each statistic can be easily misunderstood. Such results might lead one to conclude, as NBA coaches and members of the media often suggest: basketball is not about the numbers.

As we note in Chapter One, though, you can't know who won the game if you don't look at some numbers. Well, that is not entirely true. You could wait to see who was happy or sad when the game ended, although for legendary Pistons coach Chuck Daly that method may not work. Daly never looked that happy, even when his team won the NBA championship. Obviously, as Allen Barra argued, statistics are crucial to understanding what happens in the games we enjoy. The problem is making sense of what is being collected.

We think one can make sense of the various statistics the NBA collects to evaluate players with a relatively simple model of team wins. The specific model we employ actually is just a variation on the work of Dean Oliver and John Hollinger.[19] Their work relies upon a very powerful concept in the study of player productivity in the NBA, "the possession."[20] Here is how Hollinger introduced the idea of possessions:

> Possessions are the basic currency of basketball. No matter what the team does with the ball—scores, turns the ball over, or misses a shot—the other team gets it when they are done. The objective of basketball is to score more points than the other team; put that in terms of possessions, and the goal is to score as many points per possession as possible while limiting the opponent to as few points per possession as possible. (2002, p. 1)

So Hollinger, and Oliver as well, argues that wins are determined by how many points a team scores per possession relative to the opponent's ability to elicit points from its possessions. Before we apply this statement to our study of productivity, though, we need to explain exactly how possessions are defined.

As both Oliver and Hollinger note, the number of possessions a team employs in a game can be calculated with four factors (listed below for additional emphasis): field goal attempts, free throw attempts, turnovers, and offensive rebounds.[21] These four elements comprise the four basic actions a team can take once it has acquired the ball. A team can turn the ball over, thus ending the possession. If a team avoids a turnover, it will have to take a field goal attempt, a free throw attempt, or perhaps both.[22] If a team misses this shot, it can prolong the possession by capturing the offensive rebound.

How Teams Employ a Possession

Field Goal Attempts

Free Throw Attempts

Turnovers

Offensive Rebounds

Possessions employed tell us what a team did once it acquired the ball. It does not tell us, though, how the ball was acquired. To address this issue we have to go beyond the work of Oliver and Hollinger. Basically, there are three actions a team can take to get the ball: force the opponent to commit a turnover, rebound an errant shot by the opponent, or take possession of the ball after the opponent has scored via a field goal or free throw attempts. These three actions are captured via the following five statistics.

How Teams Acquire the Ball

Opponent Turnover

Defensive Rebound

Team Rebound

Opponents Made Field Goal Attempt

Opponent Made Free Throw Attempt

Of these statistics, rebounding needs just a bit more explanation. If an individual player rebounds an errant shot by the opponent, this is called a defensive rebound. If a team takes possession of the ball after an errant shot, but no individual player is responsible, then this is called a team rebound.[23] In the endnotes we offer a lengthy discussion of how we estimate for each team how many team rebounds actually gave the team possession of the ball.[24] As we explain, team rebounds that change possession are not reported by the NBA, but can be estimated. The other four statistics are tracked by the NBA, so with these measures in hand, we can now determine the number of times a team acquires the ball.[25]

As Hollinger and Oliver emphasize, the number of possessions each team employs basically equals the number of possessions used by the opponent. Repeating Hollinger: "No matter what the team does with the ball—scores, turns the ball over, or misses a shot—the other team gets it when they are done" (2002, p. 1). Likewise, the number of possessions a team employs must equal the number of possessions a team acquires.[26]

The importance of possessions employed and possession acquired can be illustrated if we think about the general method often used to evaluate offense and defense in the NBA.

TABLE 6.2

Teams with the Highest Offensive Efficiency in 2004–05

Team	Rank: Points Scored per Possession Employed	Points Scored per Possession Employed	Rank: Points Scored per Game	Points Scored per Game
Phoenix	1	1.12	1	110.4
Miami	2	1.08	4	101.5
Seattle	3	1.08	11	98.9
Sacramento	4	1.07	2	103.7
Dallas	5	1.07	3	102.5
Minnesota	6	1.05	16	96.8
LA Lakers	7	1.05	12	98.7
San Antonio	8	1.05	18	96.2
Boston	9	1.05	5	101.3
Toronto	10	1.04	7	99.7
Washington	11	1.04	6	100.5
Milwaukee	12	1.03	15	97.2
Denver	13	1.03	8	99.5
Houston	14	1.03	20	95.1
Cleveland	15	1.03	17	96.5

People often label the team that scores the most per game as the best offensive team and the team that surrenders the fewest points per game as the best defensive team. Hollinger and Oliver note that such analysis ignores game pace. Basically teams can play at different speeds. The Phoenix Suns in 2004–05 played at a faster pace than other NBA teams. So the Suns and their opponents used more possessions per game, and consequently, the Suns and their opponents tended to score more than teams that played at a slower pace.

Because teams can play at a different pace, in other words, average different numbers of possessions per game, points scored per game is not the best measure of offensive ability. To see this point, let's look at the top teams during the 2004–05 season in terms of offensive efficiency (points scored per possession employed) and defensive efficiency (points surrendered per possession acquired).

If we look at Table 6.2, we see that the Phoenix Suns were the best offensive team in both efficiency and scoring per game. Beyond Phoenix, though, we see why scoring per game can be misleading. The offenses of both Minnesota and San Antonio are significantly underrated when one looks at scoring per game. Seattle and Houston also had offenses that would be underrated by the traditional metric.

A similar story is told in Table 6.3, where the best defensive teams are ranked for 2004–05. San Antonio was the best defensive team in both efficiency and points al-

TABLE 6.3

Teams with the Highest Defensive Efficiency in 2004–05

Team	Rank: Points Allowed per Possession Acquired	Points Allowed per Possession Acquired	Rank: Points Allowed per Game	Points Allowed per Game
San Antonio	1	0.96	1	88.4
Chicago	2	0.97	7	93.4
Detroit	3	0.98	2	89.5
Houston	4	0.99	3	91.0
New Jersey	5	1.00	6	92.9
Memphis	6	1.00	4	91.1
Miami	7	1.01	8	95.0
Denver	8	1.01	17	97.5
Dallas	9	1.01	14	96.8
Philadelphia	10	1.01	19	99.9
Indiana	11	1.01	5	92.2
Cleveland	12	1.02	11	95.7
LA Clippers	13	1.03	12	96.5
Minnesota	14	1.03	9	95.3
New Orleans	15	1.03	10	95.5

lowed per game. Beyond San Antonio, the rankings again diverge. Perhaps the best story can be told about Denver. In terms of defense, the Nuggets were seventeenth in points allowed per game. Denver's defensive efficiency, though, was eighth in the league. Hence, in terms of defense, the Denver Nuggets were the most under-rated team in 2004–05. A very different story is told when we look at Denver's offense. In terms of points scored per game, Denver is listed as the eighth-best team in Table 6.2. The Nuggets, though, were only thirteenth in offensive efficiency. Consequently, if we only considered points scored and allowed per game one would argue that Denver needs to focus more on defense than offense in 2005–06. The efficiency measures, though, teach the exact opposite lesson.

All of this is interesting—we think—but how does this help us evaluate individual players? Let's walk through what we know and what we have learned about wins in the NBA.

Wins are determined by how many points a team scores and allows. This obvious point was made in Chapter One. At the end of the game the team with the most points gets to be happy and the team with the fewest points needs to find something else to make them happy. Now we might be tempted to stop right here. If we know how many points a player scores and surrenders, don't we know the player's contribution to wins? Unfortunately, we really do not know how many points an individual player allows. Even if we had such information, is a player's value captured entirely by noting his ability to score and play defense? If you believe this is true, then what you are saying is that the NBA game is really five games of one-on-one basketball. If my five guys tend to win their individual battles, then my team wins. Basketball, though, is not a collection of five one-on-one contests but one game of five-on-five. If we focus solely on scoring and defense, we ignore the impact of rebounds, turnovers, and steals. In fact, if the NBA measured productivity by focusing solely on scoring and defense, the players would only focus on these two facets of the game and ignore rebounding, passing, and effective ball-handling. As we will see in Chapter Ten, research on player salaries suggests—well, we get ahead of ourselves. For now, we will simply say that we think there is more to player productivity than scoring and defense and we will have to go beyond the obvious observation that wins are determined by points scored and points allowed.

Points scored are determined by how often a team has the ball and its ability to convert possessions into points. In other words, points scored are determined by the number of possessions the team employs and the team's offensive efficiency. We hope this statement is just as obvious as what we said about wins and scoring. In 2004–05 Phoenix led the NBA with 98.9 possessions employed per game. Phoenix also led the NBA in offensive efficiency, averaging 1.12 points per possession employed. If we multiply possessions employed by points per possessions—98.895 × 1.116—we see that the Suns averaged 110.4 points per game. In other words, how many points you score is determined by how many points you score per possession and how many possessions you have at your disposal. The same painfully obvious observation can be made about points allowed. The number of points allowed is determined by defensive efficiency—points allowed per possession acquired—and the number of possessions acquired.

Now why do we bother with such obvious statements? Well, if points scored are determined by offensive efficiency and possessions employed, and points allowed are determined by defensive efficiency and possession acquired, we now know something more about wins. It must be the case that wins are determined by four factors: offensive efficiency, possessions employed, defensive efficiency, and possessions acquired. However, because possessions employed equals possessions acquired, these two factors cancel each other out. Therefore, at the end of the day, we have a very simple model of team wins which we summarize in the following sentence: *Wins are solely a function of offensive and defensive efficiency.*[27]

We would emphasize, Hollinger and Oliver have already made this statement. Neither writer, though, decided to avail himself to the wonders of regression analysis. If we regress team wins on each team's offensive and defensive efficiency, or each team's points scored per possession employed and points allowed per possession acquired, we learn that 95% of wins can be explained by the team's efficiency measures.[28] More importantly, we can use this regression to determine the value of almost every statistic tabulated for the individual and the team.[29]

The Value of Each Statistic

From our regression we can determine the value of an additional point scored, point allowed, possession employed, and possession acquired.[30] We report these values in Table 6.4. From our analysis, each additional point a team scores, holding all else constant, increases wins by 0.033. Yeah, we know, who likes decimals. Let's think about it this way. If a team scores 100 more points in a season, and nothing else changes, the team can expect to win about three more games. If a team allows 100 more points, and again nothing else changes, a team can expect to lose about three more games. A similar argument can be made for possessions employed and possessions acquired.

With these values in hand, we can now estimate the value of a player's actions associated with scoring, acquiring and maintaining possession of the ball, as well personal fouls and blocked shots. Let's say a few words about the specific statistics we can now value in terms of wins.

- Scoring statistics

Three-point field goals: From our regression we learn that each additional point scored creates 0.033 wins. One might think that a shot from beyond the arc must be worth three times this value. Unfortunately, to take the shot you must use a field goal attempt. This is a key point in our evaluation of players. When a shot is made, a resource, specifically a shot attempt, has been used. The cost of this resource must be noted. A possession employed costs a team 0.034 wins, and a field goal attempt is worth one possession. Consequently, the net value of making a three-point shot is worth 0.066 wins.[31] One should note that when an opponent makes a three-point field goal it costs the team the same number of wins.

Two-point field goals: This is the same story as a three-point field goal. The net value of a two-point shot, once one accounts for the value of two points and the cost of the shot attempt, is 0.033 wins. Again, an opponent making a two-point shot subtracts virtually the same number of wins.

Free throws made: A made free throw gives a team one point, but costs the team a free throw attempt. If you are reading the endnotes as we go along you know that a free throw attempt is only worth a fraction of a field goal attempt. Our results in-

Table 6.4

The Value of Points and Possessions in Terms of Wins

Variable	If each variable increased by one, and nothing else changed, wins would change by . . .	If each variable increased by 100, and nothing else changed, wins would change by . . .
Point scored	+0.033	+3.3
Point allowed	−0.033	−3.3
Possession employed	−0.034	−3.4
Possession acquired	+0.034	+3.4

dicate that each free throw attempt, by itself, costs a team 0.015 wins. When one takes into account the value of the point and the cost of the free throw attempt, we see that a made free throw adds 0.018 wins. Again, a made free throw by the opponent costs the team the same number of wins.

Missed field goal: When a player misses a shot he has used a resource without generating any return. So a missed field goal costs a team the value of a field goal attempt,[32] or 0.034 wins.

Missed free throw: Like a missed field goal, a missed free throw results in a loss of a resource with no corresponding gain. So a missed free throw cost a team the value of a free throw attempt, or in other words, this costs a team 0.015 wins.

- Possession statistics

Offensive rebounds and turnovers: We noted that a field goal attempt is worth one possession employed. An offensive rebound erases the negative consequence of a missed field goal. In other words, it allows a team to continue to employ its possession. Hence the value of an offensive rebound is 0.034 wins. A turnover, though, costs a team possession of the ball and a loss of 0.034 wins.

Defensive rebounds, team rebounds, turnovers by the opponent, and steals: If the opponent does not make a shot, the team can acquire the ball via a defensive rebound, team rebound, or by forcing a turnover. Each of these actions is worth a possession acquired, or from the estimation of our model, generates 0.034 wins. The value of a steal can be derived from the value of an opponent's turnover. Stealing the ball is one method a team can use to force the opponent to commit a turnover, so the value of one steal is equal to the value of one turnover by the opponent. In other words, one more steal is worth 0.034 wins.

- Personal fouls and blocked shots

Personal fouls: When a player has violated specific rules of the game he is charged a personal foul.[33] Our measurement of possessions employed or acquired did not explicitly include this statistic. Still, with a bit of work, we can estimate the impact of committing a basketball crime. There are two approaches you can take:

1. If you regress the opponent's free throws made on personal fouls you learn that each personal foul is worth about one free throw made by the opponent.[34] Consequently, the value of a personal foul can be considered to be approximately the same as the value of a made free throw by the opponent, which we have already said costs a team 0.018 wins.

2. There is another way to include a player's propensity to commit crimes on the basketball court in our player evaluation. We begin by simply noting the percentage of team personal fouls committed by the player. We can then multiply this percentage by the number of opponent's free throws. What do we get for this? Well, we now have estimated the number of free throws made by the opponent that we can credit (or blame) on a specific player. This is the actual approach we took in the evaluation of individual players.

Blocked shots: Like personal fouls, blocked shots are not part of possessions employed or possessions acquired. Once again, though, we can connect this statistic to a factor included in our model. Specifically, we have learned that each additional two-point field goal made by the opponent leads to a 0.033 reduction in team wins. If we regress the opponent's two-point field goals made on blocked shots, we learn the value of a player rejecting a shot.[35] Specifically, each blocked shot reduces the opponent's two-point field goals made by 0.65; consequently, we estimate each additional blocked shot leads to a 0.021 increase in team wins, or 65% of 0.033 wins.[36]

To summarize, each statistic's value, in terms of wins,[37] is listed in Table 6.5.

We now have a value for every action a player takes on the court, except assists. Assists are like personal fouls and blocked shots. An assist is not part of our calculation of possessions employed or acquired. Although assists impact how efficiently a team elicits points from its possessions, once we know a team's offensive efficiency assists do not provide any additional information. In other words, if a team scores 1.1 points per possession employed with 10 assists per game, and another team scores 1.1 points per possession employed with 20 assists per game, neither team is better off. Once you know offensive efficiency, assists do not provide any more information. And since we know offensive efficiency when we estimate our wins model, adding assists would not further our ability to explain wins. Consequently, we might feel comfortable evaluating player productivity without acknowledging assists. After all, baseball has measures of productivity such as slugging percentage and on-base percentage that do not incorporate all the statistics

TABLE 6.5

The Value of Various NBA Statistics in Terms of Wins

Various Statistics Tracked for Players and Teams	If each variable increased by one, and nothing else changed, wins would change by . . .	If each variable increased by 100, and nothing else changed, wins would change by . . .
SCORING STATISTICS		
Three-point field goals made	+0.066	+6.6
Opponent's three-point field goals made	−0.066	−6.6
Two-point field goals made	+0.033	+3.3
Opponent's two-point field goals made	−0.032	−3.2
Free throws made	+0.018	+1.8
Opponent's free throws made	−0.018	−1.8
Missed field goals	−0.034	−3.4
Missed free throws	−0.015	−1.5
POSSESSION STATISTICS		
Offensive rebounds	+0.034	+3.4
Turnovers	−0.034	−3.4
Defensive rebounds	+0.034	+3.4
Team rebounds	+0.034	+3.4
Opponent's turnovers	+0.034	+3.4
Steals	+0.034	+3.4
PERSONAL FOULS AND BLOCKED SHOTS		
Personal fouls	−0.018	−1.8
Blocked shots	+0.021	+2.1

baseball tracks. So we might feel comfortable using a measure of productivity that ignores one statistic the NBA tabulates.

Unfortunately, the data tell a different story. As we detail in the next chapter, assists clearly matter. The more assists a team accumulates, the more productive its players will be. How do we know this? Well, we connected a player's unassisted productivity to team assists. Of course, we get ahead of ourselves. How do we measure a player's unassisted productivity?

UNASSISTED WINS PRODUCTION

Let's continue with our story of Kobe and Shaq. We wish to know if the Lakers should have kept the Diesel or built the team anew around Kobe. To answer this question, we first need to measure each player's unassisted wins production, or the production of wins these players offered in 2003–04 without any consideration of assists.

The basic steps are as follows: To determine a player's value, we begin with his player statistics—which are comprised of scoring, his ability to gain and maintain possession, personal fouls, and blocked shots. We then make a few adjustments involving primarily the position played and the statistics that are only tracked for the team. As we note, following these steps reveals that Kobe's unassisted wins production was 10.7, while Shaq's unassisted production was worth 14 wins. How do we get to this answer? Let's offer a few details of each step.

Step One: Determine the value of a player's statistics. We begin with the value of statistics tracked for the individual player. Estimating our simple model of team wins allowed us to determine the value of a player's scoring, his ability to acquire and maintain possession of the ball, his propensity to commit personal fouls, and the value of blocked shots. In terms of scoring we have learned the value of three-point and two-point field goals made, missed field goals, and made and missed free throws. If we simply multiply each player's production of each of these statistics by the value in wins we noted in Table 6.5, we see that Kobe's scoring ability was worth 3.8 wins. Shaq, who did not take a single three-point shot attempt and is a notoriously poor free throw shooter, produced 5.4 wins from his scoring. Why was Shaq more valuable? As we noted above, the number of points O'Neal created from his shots from the field exceeded the point production Bryant elicited from his field goal attempts.

Although both players are prodigious scorers, their real value comes from their ability to gain and maintain possession of the ball. When we talk about a player's impact on possession we are talking about offensive and defensive rebounds, steals, and turnovers. Bryant was able to add 10.1 wins from his impact on team possession. Again, though, his productivity was eclipsed by O'Neal, whose accumulation of these statistics was worth 20.5 victories.

The last two player statistics we consider are associated with crimes and rejections. Specifically, Shaq's ability to block shots offsets his personal fouls. Kobe, who does not block many shots, was unable to eliminate the impact of his crimes on the court.

If we put the value of scoring, possession, personal fouls, and blocked shots together for each player, though, it looks like O'Neal is easily the better player. O'Neal's player statistics were worth 26.0 victories while Bryant's were valued at 11.8 wins. In other words, as Table 6.6 summarizes, just in terms of player statistics, Shaq was worth more than twice as much as Bryant.

Step Two: Position adjustment. So even an old Shaq is better than a young Kobe? The story is not quite that simple. We need to say a few words about the positions on the court. Shaq is a center. That places him in the frontcourt with a power for-

TABLE 6.6

Evaluating the Player Statistics for Kobe Bryant and
Shaquille O'Neal, 2003–04

Aspect of Performance	Kobe's Value	Shaq's Value
Scoring	3.8	5.4
Gaining and maintaining possession	10.1	20.5
Crimes and rejections (personal fouls and blocks)	−2.1	0.1
Scoring + Possession + Crimes and Rejections	11.8	26.0

ward and a small forward. Kobe is a shooting guard, which places him in the back court with the team's point guard. When we analyze player productivity we learn one clear lesson. Because responsibilities vary across positions, the productivity of a player depends upon the position the player plays.

Let's consider the guards. These players are primarily responsible for handling the ball. When compared to frontcourt performers, these players accumulate a relatively large number of turnovers. Furthermore, guards tend to be shorter players and play farther from the basket, which means these players gather few rebounds. In contrast, the bigger players in the front court play closer to the basket and handle the ball less. So frontcourt players get more rebounds and commit fewer turnovers. All of this means the average frontcourt player produces more than the average backcourt player.

Now if we did not consider this in our analysis, the measurement of productivity we offer would clearly indicate that most of the wins on the team were created by the frontcourt players. As a consequence, if NBA teams paid attention to our work, they might only want to hire front-court players. The problem with this approach is that we think basketball requires all five positions. In other words, we don't think teams would be better off taking their back-up center and playing him at point guard. In fact, given our unscientific observation that many of the game's giants seem to have trouble walking and dribbling the ball, we are fairly certain placing a back-up center at point guard would result in many more turnovers than what we see from an average point guard.

As economists, we would argue that backcourt and frontcourt players are complements in production, in other words, these players work together to produce wins. Backcourt players handle the ball more, because this job must be done and the guards are relatively better at completing this task. Frontcourt players rebound, because this job must also be done and forwards and centers have an advantage with respect to hitting the boards. We would argue that all these players are necessary to produce wins. Therefore, player evaluations must be weighted by the position the player plays.[38]

What does all this mean for our evaluation of Kobe and Shaq? As we stated, to truly assess their impact, we need to measure their value in the context of the position each player plays. The average center in the NBA in 2003–04, if he was on the court the same amount of time as Shaq, would have produced 17.3 wins. O'Neal produced 26 wins, and if we compare this to the production of an average center, we see that Shaq produced 8.7 wins more than the average player at his position.

If we turn to Bryant we would consider the average shooting guard. The average shooting guard would have produced only 6.4 wins. Kobe's statistics were worth 11.8 wins. Consequently, compared to the average shooting guard, Kobe produced 5.3 more wins than the average player at his position. So Shaq's relative wins production was a bit less than 9, while Kobe's relative wins produced was a bit more than 5. When we look at each player relative to his position, we see that the productivity difference between Shaq and Kobe is no longer quite as great as our strict analysis of player statistics suggested.

You will note we still have two steps to go to reach our final calculation of wins produced. At this point we would emphasize, the final steps do not tend to alter our rankings of the players. As we will mention below, a player's ranking by our measure is almost entirely determined by his statistical production and the position he plays. Still, if we want to move from a player's *relative* wins production to his *total* wins production, there are two more steps.

Step Three: Moving from relative wins toward total wins. Determining each player's relative wins production is revealing, but what we really want to know is how many total wins can we attribute to each player.[39] To move from relative wins to total wins, it is useful to think about this at the level of the team. An NBA team plays 82 regular season games. So an average team will win 41 games. The Lakers in 2003–04 won 15 more games than the average team. Quickly, how many games did the Lakers win? Obviously if the average team wins 41, and a team won 15 more than average, then we are saying that team won 56 games. To move from relative wins to total wins, one simply adds the average to the relative value.

This same logic applies to players. If we wish to move from Shaq's production relative to the average center, to Shaq's total wins production, we simply have to add the average player's production of wins to Shaq's relative output. Now this might seem like we are taking one step forward and one step back. Remember, though, that the average center, or if we look at Kobe, the average shooting guard, is not the same as the average player.

How many wins will the average player produce? If an average team wins 41 games, and it takes five players to play basketball, then an average player who plays all the time will produce 8.2 wins. Now both Shaq and Kobe played only 62% of the available minutes at their respective positions. So an average player who is on the court 62% of the time would produce 5.1 wins. This number is added to both Shaq and Kobe's *relative* wins production. When we do this, we determine each player's *total* wins production. As we mentioned, this adjustment has no impact on either player's ranking. We are making the same adjustment to each player, so the argument that Shaq is more productive than Kobe still remains.

Step Four: Adjusting for team statistics. We are just about finished. So far we have not discussed the various statistics tracked for the team. These include three-point and two-point field goals made by the opponent, turnovers by the opponent that are not steals, and team rebounds.[40] For the most part these are measures of defense that we do not track for individual players.

Before we say how we incorporate these factors, let's make a brief comment about how defense is assessed in the NBA. We often hear that this player or that player is good at defense. Such players, therefore, must be difficult to score upon. Given that we hear such accolades, it must be the case that someone has tracked how many times an opponent scores when a specific player is playing defense. After all, without this kind of data, how would you know? Can you tell if a player is good at defense just by staring real hard at the player? If staring worked, why are we keeping any of these other numbers?

As Barra notes, we keep numbers because we can't watch all the players all the time. If we follow that argument, then people who claim that one player is better than another defensively need to tell us where they found the time to constantly watch these players.[41] The problem is even more complicated because the NBA now allows zone defenses, which means players are no longer technically assigned the responsibility to guard specific players. In the end, we think assessing defense would be difficult by just staring at the players. However, if anyone has actually collected the data, these numbers could then be easily incorporated in our player evaluation.

While we wait for each player's defensive measures, we have constructed what we call the team's statistical adjustment. We then follow a convention we have observed and personally employed in the economics literature. Specifically we allocate the impact of the team statistical adjustment according to the minutes each player was on the court.[42]

What matters in this calculation is the team's measure relative to the average team. The Lakers were slightly better with respect to our team statistics than the

TABLE 6.7

Evaluating the Unassisted Wins Produced: Kobe Bryant
and Shaquille O'Neal, 2003–04

Steps	Aspect of Performance	Kobe's Wins Production	Shaq's Wins Production
Step 1	Scoring + Possession + Crimes and Rejections	11.8	26.0
Step 2 & Step 3	Adjustment for averages	1.4	12.2
Step 4	Adjustment for team statistics	0.3	0.3
	UNASSISTED WINS PRODUCED: Step 1 – Step 2 + Step 3	10.7	14.0

average team. Consequently we end up adding to each player's production value, as determined in steps one through three, each player's contribution to the Lakers' team statistical adjustment.[43] Specifically, incorporating the team statistical adjustment for Bryant and O'Neal involves adding about 0.3 to both Kobe's and Shaq's total wins production. In general, the team statistical adjustment is quite small for each player and therefore this adjustment does not substantially alter our rankings of players across teams. To illustrate this point, the correlation coefficient between player production unadjusted for team statistics and then adjusted for team statistics is 0.99. In simple words, whether you adjust for the team statistics or not, the player rankings are essentially the same.

We summarize all of our steps in Table 6.7. We began with the value of each player's statistical production. This value was then weighted in steps two and three by the two averages we noted above. For simplicity, we added these steps together. Finally, we adjusted for team statistics, resulting in our final measure of unassisted wins production.

After completing all these steps we learn that Shaq was worth 14 wins and Kobe contributed 10.7. As we said, the older Shaq was slightly better than the younger Kobe. Now we must note, we do not believe the Lakers followed any of these steps. Given that our book is being published two years after the decision was made, unless the Lakers have access to time travel, this was probably not exactly how these players were evaluated. Still, our analysis indicates that if the Lakers did follow these methods they might have come to the same conclusion. A younger, slightly less productive Kobe, could be thought of as a better bet than an older, slightly more productive Diesel. This will also be true once we account for assists, a step we take in the next chapter.

Summarizing All of Our Steps

Before we move to the next chapter, though, let's review what we have learned thus far. We start at the very beginning. To determine a player's wins production you:

1. Regress team wins on offensive efficiency—points scored per possession employed—and defensive efficiency—points allowed per possession acquired.

2. From this regression, determine the value of a collection of statistics tabulated for the individual player and team, in terms of wins.

3. The player statistics can be separated into the following: scoring, possession, personal fouls, and blocked shots. If we multiply each player's accumulation of each statistic by its corresponding value in terms of wins, we can determine the value of each player's statistical production.

4. We argued that position matters, so each player's statistical production needs to be considered relative to what the average player at his position would produce.

5. The previous step gives us a player's relative wins production, but we want total wins. To move from relative wins to total wins, simply add the number of wins an average player would produce. It is important to note that this step does not alter how we rank the players.

6. We also need to adjust for the statistics only tabulated for the team. These are allocated according to the amount of time the player was on the court. Such an adjustment is generally quite small and also tends not to alter our ranking of players.

After all these steps what do we learn? Once again we repeat ourselves: Where we rank players according to our measure is driven almost entirely by each player's statistical production relative to the position the player plays.

See, pretty easy stuff. Okay, not so easy stuff. We promised simple and accurate, and so far we don't seem to have simple. We will make this simple in the next chapter (we promise). For now, though, let's talk about accuracy.

THE ACCURACY OF OUR METHODS

How accurate is this approach? We have already said that our model explains 95% of team wins. Unfortunately, this basic statement has little meaning for those not versed in regression analysis. To put the accuracy of our methods in perspective, we measured the wins produced by each player employed by the NBA for the

TABLE 6.8

Evaluating the Accuracy of Wins Produced, 2003–04 Regular Season

Teams	Summation of Player Wins Produced	Actual Team Wins	Difference in Absolute Terms
San Antonio	60.4	57	3.44
Detroit	56.7	54	2.75
Indiana	56.6	61	4.41
Minnesota	55.8	58	2.21
Sacramento	54.6	55	0.38
Dallas	53.1	52	1.15
LA Lakers	51.7	56	4.31
Memphis	47.8	50	2.23
New Jersey	47.5	47	0.52
Houston	45.9	45	0.90
Milwaukee	43.8	41	2.85
Denver	43.7	43	0.73
Miami	42.3	42	0.28
New Orleans	40.7	41	0.26
Seattle	39.3	37	2.31
Golden State	39.1	37	2.10
Portland	37.9	41	3.10
Utah	37.6	42	4.41
New York	37.1	39	1.89
Boston	36.8	36	0.82
Philadelphia	34.3	33	1.27
Cleveland	33.9	35	1.06
Toronto	33.1	33	0.09
Phoenix	30.6	29	1.64
Atlanta	28.5	28	0.55
LA Clippers	28.5	28	0.53
Washington	25.7	25	0.68
Chicago	23.7	23	0.70
Orlando	22.0	21	0.96
		AVERAGE ERROR	1.67

2003–04 season. We then summed wins produced by each player for each team. How does our summation of player wins produced compare to actual team wins?

The answer is reported in Table 6.8. The average difference between the summation of player wins produced and team totals is 1.67 wins.[44] How does it do for the Lakers? The team won 56 games, yet our model predicts only 51.7 victories. The difference of 4.3 wins is actually one of the largest we observe. The team the Lakers played in the finals, the Pistons, had a predicted win total equal to 56.7. Remember our model is based on offensive and defensive efficiency. Given these results, perhaps people should not have been surprised when the Pistons defeated the Lakers in five games. Although playoffs are not a perfect test for determining the identity of the best team, our analysis of player production indicates that contrary to popular perception, the Lakers were not necessarily better than the Pistons in the regular season and should not have been heavy favorites prior to the 2004 NBA Finals.

So we may not have simple, but it looks like we have accurate. Of course, having an accurate model can provide much joy, but simple and complete would certainly increase our happiness. And that is what we will work toward next.

7 | WHO IS THE BEST?

In introducing our approach to measuring productivity we stated our goals. We wanted a metric that was accurate, simple, and complete. So far we are batting one for three. If this were baseball, we would be all-stars. Unfortunately, one for three is a lousy average in the life that exists outside of baseball. So we take the field in this chapter with the goal of producing a model that is not only accurate, but also simple and complete.

A SIMPLE MODEL OF UNASSISTED PRODUCTIVITY

To build a truly simple model we need to return to our simple statement describing wins: *Wins are solely a function of offensive and defensive efficiency.* In general, what do we see when we look at an NBA team's level of efficiency? In 2003–04 the average team managed to score one point per possession employed, and conversely, allow one point per possession acquired. Over the years we examine (1993–94 to 2004–05) this ratio tended to hover around one, hitting a high of 1.05 points per possession in 1994–95 and a low of 0.99 points per possession in 1998–99. In general, though, one can argue that the average team gets one point per possession.[1]

Why is this important? If each possession yields one point, then the value of a point scored equals the value of each factor that comprises possessions employed and possessions acquired. In other words, the value of scoring one point must equal, in absolute terms, the value of a field goal attempt, offensive rebound, turnover, defensive rebound, and steal. We have also learned that a free throw attempt is worth a bit less than half a point, while personal fouls and blocked shots are worth a bit more than half a point. Knowing all this, we can create a very simple model of unassisted productivity. Basically a player's unassisted productivity can be calculated as follows:

Points + Total Rebounds + Steals + ½ Blocked Shots − Field Goal Attempts
− ½ Free Throw Attempts −Turnovers − ½ Personal Fouls

MAKING YOUR TEAMMATES BETTER, THE VALUE OF AN ASSIST, AND OTHER SHORT STORIES

Our very simple model is missing both a catchy label and recognition of a player's assists. The next step in our discussion is to correct both shortcomings. Before we take this step, though, let's discuss the story that great players improve the performance of their lesser teammates.

Making Your Teammates Better?

There is a standard argument offered about what makes a player truly great. Truly great players don't just play well, they also make their teammates better players. Following this line of reasoning, Michael Jordan was not just a great player because he scored, rebounded, and generated steals, but also because he was able to lead a team of lesser players, often called the Jordanaires, to six championships in eight seasons.

Is it true that Jordan made his teammates better? We have noted that Jordan not only was a record-setting performer on the court, but also may have established the NBA record for retirements, exiting the game on three occasions. The first retirement occurred after the 1993 NBA Finals. After leading the Bulls to championships in three consecutive seasons, Jordan decided to give baseball a try. Eventually Jordan learned that greatness on the diamond was not likely to happen. As a result, after a bit less than two years, Jordan again returned to basketball. Although Jordan's time in baseball was not successful, it did provide a wonderful opportunity for us to see the impact MJ had on the Bulls. The Bulls in 1992–93 won 57 regular season games. Of these 57 wins, we estimate Jordan produced nearly 25 victories.[2] With this level of productivity learning to hit curveballs, people expected the Bulls to fade considerably.

Surprisingly, though, this did not happen. In 1993–94 the Bulls managed to win 55 games. Jordan was replaced on the Bulls roster by two players, Pete Myers and Steve Kerr. It's possible that Myers and Kerr were able to offer a contribution similar to Jordan. Okay, possible, but not likely and indeed, that is not what happened.

We estimate that the difference between Jordan and these two players was about twenty wins. So something seems quite odd here. How can losing one of the greatest players to ever play the game have so little impact on a team's won-loss record? Although the statistics say Jordan was worth more than twenty wins, the won-loss record suggests the number is closer to two.

To answer this question, we examined the Bulls roster in 1993–94 and 1992–93. The results suggest a few answers. Part of the answer lies in the ability of the Bulls to elicit wins from its offensive and defensive efficiency. In 1992–93 the Bulls won 57 games, but the model predicts 58.1. In 1993–94 the Bulls won 55 games, but the model says the team should have won 49.4. In other words, from a statistical perspective, the Bulls were nearly nine games worse without Jordan. So the data tell us that the Bulls should have been twenty wins worse without Jordan. Reality says the team was only two wins worse. About half of the difference between twenty and two can be explained by the 1993–94 team getting more wins out of its statistics then we might expect.

What of the other half? The media often referred to the Bulls as Jordan and the Jordanaires. Although it is certainly the case that Jordan was the Bulls' best player, Chicago's success was due to more than Jordan. In 1992–93 the Bulls received nearly 27 wins from Scottie Pippen and Horace Grant. Although these players were not the equal of MJ, each was clearly an above average performer.

In 1993–94 the Bulls were led by these "other" two stars. Both Pippen and Grant, without MJ, suddenly played much better. How much better? We can see this if we look at Pippen and Grant on a per-minute basis. In 1992–93 both Pippen and Grant were above average NBA players. In 1993–94, though, both were quite a bit better. To illustrate the difference, had each player maintained their per-minute productivity from 1992–93 the next season, these two would have produced eleven fewer wins in 1993–94. In sum, Pippen and Grant both went from being good players with MJ, to being among the very best in 1993–94. Specifically, Pippen was the most productive small forward, and the sixth most productive player overall. Grant ranked fifteenth overall in the league, and among power forwards, placed fifth.

Now we want to emphasize that this story is purely anecdotal. Still, this anecdotal evidence suggests something odd about Jordan's performance. People often say that the truly great players in basketball can make their teammates better. Yet both Pippen and Grant played much better without his Airness. Does this mean Jordan is not a great player? Before we jump to such a silly conclusion, let's consult a bit of economic theory.

The Law of Diminishing Returns

There are two fundamental laws to the economics of a business. The Law of Demand we mentioned in Chapter Five. The other is the Law of Diminishing Returns. This law simply states that if a firm keeps hiring more workers, and nothing else about a firm's manufacturing process changes, the productivity of each worker must decline. After all, if more workers have less machinery and land to work with, then the workers must be less productive. In basketball this can be illustrated by one simple statement: "There is only one ball!" When Jordan has the ball, Pippen and Grant do not have the ball. So if you add Jordan, a certain number of shot attempts and rebounds that would go to Pippen and Grant, now go to Jordan.

To further illustrate this point, consider a team comprised of the top five players at each position in 1993–94. Such a team would have John Stockton (22.0 wins produced) at point guard, Nick Anderson (13.3 wins produced) at shooting guard, Scottie Pippen (20.4 wins produced) at small forward, Dennis Rodman (29.6 wins produced) at power forward, and Shaquille O'Neal (26.8 wins produced) at center.[3] These players combined to produce 112 wins. If all these players were on the same team, though, their wins produced could not exceed the length of the regular season, or 82 victories. Hence, if we put all five players on the same team someone would have to play worse.

This simple example illustrates a basic lesson economic theory teaches. If you add more productive players to your team, you can expect either the productivity of the new players, or the productivity of existing players, to decline. According to simple economic theory, it must be a myth that great players make their teammates better.

Now we wish to clarify exactly what we are saying. It is possible that having a great scorer who attracts the attention of defenses opens up some easier shots for other players. It is also true that passing, which is noted by the tracking of assists, also enhances the productivity of teammates. What our simple story illustrates, though, is just the idea that there is only one ball, and therefore the total productivity of one player often comes at the expense of other members of the team.

Of course we will not simply appeal to theory in making this argument. Is there any more evidence of our contention beyond our simple analysis of the Chicago Bulls from the early 1990s?

Finally, the Value of an Assist

To do better, we need to understand what determines a player's level of productivity. So far we know much about the measurement of player performance. We know

TABLE 7.1

What Explains Current Per-Minute Productivity in the NBA?

Factors we found to be statistically related to current per-minute productivity	How the factor is measured (more details in endnotes)
Player's talent and ability	Per-minute productivity last season
Player health	Games played
Player's level of experience	Two variables, one for young players, another for old players
Coaching ability	The head coach's lifetime winning percentage
Stability of a team's roster	Roster stability measure (detailed in Chapter Five)
Productivity of teammates	Wins produced by teammates, per-minute played
Team assists	Assists totaled by teammates, per-minute played

that a player increases his value via scoring, rebounding, etc., and he decreases his value by spending shot attempts and committing turnovers. Now we need to work on an explanation. Specifically what we wish to know is what factors cause a player to be more productive, and which factors lower his productivity.

It is important to note that we measured productivity with the simple unassisted model we listed above. We actually did a bit more, measuring productivity, via our simple unassisted model, on a per-minute basis. With this measure in hand, we then tried to understand why a player achieved the per-minute production we observed. Once again, we employed regression analysis. Specifically we regressed a player's per-minute performance on a variety of factors we believed could explain performance.[4] Certainly this list of factors would begin with a player's talent and ability. This we can capture by noting the player's past productivity. What will cause a player's performance to deviate from what we observed in the past?

We began with a sample of player performance that began with the 1993–94 campaign and ended with the 2003–04 season.[5] With sample in hand, we then regressed[6] current player performance on the factors we listed in Table 7.1. The first factor listed is past productivity, which is clearly the dominant factor. Past productivity alone explains 72% of the variation in current performance. When we include additional factors, our explanatory power only rises to 76%. As we expected, what a player did in the past is the key factor one needs to understand if you wish to predict current performance.

Beyond past productivity, though, we did consider six additional factors. From our model we learned that player health matters. Specifically, the more games a player plays, the greater his per-minute productivity.[7] We also learned that being an older player hurts performance. Unexpectedly, though, we did not find much evidence that younger players systematically get better. At least, the statistical evidence that players get better early in their careers was weak.[8] Coaching ability, which we measured via the head coach's life-time winning percentage, was also found to be important. Coaching experience, though, was not found to be statistically important.[9] Finally, the stability of a team's roster, which was the same factor we employed in our study of gate revenue, was found to statistically impact performance. The more stable a team's roster from year to year, the better the team's players will perform.

All of this is very interesting, but our main focus is the productivity of a player's teammates and the impact of assists. As our story of Jordan suggests, the productivity of a player's teammates matters. If a player is blessed with productive teammates, which we measured via the number of per-minute unassisted wins his teammates produced, then we can expect a player's performance to suffer.[10] So the Law of Diminishing Returns does apply to the NBA.

What about assists? Again, when we constructed our measure of productivity based upon scoring per possession, assists did not fit into our story. In fact, we were prepared to tell a clever story for why assists are not important. Unfortunately, as is often the case when we look at the numbers, the data told a different tale. Specifically, the last factor we included in our model of per-minute productivity was the number of assists a player's teammates accumulated per-minute played.[11] We found clear evidence that the more assists a team accumulates the better the players on the team will perform. In other words, assists matter.

We were also able to use our results to determine the specific value of an assist. After a bit of work,[12] we found that each additional assist was worth about 0.67 points, or about 0.022 wins. In other words, for every 100 assists a player accumulates, his teammates' productivity rises by 2.2 wins. With this information, we can now complete our simple model. Again, we choose to simplify. We could go with the precise valuation of an assist we estimated, but we found our rankings of players were unaffected if we simply said an assist was worth half a point.[13] Hence, our final simple model of player productivity, which we will call Win Score,[14] is as follows:

$$\text{Points} + \text{Total Rebounds} + \text{Steals} + \tfrac{1}{2} \text{ Blocked Shots}$$
$$+ \tfrac{1}{2} \text{ Assists} - \text{Field Goal Attempts} - \tfrac{1}{2} \text{ Free Throw Attempts}$$
$$- \text{Turnovers} - \tfrac{1}{2} \text{ Personal Fouls}$$

So now we have a measure that incorporates assists, giving us a metric that is simple, accurate, and complete. Plus we think it has a catchy label.

EVALUATING EFFICIENCY WITH NBA EFFICIENCY

At first glance, though, this might look like the NBA Efficiency model. It certainly is as easy to use as the NBA's metric. Beyond ease of use, there are other similarities.[15] Because points and possessions are virtually equal, it is then true, as the NBA Efficiency model asserts, that points, rebounds, steals, and turnovers are worth the same. Differences lie in our inclusion of personal fouls and our argument that a blocked shot and an assist are not equal in value to the statistics associated with scoring and possession.

The crucial difference, though, is seen in how we value field goal and free throw attempts. We have already noted that the NBA Efficiency model treats a missed field goal and missed free throw the same. Certainly the value of missing these different types of shots is not the same in terms of points scored, or more importantly, in terms of wins. Although this is an important issue, the bigger issue is the impact of made shot attempts. Whether a player makes or misses a shot, a resource is used when a shot attempt is taken. According to the NBA's method, though, the cost of the shot attempt is not imposed if the shot goes in. Consequently, if a player is evaluated according to the NBA model, he only needs to make 25% of his three-point shots for the benefit of these shots to equal the costs the NBA actually charges. To illustrate, consider a player who takes four three-point shots and makes one. As a result, his NBA Efficiency measure will rise by three, because this is the number of points he scored; and fall by three, because this is the number of missed shots the player accumulated. So we see that if a player converts 25% of his shots beyond the arc, then the value of the points he accumulates equals the cost of his missed shots. If he shoots better than 25%, his NBA Efficiency value will rise. For two-point attempts, the break-even point is 40%. Any player who exceeds this threshold on two-point shots will increase his NBA Efficiency value as he increases his shot attempts.

The story of Antoine Walker illustrates our point. According to the NBA Efficiency model, Walker was the 35th most productive player in the NBA in 2004–05. Given that more than 450 players played that season, if we believe the NBA model, Walker was ranked in the top 10% of all players. A key reason for Walker's lofty ranking was his scoring totals. With an average of 19.1 points per game, he also ranked in the top 40 among scorers. Although Walker achieved a high scoring average, a bit of inspection reveals he was not a very efficient producer of points. In the 2004–05 campaign, 35 players took more than 300 shots from the three-point range. Walker took 341, and with a three-point field goal percentage of 32%, his accuracy from this distance among the 300 plus shooters ranked 34th, or second to last. His two-point field goal percentage was also relatively poor. Walker was one of twenty players who took at least 1,000 shots from two-point range. Given a shooting percentage of 45%, he ranked fifteenth—out of twenty—in accuracy among prolific shooters from two-point range. So Walker shot relatively poorly from both inside and outside the arc. Still, his percentages exceeded the thresholds imposed by the NBA model, and consequently Walker earned high marks in NBA Efficiency despite his inefficient scoring.

What happens when we view Walker through the lens of the productivity model we employ? The Win Score measure we propose imposes the cost of the shot attempt regardless of whether or not the shot is made. As a result, a player must connect on at least 50% of two-point shots and 33% of three pointers for the benefit of shooting to equal the cost. Walker failed to achieve these levels; consequently, his Win Score was below the average player at his position. Specifically, Walker posted a Win Score of 493.5 in 2004–05, while an average player at his position playing his minutes would have posted a Win Score of 635. So the NBA Efficiency model, which does not value shot attempts correctly, argues that Walker is an above average performer. When we take into account the cost of Walker's many field goal attempts, we see that Walker is actually below average.

One should note that in evaluating Walker we looked at his performance relative to the average at his position. As we have previously emphasized, the position a player plays determines the relative worth of his performance. To see this again, consider the average per-minute value of Win Score at each position. From 1993–94 to 2004–05 the average center had a per-minute Win Score of 0.22, while the power forwards averaged 0.21. Small forwards only averaged 0.15, while shooting guards and point guards offered an average of 0.13. Although frontcourt players generally post higher Win Score values, it again does not mean that these players are worth more than guards. Again, centers cannot typically play point guard. Given the realities of basketball you need to consider a player's performance relative to the average at his position if you wish to compare players at different positions.

Of course, if you just wish to see if a specific player improved or declined, then Win Score is perfectly suitable to the task. In other words, if you wish to compare a player to himself the simple model unadjusted for position played is fine. You can also use the Win Score model if you wish to compare players playing the same position.

If you wish to address the issue of "Who is best?" we need to make comparisons across positions. And as long as we are going to make an effort, why not go all the way and think about each player's production of wins? Now that we know the value of an assist, we can construct each player's assisted wins production, or what we will just call Wins Produced.[16] With this metric in hand, we can now return to our story of Shaq and Kobe as we progress toward identifying the best player in the NBA.

SHAQ AND KOBE, THE SEQUEL

When we left our story we had learned that without considering assists, Shaq had produced 14 unassisted wins in 2003–04. Kobe's unassisted wins production was 10.7. Kobe was credited with 330 assists that season, surpassing Shaq's total of 196. It would seem that once assists are noted Kobe would erase some of the distance between his level of productivity and O'Neal. One must remember, though, that players are evaluated relative to their position. Shooting guards tend to accumulate more assists relative to centers. So Kobe's advantage in assists will be muted substantially.

As seen in Table 7.2, once assists are noted, Kobe's wins production did rise to 12.2. Shaq also is more productive once assists are included in our calculations. His wins production rose to 15.4. Thus the difference between the two players is still basically the same with and without assists. Shaq is still a bit more productive, and Kobe is still quite a bit younger.

We should emphasize that the accuracy of our methods is unchanged. The summation of player wins with and without assists is the same. When we say that with assists Kobe and Shaq were better, we should add that players who do not accumulate many assists, relative to the positions they play, look worse once assists are incorporated in our analysis.

TABLE 7.2

Evaluating Wins Produced: Kobe Bryant and
Shaquille O'Neal, 2003–04

Steps	Aspect of Performance	Kobe's Wins Production	Shaq's Wins Production
	Scoring	3.8	5.4
	Gaining and maintaining possession	10.1	20.5
	Crimes and rejections (personal fouls and blocks)	−2.1	0.1
	Assists	7.4	4.4
Step 1	Scoring + Possession + Crimes and Rejections + Assists	19.1	30.4
Step 2	Adjustment for averages	6.7	14.7
Step 3	Adjustment for team statistics	−0.3	−0.3
	WINS PRODUCED: Step 1 − Step 2 + Step 3	12.2	15.4

With the productivity of Shaq and Kobe accurately measured, let's return to the summer of 2004. At that time the Lakers made their choice. Shaq was traded to the Miami Heat, and the Lakers became Kobe's team. Unfortunately for Kobe, the Lakers did not have a good season in 2004–05. Making matters worse, Shaq's new team suddenly became quite successful. Did the Lakers make the wrong choice? To answer this question, let's see what really happened in 2004–05.

Shaq's Story

In 2003–04 Shaq produced 15.4 wins for the Los Angeles Lakers. He left the Lakers and joined a Heat team that had only won 42 games. In 2004–05, though, O'Neal's new team improved to 59 victories. Consequently, one might think O'Neal was worth 17 wins to his new team. As we mentioned in our discussion of plus-minus, evaluating a player in terms of how a team is with and without his services is problematic. Of course we now have a measure of each player's wins production that can tell us what Shaq meant to the Heat.

Before we discuss our results, we want to introduce one more performance metric. Shaq and Kobe played virtually the same number of minutes in 2003–04, so a comparison of total wins production was valid. When one discusses players who play different minutes, though, one needs to consider productivity per time spent on the court. Specifically, we wish to consider each player's wins production per 48 minutes played. So far in this book we have minimized our use of acronyms. We do not want to keep saying "wins production per 48 minutes played" so for the rest of the book we will simply use "WP48."

How do we calculate WP48? We begin with a player's production of wins. We then divide Wins Produced by minutes played. This calculation gives you a very small number, which we multiply by 48 to give us WP48. As with much in life, an example would help. Shaq produced 15.4 wins in 2,464 minutes in 2003–04. If you divide 15.4 by 2,464, you get a really, really tiny number.[17] If you multiply this tiny number by 48 you get 0.300. As a result we learn that per 48 minutes Shaq's statistical output was worth about .3 wins. Kobe Bryant produced 12.2 wins in 2,447 minutes. Follow the same calculations and we see that Kobe's WP48 was 0.239, or a bit less than one-fourth a win per 48 minutes played.

The next question is: What does this mean? If a baseball player had a batting average that was 0.239, that would not be good. The average Major League Baseball player hit 0.266 in 2004, so 0.239 would be thought of as bad. Of course, WP48 is not a batting average. Still, the same lesson applies. We need to know the average WP48 to know whether Shaq and Kobe were good or bad.

To understand average wins production in the NBA, let's begin by saying that

TABLE 7.3

Connecting Player Wins to Team Wins:
The Miami Heat, 2004–05

Miami Heat 2004–05	Wins Produced	WP48
Shaquille O'Neal	15.9	0.306
Dwyane Wade	12.2	0.197
Damon Jones	10.6	0.197
Udonis Haslem	10.1	0.181
Eddie Jones	7.4	0.124
Shandon Anderson	2.2	0.092
Christian Laettner	1.7	0.111
Alonzo Mourning	1.1	0.223
Wesley Person	0.3	0.062
Malik Allen	0.1	0.011
ZhiZhi Wang	0.0	0.017
Steve Smith	0.0	0.012
Qyntel Woods	0.0	−0.052
Dorell Wright	−0.1	−0.266
Keyon Dooling	−0.6	−0.023
Michael Doleac	−0.9	−0.036
Rasual Butler	−0.9	−0.035
SUMMATION OF PLAYER WINS	59.1	
ACTUAL WINS	59	

the average team wins half its games. So in each regulation game, which is 48 minutes long, the average team will produce 0.500 wins. Basketball is a game of five-on-five, so an average player over 48 minutes will produce one-fifth the wins production of an average team. In other words, the average player will have a WP48 of 0.100. From all this we see that Shaq was three times more productive than the average player. Kobe was more than twice as productive, per 48 minutes, as the average player in the NBA. In other words, Shaq and Kobe were both very good in 2003–04.

What about 2004–05? This is Shaq's story, so let's look at his impact on the Heat. We measured the Wins Produced and WP48 of each player Miami employed in 2004–05. Our analysis is reported in Table 7.3, where the players are ranked in terms of wins.

From Table 7.3 we see that Shaq offered the Heat virtually the same level of productivity he gave the Lakers. In 2003–04 O'Neal produced 15.4 wins. In 2004–05 he led the Heat with 15.9 Wins Produced. His WP48 was also quite similar in each season, rising from 0.300 in 2003–04 to 0.306 in 2004–05.

It is important to note that although Shaq was the most productive player with

Miami, he was not a one-man team. Three other players, Dwayne Wade, Damon Jones, and Udonis Haslem, each reached double digits in victories produced. Overall Wade was the third most productive shooting guard in the league, D. Jones ranked sixth among point guards, and Haslem was the tenth highest rated power forward. In fact, 83% of the Heat's 59 wins can be traced to the productivity of O'Neal, Wade, D. Jones, and Haslem.

Let's put this productivity in perspective. In 2003–04 Shaq played with a star-laden Lakers team, whose statistical production was worth about 52 wins. Of these wins, 44 wins can be traced to the productivity of the teams four stars: Shaq, Kobe, the Mailman—Karl Malone—and the Glove—Gary Payton. In 2004–05 Shaq was virtually the same player. His teammates with the Heat also offered a similar level of productivity to O'Neal's teammates in Los Angeles. Dwayne Wade, D. Jones, and Haslem offered nearly 33 wins. In 2003–04, Kobe, Payton, and Malone offered 29 wins. From all this we see that in both seasons Shaq played on one of the better teams in the league.

Kobe's Story

Let's now move on to Kobe's story. Our analysis of Shaq and Kobe in 2003–04 suggested the Lakers could not be faulted for building around Bryant. We are writing in the summer of 2005, so we already know how the 2004–05 season played out. The Lakers, without Shaq, only won 34 games and completely missed the playoffs.

So what happened to Kobe and the Lakers? We have already observed Bryant's productivity in 2003–04. Kobe produced 12.2 wins, or a bit more than 20% of the Lakers' overall win total. In 2004–05 Kobe produced nearly 30% of the Lakers' wins. Of course, 20% of 56 is a bit more impressive than 30% of 34. As we note in Table 7.4, Kobe did play worse in 2004–05. His WP48 declined from 0.239 to 0.175. Unfortunately, even if Kobe had maintained his 2003–04 productivity, the Lakers would have won fewer than four more games. This might have allowed the team to post a better record than the cross-town rival LA Clippers, but the team would have still missed the playoffs.

Clearly the problems the Lakers experienced in 2004–05 were not entirely about Kobe playing worse. If we look at the productivity of the players the Lakers lost from 2003–04, and compare this output to what the team added for 2004–05, we start to see a bigger problem. In the summer of 2004 the Lakers lost three stars likely destined for the Hall of Fame, the aforementioned Shaq, Mailman, and Glove. These three players combined for about 32 wins in 2003–04. The ten players new to the Lakers in 2004–05 only produced about 23 victories. Furthermore, none of the new players who played substantial minutes for the 2004–05 Lakers

TABLE 7.4

Connecting Player Wins to Team Wins:
The Los Angeles Lakers, 2004–05

LA Lakers 2004–05	Wins Produced	WP48
Kobe Bryant	9.8	0.175
Lamar Odom	8.4	0.173
Caron Butler	5.2	0.091
Jumaine Jones	4.6	0.122
Chris Mihm	3.3	0.084
Chucky Atkins	2.7	0.045
Luke Walton	1.8	0.115
Sasha Vujacic	0.1	0.017
Devean George	0.1	0.015
Tony Bobbitt	0.0	0.152
Vlade Divac	−0.1	−0.049
Brian Grant	−0.3	−0.012
Brian Cook	−0.3	−0.012
Kareem Rush	−0.4	−0.192
Stanislav Medvedenko	−1.1	−0.120
Tierre Brown	−1.1	−0.051
SUMMATION OF PLAYER WINS	32.9	
ACTUAL WINS	34	

were as productive per 48 minutes as the future Hall-of-Fame players the team lost. So the story of the Lakers' decline is driven by the departure of several stars the team had employed.

We still might ask, though, what happened to Kobe? One might think the key to Kobe's decline was the departure of Shaq, but we think it was more about Gary Payton. Payton has consistently been one of the best point guards in the game. When Payton left, the job of starting point guard went to Chucky Atkins. Atkins is not really a pass-first point guard, but primarily plays the role of designated three-point shot specialist. Without a traditional point guard, Bryant became the de facto ball handler. The result was Bryant's turnovers per game rose from 2.6 in 2003–04 to 4.1 in 2004–05. The increase in turnovers is the primary reason Bryant's overall productivity declined.

Should the Lakers have kept Shaq and let Kobe go? Our analysis suggests that Kobe might have remained a top shooting guard had the Lakers bothered to keep the Glove, or at least replaced Payton with a traditional point guard. Without the acquisition of a true point guard in the future, we might expect Kobe's turnovers to remain high, and his overall contribution to continue to suffer.

Before moving on, let's observe that Kobe's story highlights a key aspect of any statistical measure of productivity: One cannot end the analysis when one has measured the value of player performance. Knowing the value of each player is only the starting point of analysis. The next step is determining why the player is productive or unproductive. In our view, this is where coaching should begin. We think we can offer a reasonable measure of a player's productivity. Although we have offered some insights into *why* players are productive, ultimately this question can only be answered by additional scrutiny into the construction of a team and the roles a player plays on the floor.

WHO IS THE BEST?

As much as we love the Shaq and Kobe stories, it is time to move on to a more important issue. Let's finally address the question "Who is the best?"

This is the one question that often seems to lead to the most passionate debate among sports fans. Again fans of sport may care very little about the major issues confronting the nation or the world. But if you say to a fan of Allen Iverson that AI may not even be the best player on the 76ers, now you are just asking for an argument. At times sports talk radio appears to be a medium devoted almost entirely to people screaming about why the player they love is better than the player loved by someone else.

As we have stated earlier, it is with some trepidation that we enter this debate. We wish to make it very clear what we are saying. We are defining "best" in terms of productivity. As we demonstrated, Shaq produced more wins than Kobe in 2003–04 and 2004–05. By our definition, this means Shaq has been better in the past and Kobe has been worse.

The Most Productive Player in 2004

Our story of Shaq and Kobe began in the 2003–04 season, and this is where we will begin our examination of the best players in the NBA. Our review of the Lakers of that season revealed that the best player on that team was Shaq. Was he the most productive player in the league?

To answer this question, let's turn to the voting for the Most Valuable Player in the league.[18] The MVP of the league can be thought of as the best player, although it is not clear that is how each sports writer defines the award. In fact, it is not entirely clear how this award is defined. Still, the MVP should certainly be one of the better players in the league, so it is useful to begin our inquiry with the opinion of the sports writers who vote for this prize.

TABLE 7.5

Analyzing the Contenders for the 2004 MVP Award

Player	Team	Voting Points	Rank: Wins Produced	Rank: NBA Efficiency	Wins Produced	NBA Efficiency	WP48
Kevin Garnett	Minnesota	1,219	1	1	30.5	2,717	0.453
Tim Duncan	San Antonio	716	3	4	19.7	1,849	0.374
Jermaine O'Neal	Indiana	523	44	10	8.8	1,681	0.151
Peja Stojakovic	Sacramento	281	11	2	15.2	1,862	0.224
Kobe Bryant	LA Lakers	212	18	27	12.2	1,474	0.239
Shaquille O'Neal	LA Lakers	178	9	12	15.4	1,670	0.300
Ben Wallace	Detroit	24	2	19	20.4	1,602	0.321
Jason Kidd	New Jersey	17	10	37	15.3	1,370	0.300
LeBron James	Cleveland	11	77	23	6.4	1,483	0.099
Sam Cassell	Minnesota	4	20	11	12.0	1,674	0.203
Dirk Nowitzki	Dallas	4	37	3	9.2	1,861	0.151
Baron Davis	New Orleans	4	60	44	7.7	1,327	0.137
Andrei Kirilenko	Utah	2	4	9	17.8	1,684	0.295
Michael Redd	Milwaukee	1	43	26	8.8	1,475	0.140
Yao Ming	Houston	1	21	8	11.8	1,687	0.211
Carmelo Anthony	Denver	1	177	34	2.0	1,383	0.032

In 2004 sports writers had little trouble naming the league's MVP. Of the 123 writers voting, 120 cast their first place vote for Kevin Garnett.[19] Again, we are not sure how one defines this award. Still, when 98% of sports writers reach the same conclusion, it suggests that Garnett was considered a pretty good player in 2003–04. What does our analysis reveal?

Throughout this book we have noted that sports writers and our statistical analysis often arrive at very different conclusions. In fact, as the subtitle of our book suggests, the purpose of this book was to expose the myths of modern sports. Our analysis, though, indicates that for this one issue we must agree. In terms of Wins Produced, Garnett was the most productive player in 2003–04.

Beyond Garnett, though, the voting by the sports writers and our analysis diverge. To see this point, we measured the productivity of more than 400 players who played during the 2003–04 campaign. We then proceeded to rank all these players in terms of both Wins Produced and NBA Efficiency. For the players who received votes from the sports writers, we report our analysis in Table 7.5.

What do we learn from this exercise? Of the sixteen players who received any votes from sports writers, only seven players were actually in the top sixteen in terms of Wins Produced; and three players, LeBron James, Baron Davis, and Carmelo Anthony, were not even in the top 10% of players in the league. In contrast, nine players receiving votes were in the top sixteen in NBA Efficiency. Furthermore, all players receiving votes were ranked in the top 10% of the NBA according to the NBA's measure. Such analysis suggests that the NBA Efficiency measure corresponds more closely to the viewpoint of the writers.

We wish to point out that this is not a surprising result. In the previous chapter we noted the similarity between the NBA Efficiency measure and Bob Bellotti's Points Created measure. Bellotti argued that his metric was very accurate. How did he reach this conclusion? In 1992 he observed:

> In the past eight years, the NBA's Most Valuable Player has finished either first or second that season in my Points Created rankings. In the past 14 years, the MVP has finished first or second 12 times in Points Created. In the other two years, the MVP finished third and fourth in Points Created, and in both years, the margin between the top three or four players was small. (p. 12)

Does the consistency between Points Created, NBA Efficiency, and the sports writers voting for league MVP establish the accuracy of these statistical methods? We would argue that accuracy depends upon your ability to connect your evaluation of players to team wins. Our ranking does not appear to be highly correlated with the media's views. Still, our ranking is based on a model that connects what the player does on the court to team wins. Consequently, when we argue that Kevin Garnett is the most productive, we are saying he is the most productive in terms of his ability to generate wins for his team. When we say Ben Wallace is the second most productive player in 2003–04, we base this on Wallace's statistical production being worth 20.4 wins according to our methods. And when we say Carmelo Anthony was not productive, we base this on Anthony's statistical production of 2.0 wins. Although Anthony is still a better player than any of us, and any sports writer we have read, his performance compared to other NBA players suggests he should not have been named on anyone's ballot for league MVP.

Let's make one final observation about our analysis of the 2004 MVP vote. It is interesting that members of the media occasionally argue that the league MVP is not necessarily the player who is statistically the best. Such arguments generally belittle statistical analysis and claim that sports writers are able to see the player who, despite the statistics, truly matters most to his team. Although this may be the sports writer's intent, our analysis suggests that this is not how sports writers vote. The NBA Efficiency measure, which may be flawed but is still a statistical measure, is still quite consistent with the sports writer's voting. Hence, at the end of the day, the voting for the MVP award appears to be at least somewhat about the statistics.

The Most Productive Player in 2005

At least this is the story we would have told before 2005. In 2004–05, though, the media's selection of MVP diverged from our rankings. The selection also surprisingly diverged even more from the NBA Efficiency measure. It appears that many sports writers did not vote for who they believed was the best player in 2005, but rather for the player they thought mattered most to his team.

To see this point, let's return to our story of Shaq. Without O'Neal the Lakers became quite a bit worse in 2004–05. In contrast, the Heat became one of the best teams in the NBA. This observation leads to the question, should Shaq have been the league MVP in 2004–05?

O'Neal did receive 58 first place votes, but this was not enough to win the award. Of the 127 sportswriters charged with selecting the 2005 MVP, 65 placed Steve Nash at the top of their ballots. Who is Steve Nash? Nash was the starting point guard for a Phoenix Suns team that improved from 29 wins in 2003–04 to 62 victories in 2004–05. This was the largest improvement posted by any NBA franchise in 2004–05, and given that Nash was considered the biggest star added to the roster, many writers concluded he was most responsible for the changes in the team's fortunes.

Was Nash the most productive player in 2004–05? He was more productive than Shaq, so if the choice was between these two players, the sports media were correct. Still, Nash was not the most productive player in the NBA. In fact, point guard Jason Kidd, who did not receive a single vote for MVP, was easily the most productive player at Nash's position. Kidd's 19.9 Wins Produced, though, only ranked third in the league.

So who was the best in 2004–05? Interestingly, as noted in Table 7.6, the NBA Efficiency model and our model agree on the identity of the best player in 2004–05. Once again, it was Kevin Garnett, who again produced 30 wins.

Despite the inability of the NBA Efficiency model to identify the player chosen by the media as MVP, the NBA's model was still quite consistent with the sports writers' voting. Of the sixteen players who received votes, thirteen were ranked in the top sixteen by the NBA Efficiency model. Only nine of the sixteen players identified by sports writers were in the top sixteen in Wins Produced. Like our analysis of the 2004 voting, the evaluation of sports writers seems to be more consistent with the NBA Efficiency approach.

When it comes to Kevin Garnett, though, the sports writers seemed to ignore the statistical measures. Garnett did not receive any first place or second place votes for league MVP. In fact, only seven writers even put him on their ballot. Yet

TABLE 7.6

Analyzing the Contenders for the 2005 MVP Award

Player	Team	Voting Points	Rank: Wins Produced	Rank: NBA Efficiency	Wins Produced	NBA Efficiency	WP48
Steve Nash	Phoenix	1,066	9	16	16.1	1,656	0.301
Shaquille O'Neal	Miami	1,032	10	11	15.9	1,784	0.306
Dirk Nowitzki	Dallas	349	7	3	17.2	2,194	0.274
Tim Duncan	San Antonio	328	5	14	17.8	1,670	0.389
Allen Iverson	Philadelphia	240	36	7	10.0	1,865	0.152
LeBron James	Cleveland	93	2	2	21.7	2,259	0.307
Tracy McGrady	Houston	44	13	8	14.2	1,850	0.214
Dwyane Wade	Miami	43	23	12	12.2	1,784	0.197
Amare Stoudemire	Phoenix	41	14	4	13.5	2,141	0.225
Ray Allen	Seattle	41	53	23	8.6	1,517	0.135
Kevin Garnett	Minnesota	15	1	1	30.0	2,621	0.462
Gilbert Arenas	Washington	4	21	13	12.3	1,761	0.181
Vince Carter	New Jersey-Toronto	3	29	15	10.9	1,665	0.185
Shawn Marion	Phoenix	1	4	5	18.6	2,073	0.284
P.J. Brown	New Orleans	1	35	34	10.1	1,371	0.172
Marcus Camby	Denver	1	18	47	12.8	1,284	0.304

our model estimates that Garnett led the league in Wins Produced, suggesting he had a pretty good year in 2004–05. Why did the defending MVP not attract more attention from sports writers in 2005?

The answer seems to lie in the changing fortunes of Garnett's team, the Minnesota Timberwolves. In 2003–04 Garnett's team won 58 games and entered the NBA playoffs as the number one seed in the Western Conference. As we have observed in the selection of Steve Nash, playing for a winning team seems to attract the attention of voters. In 2004–05, Garnett did not have this advantage as the fortunes of his team declined. When the 2004–05 season concluded the Timberwolves only had 44 wins, a total that left the team entirely out of the sixteen-team playoff field.

Why did Minnesota perform worse in 2004–05? To answer this question we turn to Table 7.7 where the Timberwolves of 2004–05 are compared to 2003–04. The results reveal that Kevin Garnett was virtually the same player in 2003–04 and 2004–05. His WP48 when he was voted MVP was 0.453. The next season his WP48 actually rose slightly to 0.462.

So what happened? We would note that unlike the Lakers, the Timberwolves decline was not tied to the players the team lost. All the players the team lost from 2003–04 produced less than zero wins. The players added were more productive,

TABLE 7.7

Connecting Player Wins to Team Wins:
The Minnesota Timberwolves, 2004–05 vs. 2003–04

Minnesota 2004–05	Wins Produced	WP48	Minnesota 2003–04	Wins Produced	WP48
RETURNING PLAYERS			RETURNING PLAYERS		
Kevin Garnett	30.0	0.462	Kevin Garnett	30.5	0.453
Fred Hoiberg	6.5	0.247	Fred Hoiberg	8.3	0.220
Wally Szczerbiak	3.7	0.069	Wally Szczerbiak	1.0	0.077
Sam Cassell	3.5	0.111	Sam Cassell	12.0	0.203
Ervin Johnson	0.2	0.027	Ervin Johnson	1.4	0.067
Ndudi Ebi	0.1	0.112	Ndudi Ebi	−0.2	−0.236
Michael Olowokandi	−0.3	−0.012	Michael Olowokandi	0.0	0.001
Trenton Hassell	−0.5	−0.012	Trenton Hassell	2.8	0.059
Mark Madsen	−0.8	−0.062	Mark Madsen	−0.5	−0.018
Troy Hudson	−1.2	−0.033	Troy Hudson	−0.4	−0.037
Latrell Sprewell	−2.4	−0.047	Latrell Sprewell	1.4	0.022
Returning Players WP & WP48	*39.0*	*0.110*	*Returning Players WP & WP48*	*56.3*	*0.154*
PLAYERS ADDED			PLAYERS LOST		
Eddie Griffin	5.5	0.175	Oliver Miller	1.2	0.110
Anthony Carter	1.0	0.062	Gary Trent	0.1	0.098
John Thomas	−0.6	−0.054	Anthony Goldwire	−0.2	−0.023
			Keith McLeod	−0.2	−0.163
			Quincy Lewis	−0.5	−0.025
			Darrick Martin	−0.8	−0.229
Players Added WP & WP48	*5.8*	*0.101*	*Players Lost WP & WP48*	*−0.5*	*−0.010*
SUMMATION OF PLAYER WINS	44.8		SUMMATION OF PLAYER WINS	55.8	
ACTUAL WINS	44		ACTUAL WINS	58	

adding 5.8 victories. From this we see that the story for Minnesota is not tied to changes in their roster. The decline we observe must be connected to the players who were with the team both seasons.

Statistically the decline in the Timberwolves' output was eleven wins, as the summation of player wins declined from approximately 56 to about 45 victories. Most of this decline can be traced to one player, Sam Cassell. Cassell posted twelve wins in 2,838 minutes in 2003–04, making him the third best point guard in the league. Injuries limited both his minutes and performance the next season. Consequently, Cassell's wins production fell to 3.5. Hence, half of Minnesota's decline can be attributed to Cassell's performance worsening.

One can also see changes with respect to other players. Although Fred Hoiberg improved from a WP48 of 0.220 in 2003–04 to 0.247 in 2004–05, he played 532 fewer minutes. So Hoiberg playing less minutes ended up costing Minnesota about two wins. Trenton Hassell and Latrell Sprewell, two below average players in 2003–04, played even worse in 2004–05. The decline observed in these two players cost the team seven additional victories. Although the team added better players, and also received additional wins from Wally Szczerbiak, the declines associated with Cassell, Hoiberg, Hassell, and Sprewell caused the team to worsen considerably.

Although one can go through the team on a player-by-player basis and track down the change in team fortunes to the individual players responsible, such an exercise will not change the basic story. Kevin Garnett was essentially the same player in 2004–05 as he was in 2003–04. Still, the sports media did not quite see it this way. Such evidence suggests that the media does not appear capable of separating an evaluation of a player from the evaluation of a team.

This is a key point we would make about evaluating players. Teams win games. We can, with a bit of work, link the team's fortunes to individual players. Our research reveals, though, that good players can reside on bad teams. For example, Kevin Garnett was a very good player in 2004–05, producing 30 wins. Unfortunately, his teammates went from producing 25 wins in 2003–04 to contributing only 15 wins the next season. Although Garnett was the most productive player in the NBA in both 2003–04 and 2004–05, the decline in his teammates' productivity caused the perception people had of Garnett's performance to decline. Despite the change in perceptions, we would still argue that Garnett was the best player in the NBA in 2003–04 and 2004–05.

Twelve Years of "Best" Players

So Garnett was the "best" player in 2003–04 and 2004–05. What about in other seasons? Let's look at twelve years of player data, beginning with the 1993–94 season. In Table 7.8 we list, for each of these seasons, the player who the sports writers selected as MVP, the player who led the regular season in Wins Produced— which we identify as "Most Productive"—and the NBA Efficiency leader. For the player identified as the leader in Wins Produced and NBA Efficiency, we identify in parentheses where this player placed in voting for MVP.[20]

Table 7.8 reveals that there were three seasons—1994–95, 1999–2000, and 2003–04—where the top-ranked person in Wins Produced, NBA Efficiency, and MVP voting was the same player. In four other seasons—1993–94, 1997–98,

TABLE 7.8

Twelve Years of the "Best" Players in the NBA

Year	Most Valuable Player	Most Productive Player	NBA Efficiency Leader
2004–05	Steve Nash	Kevin Garnett (11)	Kevin Garnett (11)
2003–04	Kevin Garnett	Kevin Garnett (1)	Kevin Garnett (1)
2002–03	Tim Duncan	Kevin Garnett (2)	Kevin Garnett (2)
2001–02	Tim Duncan	Ben Wallace (10)	Tim Duncan (1)
2000–01	Allen Iverson	Shawn Marion	Shaquille O'Neal (3)
1999–00	Shaquille O'Neal	Shaquille O'Neal (1)	Shaquille O'Neal (1)
1998–99	Karl Malone	Jason Kidd (5)	Shaquille O'Neal (6)
1997–98	Michael Jordan	Dennis Rodman	Karl Malone (2)
1996–97	Karl Malone	Grant Hill (3)	Karl Malone (1)
1995–96	Michael Jordan	David Robinson (2)	David Robinson (2)
1994–95	David Robinson	David Robinson (1)	David Robinson (2)
1993–94	Hakeem Olajuwon	Dennis Rodman (11)	David Robinson (2)

1998–99, 2000–01—we would note that these three rankings reached a completely different conclusion, indicating that differences exist with respect to these evaluations.

As we argued when we examined 2003–04 and 2004–05, there seems to be greater consistency between the MVP voting and the NBA Efficiency rankings relative to what we observe between the media's rankings and Wins Produced. In ten of the twelve seasons we examined, the MVP in the league was one of the top three players in NBA Efficiency. In contrast, for two seasons the leader in Wins Produced was not named on a single ballot for MVP. In three other seasons, the most productive player did not place higher than tenth in MVP voting. As we stated earlier, there is a clear difference between popular perception and our statistical analysis of wins. We would note once again, our measure of performance is well connected to team wins. As a result, one might question the validity of popular perception.

Beyond the discrepancy between perception and our measurement, what else do we learn from our list of most productive players? Point guard Jason Kidd was the only player to lead the league in Wins Produced and also play in the backcourt. In other words, the biggest players always tend to be the most productive. It is important to note that how we calculate wins assumes that the number of wins produced at each position across the league is the same. In other words, if you add up all the wins produced by the centers in the league it will equal the number of wins created by all the point guards. This will not be true on any particular team, but it is true for the league. Yet, despite the equality of wins across positions, big men dominate the top of our rankings.

The reason for this result is "the short supply of tall people"—yes, we still love saying that. Because big men are relatively scarce in the population, the supply of these players is quite small. As we noted when we discussed the work of Gould, when the supply of athletes is relatively small, teams are forced to employ players that are not as talented. Consequently, the variation in player performance tends to be very large. When this happens, the best players perform well above the average. What does all this mean for our player rankings? The best power forwards and centers will perform further from the average at their position. The best guards will perform closer to the average at their position. When you rank players relative to position average—which we do—the very top of your rankings will be dominated by frontcourt performers.

In 2005 Shaq finished second in voting for MVP. People claimed in the summer of 2005 that it was absurd that a player of O'Neal's obvious skills was only able to secure one MVP prize over the course of his illustrious career. On this point, though, our rankings and the sports writers agree. Although Shaq has consistently been one of the top players in the league, the year he was named MVP was the only year he led the league in Wins Produced. It is interesting that given the lack of talent at the center position, a player like Shaq has been unable to consistently distance himself far enough from the average at his position to claim the highest ranking in Wins Produced. Still, this is the story the data tell.

Who Is the Best? One Answer

So who is the best? Over the past ten years, our answer is Kevin Garnett. Let's spend a few moments reviewing Garnett's career. Although he was named MVP in 2004, Garnett's team has never come close to winning an NBA championship, an accomplishment many feel is a prerequisite to be considered the best in the game. Consequently, Garnett is not known for finding ultimate success on the hardwood. In fact, his career might be best known for what has happened to Garnett off the court.

Garnett has made headlines in his career for two accomplishments. In 1995 he became the first player in twenty years to make the jump from high school to the NBA. This move began a wave of players going from high school directly to the NBA, a practice that has ended with the age limit imposed by the 2005 collective bargaining agreement between the league and its players.

The 2005 collective bargaining agreement was not the first impacted by Garnett. In 1997 Garnett signed an unprecedented $126 million, six-year contract, with the Timberwolves. Primarily because of this contract the NBA became the first major North American sports league to actually impose a salary cap. Whereas the NBA and NFL had previously enacted caps on team payrolls, in 1999 the NBA

TABLE 7.9

Ten Years of Kevin Garnett

Year	RANK Wins Produced	RANK NBA Efficiency	Wins Produced	WP48
2004–05	1	1	30.0	0.462
2003–04	1	1	30.5	0.453
2002–03	1	1	31.5	0.455
2001–02	3	2	23.0	0.347
2000–01	6	2	18.2	0.273
1999–00	4	2	20.6	0.305
1998–99	9	7	10.1	0.272
1997–98	9	5	16.8	0.250
1996–97	25	23	12.0	0.193
1995–96	50	74	8.1	0.169
AVERAGES			20.1	0.326

enacted a cap on individual player salaries, preventing players from gaining a contract like the one offered Garnett.[21]

Beyond his impact on labor relations, Garnett has also been extremely productive. As detailed in Table 7.9, Garnett led the NBA in Wins Produced for three seasons and placed in the top ten every season from 1997–98 to 2004–05. If one compares our ranking to the NBA Efficiency rankings, we see a great deal of similarity. So for at least Garnett, the NBA's measure and our measure tend to agree.

Still, is Garnett the best? Garnett produced 200 wins over his first ten years, a total that leads all players across this time frame. To put this in perspective, Shaq only produced 168 win in this time period. Tim Duncan comes close to Garnett's per year average of 20 wins, averaging 19.6 wins from 1997–98 to 2004–05. In fact, Duncan's WP48 was 0.335 over his first eight seasons, which slightly exceeds Garnett's career production. Therefore we could argue that Duncan is the best. Actually, if we consider Shaq's career up until the 2004–05 season, his WP48 was 0.344. So we guess one could claim he is also the best. Still, if the question is "Who is the best?," you have to pick a criterion. Our criterion is most Wins Produced since 1995–96, and by this measure, Garnett is the tops. As we will see in the next chapter, though, we are not married to our criteria or our answer.

How about "The Answer"?

President Harry Truman reportedly once asked for one-armed economists. His request was motivated by the tendency economists have for saying "On the other hand . . ." As economists we suffer from this affliction. We just stated that Garnett is the best in terms of Wins Produced, but then quickly note that if we look at

WP48 we could make a case for Tim Duncan or maybe Shaquille O'Neal. Such wishy-washiness might lead one to believe that if you tweaked the numbers enough our answer could be just about anyone.

Let's address this concern by looking at "The Answer," Allen Iverson. We observed in Chapter Five that Iverson's production for the entire 2003–04 campaign was worth less than one win. We also noted that this was his worst season, and as we report in Table 7.10, whether one considers Wins Produced or NBA Efficiency, this is the conclusion you reach.

So Iverson was at his worst in 2003–04. When was he at his best? According to Wins Produced and the NBA Efficiency model, 2004–05 was his best campaign. The sports writers, though, tell a different tale. In 2000–01 the writers gave Iverson the league's MVP award. This particular season may illustrate best the greatness and weakness of Iverson. That season AI led the NBA in both points scored and steals per game. In other words, by these two metrics, it appeared that Iverson dominated the game at both ends of the court. Furthermore, his team finished with 56 wins, the best record in the Eastern Conference and the second best mark in the league. If these were the only numbers one looked at, you might conclude that Iverson was at least one of the best players in the league.

Unfortunately there are other numbers. We have already noted Iverson's propensity to commit turnovers. Unlike other seasons, he did not lead the league in this category, although his 3.3 turnovers per game did rank fifth. His prodigious scoring is also suspect, since his shooting efficiency was again quite low. From beyond the arc he only converted 32% of his shots. His range from two-point range was only 44%. As we said before, Iverson achieves his scoring totals by taking a large number of shots. His 25.5 field goal attempts per game represented nearly a

TABLE 7.10

Nine Years of Allen Iverson

Year	Rank: Wins Produced	Rank: NBA Efficiency	Wins Produced	WP48
2004–05	36	7	10.0	0.152
2003–04	227	111	0.9	0.020
2002–03	72	15	6.2	0.086
2001–02	160	45	2.6	0.047
2000–01	91	52	5.2	0.083
1999–00	188	44	1.7	0.029
1998–99	47	18	5.6	0.136
1997–98	40	20	9.2	0.140
1996–97	187	37	1.5	0.023
AVERAGES	116.4	38.8	4.8	0.081

third of the shots Philadelphia took per game that season. If this were baseball, a sport where efficiency is king, people would have trouble arguing that Iverson is one of the best players. Simply stated, his efficiency measures are below average. Consequently, when we look at all the numbers we see that Iverson's MVP season was not one of his best. And this is the answer you reach whether you consider the NBA Efficiency metric or Iverson's Wins Produced.

At the end of the day, by some numbers Iverson is truly great. By other numbers, though, he is very far below the average player. When you summarize the great and the not-so-great into one metric, the net value of Iverson during his career is a bit below the average NBA player. We would add that not only is Iverson not one of the best players in the league, he has generally not been the most productive player on his own team. Only in the 1997–98 campaign did he lead his team in Wins Produced.[22]

CATCHING A DRAFT IN 1996

Let's tell one more Iverson story before moving on. In 1996 Philadelphia took Iverson with the first choice in the NBA draft. Was this a wise choice? To answer this question, let's examine the first round of that draft.

In Table 7.11 we examine how the players chosen in the first round fared across the first nine years of their careers. In this table we report where the player was taken in the draft and where the player ranks in career Wins Produced, NBA Efficiency, and salary. Finally, we report Wins Produced, WP48, and career earnings for each player.

What stands out in this table? The first item of interest is that these 29 players earned over $1 billion in their careers after the 2004–05 campaign. On average each player has earned more than $35 million. Clearly, being an NBA player is a fairly lucrative job. Of course each year less than 500 people in the world get to have such a job. Given the population of people living in the United States and the world, odds are heavily against any person achieving his dream of playing hoops in the NBA.

Beyond noting the amazing amounts of money these athletes earn, how would the draft have been played out if NBA decision makers (a) knew how many wins each player would produce in the first nine years of their career and (b) actually considered Wins Produced in making decisions?

Given these two conditions, Philadelphia would have selected with the first pick its own native son, Kobe Bryant. Bryant, following in the footsteps of Kevin Garnett, was only seventeen years old when the 1996 draft was held. Coming straight

TABLE 7.11

Reliving the First Round of the 1996 NBA Draft:
Career Performances from 1996–97 to 2004–05

Name	Draft Position	Rank Career Wins Produced	Rank Career NBA Efficiency	Rank Career Salary	Wins Produced	WP48	Career Salary
Allen Iverson	1	11	6	1	42.9	0.081	$79,812,640
Marcus Camby	2	4	10	10	68.5	0.230	$49,197,240
Shareef Abdur-Rahim	3	3	1	2	80.8	0.156	$78,421,760
Stephon Marbury	4	7	3	3	60.0	0.112	$77,625,320
Ray Allen	5	2	5	4	87.0	0.172	$77,037,360
Antoine Walker	6	12	2	5	29.3	0.053	$76,471,080
Lorenzen Wright	7	14	11	13	25.4	0.078	$39,754,720
Kerry Kittles	8	9	14	8	52.2	0.148	$55,580,373
Samaki Walker	9	17	19	20	15.7	0.100	$14,980,633
Erick Dampier	10	15	13	11	25.0	0.083	$43,434,380
Todd Fuller	11	28	23	23	−2.1	−0.040	$4,975,240
Vitaly Potapenko	12	26	17	14	−1.1	−0.005	$33,643,060
Kobe Bryant	13	1	4	6	90.0	0.197	$73,929,240
Predrag Stojakovic	14	8	9	16	54.2	0.157	$26,827,900
Steve Nash	15	5	7	12	67.9	0.178	$40,160,120
Tony Delk	16	18	18	19	11.2	0.047	$16,536,680
Jermaine O'Neal	17	10	8	9	46.0	0.147	$54,798,640
John Wallace	18	21	21	22	0.2	0.002	$10,352,799
Walter McCarty	19	29	20	21	−6.4	−0.030	$14,082,495
Zydrunas Ilgauskas	20	13	12	7	26.4	0.105	$73,364,000
Dontae Jones	21	25	29	25	−0.8	−0.410	$2,439,736
Roy Rogers	22	22	24	24	0.0	0.000	$3,298,140
Efthimios Rentzias	23	24	28	29	−0.4	−0.138	$903,360
Derek Fisher	24	16	16	17	17.0	0.054	$22,393,200
Martin Muursepp	25	23	25	28	−0.1	−0.003	$1,839,320
Jerome Williams	26	6	15	15	64.4	0.242	$29,216,180
Brian Evans	27	20	26	27	1.0	0.042	$1,845,325
Priest Lauderdale	28	27	27	26	−1.5	−0.134	$1,890,200
Travis Knight	29	19	22	18	3.0	0.032	$18,220,000
TOTAL					855.8	—	$1,023,031,141
AVERAGES					29.5	0.115	$35,276,936

to the NBA from high school, there was a fair amount of uncertainty about his future prospects. The game we are playing here is one where the decision maker knows exactly what these players would do in the NBA. If the people drafting these players knew the future, and if career Wins Produced were the criterion used to make the selection, then Bryant would have been chosen number one.

Of course people did not have perfect foresight. Bryant was ultimately selected thirteenth by the Charlotte Hornets, who traded him to the Los Angeles Lakers. As we noted, there he teamed with Shaq to win three titles. That story we have told. What other stories can we tell about the 1996 draft?

Following the condition of perfect foresight, the players following Bryant in the draft would have been Ray Allen, Shareef Abdur-Rahim, Marcus Camby, and Steve Nash. Allen Iverson would have been selected eleventh, one spot before the afore-mentioned Antoine Walker was chosen.

What if decision makers could see the future but used the NBA's Efficiency metric to rank the players? By this measure, Abdur-Rahim would have been selected first, followed by Walker, Stephon Marbury, Kobe Bryant, and Ray Allen. Under this scenario, Iverson would have been chosen sixth. Interestingly all these players have received the maximum salary the NBA's rules allow. Each of the six players earned more than $70 million through the 2004–05 season, with the differences in compensation due entirely to differences in each player's actual draft position. The NBA imposed a strict rookie salary scale in the 1995 collective bargaining agreement, which set the salary each of these players earned the first three years of their respective careers. One should note that Zydrunas Ilgauskas is the only other maximum salary player on this list. Injuries have limited his playing time, hence in terms of Wins Produced and NBA Efficiency he only ranks thirteenth and twelfth, respectively.

Despite the case of Ilgauskas, NBA Efficiency and career salary are highly correlated in our sample. The simple correlation coefficient between these two measures is 94%. Although the initial salary paid these players was set by their draft position, the money these players earned after three years, which for most players is the bulk of their career salary, was set by decision makers in the NBA who had seen these players play. The strong correlation between NBA's performance metric and career salary suggests that decision makers evaluate talent in a fashion consistent with the NBA Efficiency measure. Consequently, players like Walker and Iverson, who are prolific yet inefficient scorers, are paid very well by the NBA although their measured contribution to team wins is relatively meager.

We will return to this story in Chapter Ten, where we examine in detail the link in the NBA between salary and performance. For now, though, let's take our Wins Produced metric for a ride and see what other stories it can tell.

8 A FEW CHICAGO STORIES

The great Frank Sinatra, in a 1962 concert in Paris, France, sang the immortal words: "Chicago, Chicago, that toddlin' town, a wonderful town, Chicago, Chicago . . ." Then he stopped and said, "What the hell I'm from Los Angeles, what am I singing about Chicago."[1]

Although none of us are from Chicago, like Sinatra we feel the need to sing about this city. Like Sinatra, we are also not sure why. Well, we have some idea why we feel the need to tell some Chicago stories. Now that we have a measure of player performance we wish to tell a few short stories. Coincidently, the stories we wish to tell seem to all be about the Chicago Bulls.

Before we commence with our Chicago storytelling, though, let's say a few more words about life in academia. The job of a college professor involves two activities: teaching and research. The latter activity generally involves writing academic articles. If you are lucky, academic articles are loved and enjoyed by as many as three or four other people living on the planet. Primarily this is because articles can only be read by people who have two characteristics: an understanding of the techniques employed—in economics this generally involves math and/or statistics— and an interest in the topic the writer examines. Few people have one of these characteristics. Hitting the daily double with an audience member is truly rare.

The size of the audience for any academic work suggests that most people living on the planet may live their entire lives and never curl up with a good academic article. For those who have missed out on this delight, what exactly have you missed? An academic article is really just a story. Sometimes it's an interesting story, sometimes it's not. Still, even the uninteresting articles, when all is said and done, are still just stories.

How do these stories get published? Typically, for these stories to be published in an academic journal, the story has to address a question of interest to others in the discipline. Consequently, when we write about sports in economics, we typically have to make an effort to convince an editor that others in economics, who are often not interested in sports, might find the article useful or interesting.

This point brings us to the subject matter we examine in this chapter. As you recall from the previous chapter, when we last left our story we had developed a method for measuring an individual player's Wins Produced in the NBA. We had also developed a simpler Win Score metric. As promised, we will employ our measures to provide answers to questions we think are of interest to people who like basketball. So in this chapter we will again address the legend of Michael Jordan, comment on perhaps the best team ever—the 1995–96 Chicago Bulls—and tell a few more stories about Chicago.

We should point out that these stories may not be of interest to economists who do not like sports, and consequently, would probably never be published in an economics journal. Despite this shortcoming, we think these stories will be both insightful and delightful, even to people who are not necessarily fans of "da Bulls." So let's commence with the greatest Bull of them all, Michael Jordan.

THE JORDAN LEGEND

In the past two chapters we have danced with the question: "Who is the best?" For fans of the NBA, especially those who came to the game in the past two decades, the answer may seem obvious. Whether you call him MJ, Air, or His Airness, for many fans the greatest player in NBA history is Michael Jordan.

Is this just another myth? In our list of most productive players from 1994 to 2005, Jordan's name failed to make an appearance. Does this mean Jordan is not the greatest?

To answer this question, let's consider the complete history of MJ. Jordan entered the league in 1984 and retired a third and final time—at least as of this writing it is the final time—in 2003. Over this time period Jordan played in fifteen seasons, playing his last season when he was 40 years old. How does Jordan's performance across all these years compare to what we have seen thus far from Kevin Garnett? As we noted, in Garnett's first nine seasons his WP48 was 0.326. Now we must remember that Garnett began his career when he was nineteen and at the conclusion of the 2004–05 campaign he was only 29 years old. So we are only looking at Garnett in his prime, while we are considering both MJ's prime years and also his time as the very elderly statesmen of the Washington Wizards. Surprisingly, MJ's WP48 across this entire career bested Garnett in his prime. When Jordan retired in 2003 his career WP48 stood at 0.346.

Now what if we only considered MJ's seasons before his first retirement? Well, in Garnett's first ten seasons he produced 200 wins. Jordan was hurt for much of his second season, and he retired the first time after only nine years. Yet despite playing only a bit more than eight seasons, Jordan produced 219 wins before giving baseball a try. Jordan's WP48 across these years was an amazing 0.406. What does that mean? With a bit of math[2] we can see that a team of average players plus Jordan would win 61 games.[3]

Let's consider the other extreme of Jordan's career. In 2002–03 His Airness finally ended his career—we think—with the Washington Wizards. Playing on a roster with teammates who were very small children when he began his career, and at a very advanced age, he still led his team in Wins Produced. MJ's ten wins ranked eighth in the NBA at his position, ahead of much younger players like Allen Iverson, Allan Houston, and Richard Hamilton.

Jordan's career productivity is even more impressive when we note that he was a shooting guard. It is important to recognize that it is harder for a guard to perform well beyond the average player at his position. Relative to frontcourt players, the supply of quality guards is higher. Therefore, the top frontcourt players are likely to perform further from the average at their position, and consequently accumulate more wins than a top guard. This can be clearly seen in 1995–96, when Jordan produced nearly 25 wins. This lofty total was eclipsed by David Robinson, a center for the San Antonio Spurs who produced 28 victories.

When we examine how many standard deviations each player is above the average at his position, we have evidence that Jordan had the better season. Robinson's WP48 of 0.449 was 2.6 standard deviations above the average center. Jordan posted a WP48 of 0.386, but given that shooting guards have a relatively small variation in performance, MJ was actually 3.2 standard deviations better than the average player at his position. When we take into account the realities of NBA production, Jordan's performance at guard is all the more incredible.

Does this mean Jordan was the greatest player ever? Once again we have two hands and we can't make such a definitive statement. There have been a few truly outstanding players in NBA history. For example, we estimate that Magic Johnson produced 312 wins in his career, posting a WP48 of 0.451. Like MJ, Magic played in the backcourt. Unlike other backcourt performers, though, Magic had the dimensions of a power forward. Standing 6 feet, 9 inches tall, Johnson passed like a little man and rebounded like a big man. Given that his production is evaluated relative to other point guards, though, his estimated wins production eclipses that of MJ. So one could make an argument that Magic is the best ever.[4]

Then again, maybe we have more than two hands. What about Wilt Chamberlain? In the 1961–62 season Wilt the Stilt averaged 50 points and 25 rebounds per game. What if Chamberlain did this today? Well, NBA teams shoot better today and play at a slower pace. Relative to teams in 2004–05, the average NBA team in 1961–62 missed seventeen more shots per game. The extra missed shots clearly helped Chamberlain achieve his impressive rebounding totals. Putting that point aside, there are a couple of additional reasons we can't know if Wilt the Stilt was truly best player to ever play in the NBA. First of all, statistics like blocked shots and steals were not tracked for individual players until the 1973–74 season. Turnovers were not tabulated for players until 1977–78. Wilt retired in 1972–73, so as we noted in Chapter One, we do not have all the information we need to fully evaluate his performance.

Still, let's imagine that he did what we know he did in 1961–62 in 2004–05. To fill in the missing data, we will say his steals, blocks, and turnovers looked like Shaq's production of these factors. Given this adjustment, we estimate Wilt's production in 1961–62 would be worth nearly 52 wins. We mentioned that there were a couple of problems with our evaluation of Wilt. The first was missing data. Now we see the second difficulty. Wilt's team won only 49 games in 1961–62. Remember, the summation of player wins tends to come quite close to team wins. Either Wilt's teammates produced nearly a negative three wins in 1961–62, or comparing Wilt's performance more than 40 years ago to the performance of the average center today is an incorrect comparison. We suspect the latter is true. In other words, we believe Wilt was very good, and maybe the best that ever played the game. Without the data we track today, though, we cannot measure the average productivity of Wilt's peers, so we don't know how good he truly was.

So what have we learned? Clearly we three economists can't come to a conclusion. Anyone who has listened to economists speak, though, already understood this point. Let's simply say that Michael Jordan, Magic Johnson, and Wilt Chamberlain were all phenomenal players. Each was likely better than any player playing today, and that means they were pretty good.

THE BEST TEAM EVER

So we are not sure Jordan was the best ever. He was, though, a key member of perhaps the greatest team in NBA history. Prior to the 1995–96 campaign, the best regular season record posted by an NBA team was the 1971–72 LA Lakers. This team, led by Wilt Chamberlain, Jerry West, and Gail Goodrich, won 69 games. The 1995–96 Chicago Bulls bested this record by three games, winning 72 contests.

Why were the Bulls so good? Was it just Jordan? To see the answers to these questions, let's think about the construction of this team. We have already detailed the Bulls' championship team of 1993, and the impact MJ's sudden career change had on the 1993–94 campaign. By the time Jordan returned to the Bulls in March 1995, Chicago's championship team had been almost completely dismantled. When MJ stepped into the locker room that spring only B. J. Armstrong, Will Perdue, and Scottie Pippen were left from the 1993 champions. Without Jordan the Bulls had already played 65 games of the 1994–95 season, and their record stood at 34–31. The addition of MJ was clearly positive, as the Bulls finished the season winning thirteen of their final seventeen contests. After a second round exit in the playoffs, though, it was not clear that the Bulls with MJ were championship contenders.

In the summer of 1995 the Bulls made a few changes to their roster. B. J. Armstrong was left unprotected in the league's expansion draft and was selected by the Toronto Raptors. Four free agents were signed, including point guard Randy Brown, and centers Jack Haley, James Edwards, and John Salley. In addition the Bulls drafted power forward Jason Caffey out of the University of Alabama. The Bulls also completed one trade, sending Will Perdue to the San Antonio Spurs for Dennis Rodman.

With the departures of Armstrong and Perdue, Pippen and Jordan were now the only players left from the 1993 championship team. Led by Pippen and Jordan, the newly designed Bulls managed to win more regular season games than any other team in NBA history. How was this record achieved? Our answer is reported in Table 8.1 where we list the Wins Produced of each player employed by Chicago in 1995–96.

We noted the many changes the Bulls made in the summer of 1995. One might suspect that the contributions of newcomers Brown, Haley, Edwards, Salley, and Caffey were key to the team's success. Okay, those who know basketball might suspect that these players made little difference. Although both Haley and Salley have had success in the sports media when their careers ended, these two players combined with Brown, Edwards, and Caffey to produced –3.9 wins. So these new players were not the reason the Bulls won 72 games.

We would note that our model, based on offensive and defense efficiency, predicts that the Bulls should have won 74 games. In other words, without the five newcomers identified above, the Bulls would be predicted to win 78 games. Who produced these wins?

TABLE 8.1

The Greatest Team Ever: The 1995–96 Chicago Bulls

Chicago 1995–96	Position	Wins Produced (WP)	WP48
Michael Jordan	Shooting Guard	24.9	0.386
Dennis Rodman	Forward-Center	18.1	0.415
Scottie Pippen	Small forward	15.8	0.269
Toni Kukoc	Forward	8.5	0.193
Ron Harper	Guard	5.6	0.143
Steve Kerr	Point guard	5.2	0.129
Jud Buechler	Guard-forward	2.2	0.143
Randy Brown	Point guard	0.1	0.010
Dickie Simpkins	Power forward	0.1	0.007
Jack Haley	Center	−0.1	−0.707
John Salley	Center	−0.1	−0.029
Luc Longley	Center	−0.5	−0.016
Jason Caffey	Power forward	−1.5	−0.136
Bill Wennington	Center	−1.7	−0.078
James Edwards	Center	−2.2	−0.393
SUMMATION OF PLAYER WINS		74.1	
ACTUAL WINS		72	

Not surprisingly, Michael Jordan led the team, producing nearly 25 victories. For his efforts, he was also named league MVP by the sports writers. What may be a surprise, though, is the contribution of Dennis Rodman. The addition of Rodman appeared to transform a team that was probably expected to contend for a title into the greatest team in league history. In only 2,088 minutes, Rodman produced 18.1 wins. Per 48 minutes played, Rodman's productivity even eclipsed Jordan. Rodman's WP48 of 0.415 was four times the production offered by an average player in the NBA, and even surpassed the 0.386 WP48 posted by Jordan. Of course when one looks at standard deviations above the average, Jordan was still more productive than Rodman.

Jordan and Rodman were not a two-man team. Five other Bulls posted a WP48 that was above average. With the exception of point guard Randy Brown, the list of above average players includes every player employed at point guard, shooting guard, and small forward. Scottie Pippen, Steve Kerr, Toni Kukoc, and Ron Harper added 35 wins to the 43 wins produced by Jordan and Rodman.

Of interest is the lack of contribution from any center and power forward besides Rodman. Traditionally NBA teams believed you needed a dominant big man to win in the NBA. The best team in NBA history did not have a single center whose wins production exceeded zero. Part of the problem may have been the rebounding prowess of Rodman. It is not unreasonable to suspect that some of the fifteen rebounds Rodman averaged per game were not taken from Chicago's opponents, but were actually captured at the expense of his teammates. In other words, had Rodman not been on the team the rebounding numbers of Rodman's fellow frontcourt performers would have been higher and this would have been reflected in their wins production. It is not clear, though, that this impact would have lifted the observed productivity of these players to such a level that we would have said any of Chicago's centers were above the average at their position. In essence, the productivity we observe from Chicago's centers leads us to conclude that the best team in the history of the NBA had little in the middle. In essence, the best team was a doughnut.

THE DECLINE AND REBIRTH OF
THE CHICAGO BULLS

So whatever happened to those Chicago Bulls? Led by Michael Jordan and Dennis Rodman, as well as Scottie Pippen, Ron Harper, etc., the team went on to win 69 games in 1996–97 and 62 games in 1997–98. In each campaign Chicago also won the NBA championship. After the 1998 season, though, the Jordan era ended in Chicago. Not only did Jordan retire, for the second time, but the Bulls also lost the services of Pippen, Rodman, and head coach Phil Jackson. With this much talent exiting the building, people expected the days of lofty win totals to be over for a time.

Such expectations were met during the lockout shortened campaign of 1999. Although the Bulls only played 50 games, the team managed to lose 37 contests. To put this in perspective, in 246 regular season contests in the previous three seasons the Bulls lost a total of 43 games. Clearly the talent drain had an impact. Still, there was a glimmer of hope in the collapse of the Bulls.

Hope springs eternal for the less successful NBA teams each May. While the sixteen best teams participate in the playoffs, the NBA's worst are gathered together for the annual NBA Draft lottery. Sports fans have become accustomed to the reverse order draft, which allows the worst teams in the league to select first among the amateur talent playing the sport. As we mentioned in our lengthy review of competitive balance, leagues institute such drafts in an effort to improve the fortunes of the less fortunate.

Unlike Major League Baseball and the National Football League the NBA puts a different spin on this event. To see this, consider the 1998–99 Chicago Bulls. Chicago only won 13 games. Both the Vancouver Grizzlies and LA Clippers, though, did even worse. In football this would have given the Bulls the third selection in the draft. The NBA, though, employs a lottery to assign the top three choices.[5] The Bulls won the lottery and were able to select first in 1999. Before we discuss the impact of this selection, allow us to digress from the story of the Bulls to explain this odd institution.

The NBA Draft Lottery

Historically the NBA operated the draft like the remaining North American sports leagues: worst teams selected first. In the 1980s, though, observers of the NBA suggested that teams were intentionally losing games to secure a better selection in the draft.

It is quite clear why teams would behave in this fashion. Although our review of the 1996 draft suggests otherwise, it is often only one or two players in a draft that are truly expected to alter the fortunes of an NBA team. Consider the 1992 NBA draft. The top three players taken in that draft were all employed by the Miami Heat in 2004–05. This tells us that all three players managed to last at least thirteen seasons in the NBA. All three players, though, have not achieved the same success.

The top prize that season was Shaquille O'Neal. After thirteen seasons O'Neal has produced 236 regular season victories and has a 0.344 career WP48. The player taken second was Alonzo Mourning. Mourning has also been a very good player, at least until a kidney ailment sidelined him after the 2001–02 season. Despite serious health problems, Mourning produced nearly 100 victories through the 2004–05 campaign. His career WP48 was also a more than respectable 0.211.

The third choice was Christian Laettner. Laettner played college ball for Duke. In his four college campaigns Duke went to the Final Four each season and captured the NCAA title in 1991 and 1992. In 1992 Laettner was named winner of the John R. Wooden Award, given to the nation's top college player. In the summer of 1992 Laettner was the only college player to play on the original Olympic Dream Team, the U.S.A. team led by Michael Jordan, Magic Johnson, Larry Bird, etc. This team won every Olympic game by an average margin of 44 points and set a standard for Olympic competition that has not been matched since.

Given this record, one might suspect that Laettner was a pretty good basketball player. Certainly he was, but for those drafting at the time he was not considered on par with O'Neal or Mourning. History has proven this evaluation to be correct. After thirteen seasons Laettner has produced 63 wins, with a career WP48 of 0.117. Although this record marks Laettner as an above average player, his career indicates he is not quite as good as O'Neal or Mourning. To put the difference in perspective, every season O'Neal has produced, on average, more than thirteen additional wins.

The NBA's lottery winner in 1992 was the Orlando Magic, who finished the 1991–92 campaign with 21 victories. The Charlotte Hornets, with 31 victories, won the second choice. The team selecting third was the Minnesota Timberwolves. If the NBA had a strict reverse order draft, Minnesota's fifteen wins in 1991–92 would have given them the first selection and the rights to Shaq. The lottery, though, left Minnesota with Laettner. In 1992–93 each player performed in a fashion similar to his career marks. O'Neal produced 21.7 wins for Orlando as the team improved to 41 wins. Mourning produced 10.6 victories for Charlotte, and the Hornets improved to 44 wins. Laettner managed to produce 6.5 wins for Minnesota, a team that only won 19 games in 1992–93. Not until the team drafted Kevin Garnett in 1996 did Minnesota ever reach 40 wins in a season. By then, though, Laettner had been traded to Atlanta and O'Neal had already played in one NBA Finals with Orlando.

Such anecdotal evidence is not unique to the 1992 draft. In essence, if a team has a poor season, yet is not truly the worst team in the NBA, a draft where selection follows a strict reverse order will result in several poor teams choosing among a collection of players who will not dramatically alter the team's fortunes. As a result, there is an incentive to lose as many games as possible to secure the rights to that one talent that might turn a franchise into a contender.

The NBA has denied that any team would ever intentionally lose. After all, trying to lose undermines the fundamental integrity of sporting competition. Still, the NBA went away from the strict reverse order draft in 1985. For this draft the seven non-playoff teams were placed in a lottery, with all teams having an equal shot at the top spot. In 1986 the league only chose the first three picks by lottery, consequently the worst team would not select worse than fourth. After a few seasons where the worst team was just never that lucky, the NBA in 1990 introduced a weighted lottery where the NBA's very bad teams would have a better shot at the number one pick.

At this point in the story we would love to turn to one of our brilliant papers and expose the behavior of NBA teams. Unfortunately, this bit of investigative economics, dare we say reminiscent of Steve Levitt's research reported in *Freakonomics*, is actually offered by Beck Taylor and Justin Trogdon (2002). Taylor and Trogdon wondered how the incentive to lose altered the behavior of NBA teams. During the 1983–84 season, the year before the lottery was established, these authors found that teams eliminated from the playoffs were, relative to playoff teams, about 2.5 times more likely to lose. This result was uncovered after they controlled for team quality. In other words, non-playoff teams were found to lose more often than one would expect even bad teams to fail. When the lottery was instituted the next season, though, the increased tendency of non-playoff teams to lose vanished.

That is not the end of the story. In 1990 the NBA instituted a weighted lottery, where the odds of landing the top pick would improve the more the team lost. Once again, teams in the NBA had an incentive to lose. Once again Taylor and Trogdon report that after controlling for team quality, non-playoff teams were more likely to lose, although the size of the effect was smaller. With a weighted lottery non-playoff teams were only 2.2 times more likely to lose. Hence, as the incentives these teams faced were changed, the behavior changed as well.

What does all this have to do with the Chicago Bulls? Well, we are not sure it has anything to do with our Chicago stories. We just thought the Taylor and Trogdon story was really neat and wanted to mention it in the book someplace.

Eddy Curry vs. Tyson Chandler

Now that we understand the intricacy of the draft lottery, let's return to our story. When we last left Chicago, the team had just won the 1999 draft lottery. With the number one pick in that draft, the Bulls selected Elton Brand. With Brand added to the team, the Bulls managed to increase their win total to seventeen, although the team played 82 games in 1999–00. So the winning percentage of the team actually declined. We would add, this was not due to Brand, whose production of ten wins his rookie campaign indicated that he was an above average player. Despite Brand's positive contribution, the Bulls were the second worst team in the league. Unfortunately, the draft lottery gods did not smile upon Chicago. Losing the lottery, Chicago picked fourth and selected Marcus Fizer. Once again the Bulls saw a further decline in their fortunes, winning only fifteen games in 2000–01.

Although the Bulls were now the worst team in the NBA, the draft lottery was again unkind. Missing out on the top three selections, the Bulls took 6'11" Eddy Curry, a local high school player with the fourth pick. In addition to adding Curry, the Bulls made a bold move to rebuild the franchise by sending Elton Brand to the LA Clippers for the second choice in the draft and Brian Skinner. The player chosen with the second choice was another high school player, 7'1" Tyson Chandler.

Given the nature of rookie contracts, the Bulls had the services of two talented, yet very young, big men for four seasons. The fortunes of the franchise did improve slightly over the next two seasons. In 2001–02 the team won 21 games, a winning percentage that still lagged behind the 0.260 offered in the lockout shortened 1999 season. In 2002–03 the team again improved, this time winning 30 games. The next season, though, even with the return of a 38-year-old Scottie Pippen, the team regressed to 23 wins. Pippen was not quite able to replicate the geriatric performance of MJ, as he played 412 minutes in 2003–04, producing only 0.7 victories. After this performance, Pippen joined Jordan in retirement.

The 2004–05 season appeared to continue the decline. After nine games the team had secured zero wins. After nineteen contests, the Bulls record was only 4–15, a pace that would give the team seventeen wins by seasons end. At this point, the Bulls became transformed. Over the remaining 63 games of the 2004–05 season, Chicago won 43 contests, for a winning percentage of 68%. Had the Bulls played at this pace the entire season the team would have won 55 games, a total that rivaled a few teams led by Jordan. In the end, their 47 regular season wins were good enough to return playoff basketball to Chicago.

The summer of 2005, though, brought a bit of a dilemma to the Bulls. Both Curry and Chandler were restricted free agents. Should Chicago keep both big men? Was one preferred, or were both equally good—or equally bad? As one might expect from us, the answer is in the numbers.

Eddy Curry averaged 16.1 points per game in 2004–05, making him the leading scorer on the Bulls. Curry, though, despite his size, was only able to capture 5.4 rebounds per game. Tyson Chandler led the team with 9.7 rebounds per game, but was only able to score eight points per contest. Both players were considered talented and young big men. And given the "short supply of tall people"—there we go again—each would command a significant salary. So who should the Bulls choose? The big man who can score but can't rebound, or the big man who can rebound but not score?

So far we have not looked at the specific numbers for each player that would tell us the answer. How many wins did each produce? What role did these players have in the Bulls' improvement? The answer is reported in Table 8.2, where we report the Wins Produced by each player the Bulls employed in 2003–04 and 2004–05.

The Bulls only returned five players from their roster of 2003–04. It is important to remember that an average player produces approximately 0.100 wins per 48 minutes played. When we consider the productivity of an average player, we see that three of the five returning Bulls were below average per 48 minutes played in 2003–04 and 2004–05. The two exceptions were Kirk Hinrich and Tyson Chandler. The improvement in the play of Hinrich added three wins to the Bulls' final season tally. Chandler's improvement was the much bigger story. Not only did Chandler improve on a per-minute basis, but because his minutes increased substantially, he also increased his overall wins production from 3.8 wins to 15.6 victories in

TABLE 8.2

Connecting Player Wins to Team Wins:
The Chicago Bulls, 2004–05 vs. 2003–04

Chicago 2004–05	Wins Produced	WP48	Chicago 2003–04	Wins Produced	WP48
RETURNING PLAYERS			RETURNING PLAYERS		
Tyson Chandler	15.6	0.341	Tyson Chandler	3.8	0.233
Kirk Hinrich	8.4	0.144	Kirk Hinrich	5.0	0.088
Antonio Davis	3.0	0.079	Antonio Davis	3.2	0.075
Eddy Curry	0.3	0.007	Eddy Curry	−1.9	−0.042
Jannero Pargo	−0.2	−0.025	Jannero Pargo	−0.1	−0.017
Returning Players Totals	*27.0*	*0.143*		*9.9*	*0.060*
PLAYERS ADDED			PLAYERS LOST		
Chris Duhon	5.8	0.127	Jerome Williams	5.1	0.199
Luol Deng	5.1	0.147	Jamal Crawford	3.7	0.063
Adrian Griffin	2.6	0.185	Corie Blount	2.1	0.133
Andres Nocioni	1.8	0.045	Linton Johnson	1.9	0.126
Othella Harrington	1.6	0.062	Donyell Marshall	1.7	0.198
Eric Piatkowski	1.3	0.073	Rick Brunson	0.9	0.102
Lawrence Funderburke	0.0	−0.040	Scottie Pippen	0.7	0.085
Frank Williams	−0.3	−0.195	Ronald Dupree	0.1	0.005
Jared Reiner	−0.4	−0.128	Eddie Robinson	0.0	0.001
Ben Gordon	−0.7	−0.016	Jalen Rose	0.0	−0.003
			Lonny Baxter	−0.1	−0.019
			Roger Mason	−0.3	−0.382
			Kendall Gill	−0.4	−0.012
			Paul Shirley	−0.4	−0.220
			Chris Jefferies	−0.4	−0.111
			Marcus Fizer	−0.8	−0.053
Players Added Totals	*16.8*	*0.075*	*Players Lost Totals*	*13.8*	*0.056*
SUMMATION OF PLAYER WINS	43.8		SUMMATION OF PLAYER WINS	23.7	
ACTUAL WINS	47		ACTUAL WINS	23	

2004–05. In terms of our model, the Bulls improved statistically by twenty wins. Our analysis of Chandler suggests that more than half of the team's improvement can be traced to Chandler's increase in Wins Produced.

What of Eddy Curry? Curry also improved. In 2003–04 his productivity actually cost the Bulls nearly two wins. In 2004–05 his output gave the Bulls 0.3 victories, indicating that Curry did not play a major role in the Bulls' resurgence. Why the disparity between these two players? The story is rebounding. The average center will get approximately one rebound every four minutes on the floor. Curry, though, takes more than five minutes to secure one rebound. So in Curry's 28 minutes of playing time, he is only able to capture 5.4 rebounds. The average center, though, in the same amount of time on the court, would secure about seven rebounds. This means that when Curry is on the floor it is harder for the Bulls to end the opponent's possessions without the other team scoring. Or, on the offensive end, the Bulls have a harder time taking more than one shot per possession. Despite Curry's scoring ability, his lack of rebounding detracts from Chicago's efforts on both ends of the floor.

In contrast, Chandler is exceptional on the boards. The average power forward also secures about one rebound every four minutes. So in the 27 minutes Chandler plays per contest, the Bulls would expect a bit less than seven rebounds from an average player. Chandler, though, provides nearly ten rebounds per game. The presence of Chandler on the floor results in more shots on the offensive end and fewer shots for Chicago's opponents. Such productivity translates into greater wins for the Bulls and is a key reason why the Bulls improved so dramatically in 2004–05. We would emphasize, though, that Chandler was not the entire story for Chicago. The Bulls also received significant contributions from Hinrich, as well as newcomers Chris Duhon and Luol Deng. In sum, Chandler, Hinrich, Duhon, and Deng accounted for 79% of the Bull's statistical production of wins.

Given this evidence, who did the Bulls choose? Before the start of the 2005–06 campaign Chandler had signed a six-year contract for a reported $64 million. Eddy Curry was also signed to a six-year contract for a reported $60 million and then was traded to the New York Knicks. On the surface it may look like the Bulls kept Chandler and let Curry depart.

The story was complicated, though, when Curry was diagnosed with a potentially serious heart ailment in the last few weeks of the 2004–05 campaign. Curry's health problems forced him to miss the last few weeks of the 2004–05 season and the Bulls' first round playoff series. We will not review the entire saga between the Bulls and Curry here, but nevertheless, Curry's health problems certainly impacted Chicago's willingness to sign him to a long-term contract. When all was said and done, Curry and Chandler, despite Curry's health problems, received similar contracts. Our analysis of each player's past performance suggests, though, that this should not have been the case.

Is Gordon the Next Jordan?

The story of the Bulls' resurgence was not only about Chandler and Curry. The media also focused much attention on rookie guard Ben Gordon. Despite generally coming off the bench[6] and averaging only 24 minutes of playing time per contest, Gordon still averaged 15.1 points per game. Had Gordon played the minutes of a starter he probably would have been "like Mike" and averaged more than twenty points per game as a rookie shooting guard for the Bulls.

The media and coaches in the NBA were clearly impressed by this effort. Gordon was named sixth man of the year by the sports media, an award given to the best non-starter in the NBA. He also finished second in the media's voting for Rookie of the Year. Finally, the NBA coaches unanimously selected Gordon to the All-Rookie team. In the opinion of both the media and the NBA coaches, Gordon played a substantial role in the success of the Bulls in 2004–05.

Our analysis tells a different story. Although Gordon was a prolific scorer, he offered very little else to the Bulls. For his position he was above average in terms of turnovers, committing nearly one more turnover per game than you would expect from the average shooting guard. Gordon's ability to accumulate rebounds and assists was also below average for his position. Despite his lofty scoring marks, he was not above average in shooting efficiency. An average shooting guard, given his field goal attempts, would have actually scored slightly more points. Although Gordon was above average from three-point range, he was below average inside the arc. In essence, Gordon seemed to have one ability, hitting three pointers, that was offset by another weakness, hitting shots closer to the basket. In the end, given Gordon's inability to maintain possession of the ball, generate assists or rebounds, and his lack of excellence with respect to turning shots into points, it is not surprising that Gordon's production of wins was actually negative. Remember, Jordan was not great just because he could score; Jordan also scored efficiently. Furthermore, Jordan was an exceptional rebounder and passer. Given our analysis, until Gordon matches MJ with respect to these aspects of the game, his performance will never produce the lofty totals we observe for Jordan.

Let's stop for a moment and summarize what we have learned from the story of the 2004–05 Chicago Bulls. Tyson Chandler, a player who does not score, is substantially more productive than two of the Bulls leading scorers. Does this pass the "laugh test"? We would note again that player salary only explains a small fraction of team wins. So the methods employed by the NBA, as we keep saying, may be suspect. Our methods, based upon offensive and defensive efficiency, explain 95% of team wins. Nevertheless, is it reasonable that a non-scorer can matter so much to the success of an NBA franchise, or put another way, that two scorers could matter so little?

One valid criticism of our approach is that a team cannot employ an entire team of Tyson Chandlers. At some point, someone has to take a shot if a team has any chance of succeeding. This is certainly true. If a team only employed non-scorers, we would see the productivity of these players decline as the accumulation of missed shots or turnovers would substantially reduce the effectiveness of these athletes. Although this is true, a team cannot employ an entire roster of players like Ben Gordon either. At some point someone has to pass the ball, rebound, create steals, and avoid turnovers. Players who only want to shoot force a team to accept only one shot per possession while allowing the team's opponent multiple opportunities to score.

Still, we agree that someone must score at some point if a team is going to succeed. In our analysis we have made it a point to compare a player relative to his position. Perhaps the same thinking applies to evaluating a scorer like Gordon. Comparing a scorer to a non-scorer might be unfair, since each plays a different role on the team. Perhaps we would be better off comparing Gordon to other scorers.

Who is a scorer? Well, obviously a scorer is someone who accumulates a large number of points. Specifically, we are going to define a scorer as a player who can score at least one point every two minutes on the floor. With this definition in mind, we looked at each NBA player who met our definition of a scorer and who also played at least 2,000 minutes during the 2004–05 campaign. This list of 33 players, reported in Table 8.3, includes each of the top scorers in the league.

How does Gordon compare to this group? As one can see, relative to other scorers, Gordon ranks last in terms of Wins Produced. One would note that these scorers are generally quite productive players by our metric. The average WP48 in this group is 0.182, well above the average player in the league. Although our measure emphasizes the importance of possession factors, scorers still generally score high in Wins Produced. Gordon, though, does not, causing us to question how he received the accolades from both members of the media and NBA coaches.

We would note that Gordon typically came off the bench in the fourth quarter. Given that many people believe games are won or lost in the final quarter of the game, scoring at this point of the contest can be thought of as quite valuable. The only problem with this logic is that points in the first quarter are actually worth the same as points in the final quarter. To see this, consider game three of the 2005 NBA Finals. The Pistons won this game 102–71. Quick question: Who was Mr. Clutch for the Pistons in this all important playoff game? The last two shots were hit by Darko Milicic and Carlos Arroyo. The clutch shot by Milicic was surprising, since this was the only basket he scored in the finals.

Of course we are again approximating humor. Milicic and Arroyo were not clutch performers in this game. By the time Milicic entered the game the Pistons were winning by 26 points. All those supposedly unimportant points the Pistons

TABLE 8.3

Evaluating the Top NBA Scorers, 2004–05

(Minimum 2,000 Minutes Played, 0.500 Points Scored per Minute Played)

Rank: Wins Produced	Scorers	Team	Wins Produced	WP48	Points per Minute	Points per Game
1	Kevin Garnett	Minnesota	30.0	0.462	0.582	22.2
2	LeBron James	Cleveland	21.7	0.307	0.642	27.2
3	Tim Duncan	San Antonio	17.8	0.389	0.609	20.3
4	Dirk Nowitzki	Dallas	17.2	0.274	0.673	26.1
5	Paul Pierce	Boston	16.7	0.270	0.598	21.6
6	Shaquille O'Neal	Miami	15.9	0.306	0.670	22.9
7	Stephon Marbury	New York	14.2	0.208	0.543	21.7
8	Tracy McGrady	Houston	14.2	0.214	0.629	25.7
9	Amare Stoudemire	Phoenix	13.5	0.225	0.720	26.0
10	Manu Ginobili	San Antonio	13.0	0.285	0.541	16.0
11	Elton Brand	LA Clippers	12.5	0.199	0.540	20.0
12	Gilbert Arenas	Washington	12.3	0.181	0.622	25.5
13	Dwyane Wade	Miami	12.2	0.197	0.623	24.1
14	Yao Ming	Houston	11.7	0.229	0.599	18.3
15	Larry Hughes	Washington	11.2	0.229	0.570	22.0
16	Vince Carter	Toronto-New Jersey	10.9	0.185	0.667	24.5
17	Mike Bibby	Sacramento	10.5	0.163	0.509	19.6
18	Allen Iverson	Philadelphia	10.0	0.152	0.725	30.7
19	Kobe Bryant	LA Lakers	9.8	0.175	0.676	27.6
20	Rashard Lewis	Seattle	8.9	0.158	0.540	20.5
21	Ray Allen	Seattle	8.6	0.135	0.609	23.9
22	Steve Francis	Orlando	8.5	0.137	0.558	21.3
23	Jason Richardson	Golden State	8.0	0.141	0.572	21.7
24	Corey Maggette	LA Clippers	7.7	0.152	0.601	22.2
25	Grant Hill	Orlando	6.9	0.141	0.563	19.7
26	Zydrunas Ilgauskas	Cleveland	6.4	0.117	0.505	16.9
27	Peja Stojakovic	Sacramento	4.4	0.084	0.524	20.1
28	Chris Webber	Sacramento-Philadelphia	4.0	0.080	0.551	19.5
29	Michael Redd	Milwaukee	2.9	0.049	0.605	23.0
30	Jalen Rose	Toronto	2.4	0.042	0.552	18.5
31	Antawn Jamison	Washington	1.2	0.021	0.512	19.6
32	Carmelo Anthony	Denver	0.2	0.004	0.597	20.8
33	Ben Gordon	Chicago	−0.7	−0.016	0.617	15.1

had scored earlier in the game rendered the points scored in the last seconds meaningless.

So is Gordon the next Jordan? The early returns are not positive. Of course, Gordon could begin to do all the things that made Jordan great. He could learn to make his shots at an above average rate, hit the boards, generate steals, and reduce his turnovers. If he did all this, he could someday approach the greatness that is MJ.

Of course one might think he already has one aspect of Jordan's greatness. Gordon can turn it on when the game in on the line. Although we have already noted that it is incorrect to value fourth quarter scoring higher than scoring at other points in the game, the concept of clutch performance brings us to our last story in this chapter. Specifically we now wish to address the myth that a player can "turn it on" when the games matter the most.

CAN ANY PLAYER TURN IT ON?

We went to a fair amount of trouble to develop a measure of player performance that was as simple as the NBA Efficiency measure yet a better representation of a player's contribution to wins. So far, though, all our stories have utilized a player's actual production of wins, not the simple Win Score measure we developed in Chapter Seven. As we mentioned, if you want to compare players at different positions the simple Win Score measure will be misleading. However, if you want to compare a player's performance today to his past performance, then the Win Score metric is perfectly suitable.

Another Jordan Myth

To illustrate this point, let's return to the story of Michael Jordan. The common perception that Jordan was one of the greatest players to play the game is supported by the evidence. We have already noted, though, that Jordan's greatness may have actually diminished, rather than enhanced, the productivity of his teammates. Now we turn to another Jordan myth.

Let's spend just a bit of time discussing Jordan's post-season exploits. Previously we examined Jordan's first retirement. Now we wish to look briefly at how he exited the NBA's stage the second time. It was Game Six of the 1998 NBA Finals. The Bulls led the series three games to two, but the final two games were to be played in Utah. With twenty seconds remaining, the Jazz had the lead and the ball. Game Seven seemed inevitable.

Still Utah needed to score if it hoped to keep the Bulls at bay. Fortunately for Utah it employed one of the greatest scorers in NBA history, Karl Malone. When the ball went to Malone, though, Jordan stepped forward and took it away. Now the Bulls had the ball, but they were still down by one point. This is how the *Sporting News NBA Guide* describes this final Chicago possession: "The defender (Byron Russell of the Utah Jazz) loses his footing and falls to the court as he tries to keep the best player in the game from blowing past him. *Michael Jordan seizes the moment*. He stops on a dime, elevates and lets fly with the shot that will win or lose the game. Nothing but net" (*Sporting News NBA Guide 1998–99*, p. 117, italics added).

What a story. At the time this was thought to be Jordan's final NBA moment. To win the championship his team needed both a defensive stop and a score, and MJ provided both. Certainly this tale proves that Jordan could, in the words of the *NBA Guide*, "seize the moment" and elevate his game to such a level that victory was inevitable.

Given how this book has gone, it may come as no surprise that a bit more investigation reveals that this view is just another NBA fable. The box score from this game states that Jordan took 34 shots and made only 14. This is a success rate of 41%. Had Jordan made 47% of his shots, his regular season average from that year, he would have already made two more shots before the drama of the final seconds unfolded. In this scenario, a last second shot may not have been necessary.

The story we hear leads us to believe that Jordan could choose to make a shot when the game was on the line. If he had this power, why did he not choose to make more shots in Game Six? Furthermore, why did Jordan only hit 35% of his shots in Game Five? This was a game that would have also given the Bulls the title, this time on their home floor. Unfortunately, the Jazz won by two points, an outcome that could have been avoided had MJ simply "chosen" to hit more shots.

Of course performances in a couple of games don't prove a point. What we wish to do is make use of our simple model, Win Score, and evaluate the entire history of Jordan's regular and post-season performances.[7] Table 8.4 reports our analysis, where we list MJ's per-minute Win Score performances. In looking at these results, we must remember that we are using our simple model. An average shooting guard will post a per-minute Win Score of 0.13. With this average in mind, we can easily see that Jordan was an above average performer in each regular and post-season we examined. This is not surprising given our previous analysis of MJ. Whether we utilize Wins Produced or Win Score, Jordan ranks as one of the best players to play the game.

We have already covered this ground. What we wish to examine now is Jordan's ability to elevate his game when it matters most. As we can see, although Jordan is easily above average in both the regular and post-season, his post-season performance was consistently below his regular season production.[8]

The only two years where Jordan actually improved on his regular season Win Score were 1985–86 and 1994–95. In each of these seasons Jordan played less than

TABLE 8.4

Michael Jordan's Playoff History

Season	Regular Season Games Played	Post-Season Games Played	Win Score per Minute, Regular Season	Win Score per Minute, Playoffs	Relative to Regular Season, Playoff Performance . . .
1984–85	82	4	0.282	0.237	DECLINED
1985–86	18	3	0.194	0.241	IMPROVED
1986–87	82	3	0.245	0.230	DECLINED
1987–88	82	10	0.323	0.280	DECLINED
1988–89	81	17	0.391	0.304	DECLINED
1989–90	82	16	0.360	0.326	DECLINED
1990–91	82	17	0.354	0.348	DECLINED
1991–92	80	22	0.311	0.243	DECLINED
1992–93	78	19	0.306	0.271	DECLINED
1994–95	17	10	0.187	0.212	IMPROVED
1995–96	82	18	0.304	0.201	DECLINED
1996–97	82	19	0.266	0.224	DECLINED
1997–98	82	21	0.196	0.179	DECLINED

NOTE: An average shooting guard from 1993–94 to 2004–05 had a Win Score per-minute of 0.128.

twenty regular season games. Also, in each of these post-seasons, Chicago failed to win a championship.

Of course one might expect performance to decline in the playoffs. Teams play better defense and at a slower pace in the post-season. So naturally players accumulate fewer points, rebounds, etc. To see how big a decline we can expect, we collected data for every player in every post-season from 1995 to 2005. On average, Win Score declines by .03. Even when we take this average decline into account, though, Jordan still doesn't consistently get better in the playoffs. Specifically, if we add .03 to Jordan's playoff performance, adjusting for the expected decline from the slower pace and better defense teams play in the post-season, Jordan's production in the post-season is still worse than his regular season output in eight of the thirteen seasons we examined.

A Few Other Stars

One should emphasize that Jordan's declines in the playoffs were not unique to him. We mentioned that the same teams contend for the NBA title year after year. From 1980 to 2005, 20 of the 26 titles won were captured by the LA Lakers, Chicago Bulls, Boston Celtics, and San Antonio Spurs. These teams were led by a collection of truly great players. In the 1980s the Lakers were led by Magic Johnson to five titles in nine seasons. Larry Bird led the Celtics to three championships over the same time period. After Detroit captured two titles in 1989 and 1990, the Jor-

TABLE 8.5

Playoff History of Five NBA Stars

(Extended Stay = 10 or More Playoff Games Played)

Player	Years of Extended Stay in Playoffs	Years with Superior Playoff Performance	Percentage of Superior Playoff Performances
Michael Jordan	10	3	30.0
Magic Johnson	10	5	50.0
Shaquille O'Neal	9	4	44.4
Larry Bird	8	3	37.5
Tim Duncan	5	3	60.0
TOTALS AND AVERAGES	42	18	42.9

dan title era began, with the Bulls capturing six titles in eight seasons. After Jordan left the scene in 1998, three titles were won by both the Spurs, led by Tim Duncan, and the Lakers again, this time led by Shaq. So how did Magic, Bird, Duncan, and Shaq perform in the post-season?

To answer this question, we looked at the extended post-seasons each player offered, which we define as one lasting at least ten games.[9] Our analysis is reported in Table 8.5.

Not surprisingly, all of these stars led their teams repeatedly deep into the NBA post-season. Like Jordan, though, none of these players could consistently raise their game in the playoffs. When we compare regular season performance to post-season output, adjusted for the lower production we tend to observe in the playoffs, these stars could only elevate their performance in the playoffs 43% of the time.

Of these it may appear that Tim Duncan is the best. In fact, in Duncan's first three extended post-season appearances, his post-season play exceeded his regular season output each time. In 2004 and 2005, though, Duncan's playoff performance was not quite as stellar. In 2005 Duncan's Spurs captured the NBA title. Duncan, though, despite his team's success, did not elevate his play in the Spurs' title run. To see this point, we measured Duncan's Win Score in the 2004–05 regular season, in the entire 2005 post-season, in just the NBA Finals, and finally, in Game Seven of the finals. Our analysis is reported in Table 8.6.

Duncan plays either power forward or center. An average player at power forward has a Win Score of 0.21, while an average center offers 0.22. Clearly Duncan was well-above average in the regular season, and if we look at the entire post-season, he was again an outstanding performer. When the games mattered most,

TABLE 8.6

Tim Duncan in 2004–05

	Win Score, per Minute
Regular Season	0.375
Post-season	0.312
NBA finals	0.281
Game Seven of NBA finals	0.060

NOTE: An average power forward from 1993–94 to 2004–05 had a Win Score per-minute of 0.215

though, Duncan's performance declined. This can be seen clearly in Game Seven, where Duncan shot 37% from the floor and committed five turnovers. Although the Spurs captured the title, Duncan's performance was well-below average.

With a bit of thought we might be able to see why Duncan did worse in the finals. His opponent was one of the best defensive teams in the league, the Detroit Pistons. The Pistons' strategy in the final game appeared to be to focus on Duncan and see if anyone else on the Spurs could win the game. As it turned out, the Pistons did effectively limit Duncan. Unfortunately for the Pistons, they found that other Spurs could win the game as both Manu Ginobili and Robert Horry played extremely well. Although Duncan was named MVP of the NBA Finals, it was Ginobili and Horry who led the Spurs to victory in Game Seven.

And Now a Larger Sample

We are beginning to see a possible reason why stars falter in the playoffs. More evidence could be uncovered if we looked at a larger sample. We collected data on each post-season performer from 1995 to 2005. To evaluate performance we need an adequate sample of both regular and post-season productivity. With that in mind, we restricted our sample to those players who played at least twenty minutes per game in both the regular season and playoffs, played at least twenty regular season games, and appeared in ten post-season contests.

In our sample were 29 players who had at least four extended post-season stays during the time period we examined. For this group we examined how often their post-season performance, which we adjusted for the tendency of post-season performance to be lower, exceeded what the player offered in the regular season. Our analysis is reported in Table 8.7.

Players like Jordan, Shaq, and Bird couldn't offer improved play in the post-season more often than not. Our research did uncover eleven players whose perform-

TABLE 8.7

Analyzing Extended Playoff Performances, 1995–2005

(*Minimum Four Extended Stays*)

Player	Years of Extended Stay in Playoffs	Years with Superior Playoff Performance	Percentage of Superior Playoff Performances
Ron Harper	4	4	100%
Mark Jackson	4	3	75
Avery Johnson	4	3	75
Bryon Russell	4	3	75
Steve Smith	4	3	75
Robert Horry	6	4	67
Chris Childs	5	3	60
Dale Davis	5	3	60
Tim Duncan	5	3	60
Derek Fisher	5	3	60
Scottie Pippen	5	3	60
Reggie Miller	6	3	50
Bruce Bowen	4	2	50
Antonio Davis	4	2	50
Eddie Jones	4	2	50
Michael Jordan	4	2	50
Shaquille O'Neal	9	4	44
Jeff Hornacek	5	2	40
Toni Kukoc	5	2	40
David Robinson	5	2	40
Tony Parker	4	1	25
Gary Payton	4	1	25
Rik Smits	4	1	25
Rasheed Wallace	4	1	25
Kobe Bryant	5	1	20
John Stockton	5	1	20
Karl Malone	6	0	0
Charles Oakley	4	0	0
Dennis Rodman	4	0	0
AVERAGE	4.7	2.1	45%

ance did improve in the playoffs more often than it declined during the time period we considered. Although this list includes the aforementioned Tim Duncan, most of these players are hardly considered the stars of the NBA.

Let's briefly consider the top five players on the list: Ron Harper, Mark Jackson, Avery Johnson, Byron Russell, and Steve Smith. After these five, every other player on the list had at least two extended post-season stays where their performance declined from the regular season. Are these five players the prime-time performers in the NBA? Are these players the "stars" that people expect to shine in the playoffs?

There is little evidence that these players are perceived by many to be the "stars" of the game. From 1988 to 2005, none of these players received as many as 500,000 votes for the mid-season All-Star game. Nevertheless, these are the people who appear to raise their game in the playoffs. How much of a lift are we talking about? In the years where these players had extensive post-season experience their average Win Score per-minute in the regular season was 0.160, while their average post-season production was 0.156. Only after we adjust for the tendency for post-season performance to decline do these players look like they actually improved in the playoffs. Of these five, only Ron Harper actually offered unadjusted post-season productivity that was better than his regular season output more often than not. Specifically, in three of the four extended stays we consider, Harper did indeed perform better in the playoffs than he did in the corresponding regular season. Once we adjust for the natural decline in post-season output, Harper looks better a perfect 100% of the time.

Before we get too excited about Harper, we should note that in 1992, a few years before our sample begins, Harper did perform worse in the playoffs than he did in the regular season. So Harper was not able to always raise his level of play. Furthermore, it is not clear that when his post-season performance actually exceeded his regular season output, the difference was very large. In the seasons where his team made the post-season, Harper's regular season Win Score was 0.170. Harper's career per-minute Win Score in the playoffs, though, was only 0.173. So even if Harper did have the ability to raise his post-season performance, the results did not lead to very much additional production.[10]

Insights into Prime-Time Performance

The story of Harper, Jackson, Johnson, Russell, and Smith, when coupled with what we learned about MJ, Magic, Bird, Shaq, and Duncan, has the makings of an interesting insight into post-season performance. The former five did not tend to score very much. The latter five were clearly the focus of their respective team's offense. Perhaps the story of Duncan in Game Seven of the 2005 NBA Finals is not that uncommon. Maybe teams in the playoffs focus much of their defensive energy on the star, and given that playoff teams tend to be good defensive teams, these scorers tend to do even worse than we would expect in the post-season.

To test this hypothesis we looked at all players who had extended post-season stays from 1995 to 2005. In all we had 418 player observations. With this sample in hand we set out to understand what determines post-season productivity. Specifically we regressed each player's post-season Win Score, calculated on a per-minute basis, on the player's regular season per-minute Win Score. Beyond regular season performance we also included in our model the health of the player, which we try to capture by noting how many games the player played in the regular season. Quality of competition is noted by including the seeding of the player's team in the playoffs.[11] Finally, we included the number of points the player scored per game in the regular season. The last factor is included to test our hypothesis that scorers suffer in the post-season.

What does our model tell us about post-season performance? The most important determinant is regular season productivity. Regular season performance by itself can explain 67% of post-season performance. Given what we have learned about consistency in performance from season to season, we now see that players are almost as consistent from regular season to post-season as we find from year to year.

When we add our other variables our explanatory power is . . . well, it is still 67%. Just like our analysis of regular season productivity in Chapter Seven, the key determinant of current performance in the post-season is past performance. In other words, if a player is good in the regular season, he will tend to be good in the playoffs. If he is bad, he will probably still be bad. This is a key point we wish to emphasize. We think there are players who play well in the post-season. What we are arguing, though, is that the players we see play well in the playoffs are generally the same players who play well in the regular season. Furthermore, those players we see playing well in the post-season tend not to consistently play any better than they played in the regular season.

In fact, as our model indicates, playoff performance tends to be a bit worse when compared to regular season output. What of games played, seeding, and scoring? Of these, only scoring was statistically significant. The impact was also found to be negative, indicating that scorers are more likely to play worse in the post-season. Although such a result supports our intuition about scorers, the actual impact is quite small. Our analysis indicates that a player who scores twenty points per game will see his productivity decline 0.009 more than a player who only scores ten points per regular season contest.

So what have we learned? There is some evidence that scorers suffer in the play-offs, although the effect is quite small. We do see that the very best stars from the past 25 years tended to perform worse when the games mattered most. Although no player could always lift his performance in the post-season, most of the small number of players who could generally perform better were actually lesser NBA players. Given all this, what can we conclude? Should Ron Harper be considered a bigger star than MJ?

Well, both were backcourt performers, so we can compare each player's Win Score per minute. Jordan's career post-season average Win Score was 0.255. Ron Harper averaged 0.173. In 1998 Jordan offered his worst playoff performance of 0.179. In only four of Harper's ten years in the playoffs did his per-minute output exceed Jordan's 1998 production. Although Harper was more likely to best his own regular season output in the playoffs, this tendency does not make him the equivalent of or better than MJ. In fact, such a suggestion would have trouble with that famous "laugh test." His Airness may have been slightly deflated in the NBA's post-season, but he was still better than virtually anyone else on the court when the games mattered the most.

9 | HOW ARE QUARTERBACKS
LIKE MUTUAL FUNDS?

We have spent a fair amount of time discussing the greatness of Michael Jordan. The data clearly suggest he was one of the greatest players of all time. Our research, though, reveals that there are two fables associated with MJ. Like all great players, as the Law of Diminishing Returns suggests, Jordan's production did not tend to make his teammates more productive. We also learned that Jordan did not consistently raise his level of play in the post-season. When the games mattered most, again like other stars, Jordan did not tend to perform his best.

Does all of this diminish the greatness of MJ? Jordan still produced close to 300 wins in his career. Furthermore, he was consistently a great player. Except for his first season with the Washington Wizards, when Jordan was 39 years old, he was always an above average performer. The same statement can be made for Magic, Bird, Shaq, Duncan, and Kevin Garnett. All of these players, year in and year out, are/were above average performers. In addition to being great on average, these players have been consistently phenomenal players.

How consistently great are these players? As always, we need a reference point to answer such questions. So now we turn to a sport we have said very little about, American football.

THERE'S SOMETHING ABOUT BRETT[1]

Football is the ultimate team game. Eleven players must work together to move the ball. Eleven players must work together to stop the other team from moving across the field. No one player can do the job alone, so no one player can be thought of as the star. At least, that is the story often told by people in football. The exception to the team focus is the quarterback position. Quarterbacks are credited when the team wins and blamed when the team loses. If there is a star in the game of football, it tends to be the quarterback.

We begin our discussion of football by focusing on one of the all-time great signal callers in NFL history. Brett Favre came to the Green Bay Packers in 1992. At Packers.com, one can learn much about the highlights of Favre's exploits on the frozen tundra. Favre is the Cal Ripken of the NFL's quarterbacks, having started 221 consecutive games at the conclusion of the 2005 campaign. Not only does he show up to work, observers are generally impressed with what they see. He was named MVP in the league after the 1995, 1996, and 1997 seasons, the only player to have won this award on three occasions. According to Packers.com, his career totals in games won, lifetime winning percentage, touchdowns, completions, attempts, and passing yards each rank in the top five all-time in NFL history.

Given this list of accomplishments it would not be a stretch to say that Favre is to the NFL what stars like Jordan, Magic, Bird, and Shaq are to the NBA. There appears to be one important difference. The stars of the NBA were consistent throughout their careers. Young or old, regular season or playoffs, these players were almost always consistently better than the average performer in the NBA.

Being above average is clearly an apt description of Favre in 2004. For the season he threw for 4,088 yards, 30 touchdowns, and only 17 interceptions. His quarterback rating of 92.4 was one of the better marks of his career. Despite such an outstanding performance, from week to week one was not sure which Favre would show up.[2] We make this point in the first table of this chapter.

In week one of 2004 Favre posted a quarterback rating of 101.1. In week two, he threw two interceptions and his rating plummeted to 62.8. Week three the star quarterback returned, as Favre threw four touchdown passes without an interception. In week four, though, his performance again declined. This was the basic pattern to Favre's season. In the odd number games, Favre threw 2,103 yards, 20 touchdowns, and 4 interceptions. In even number games Favre threw 1,985 yards, 10 touchdowns, and 13 interceptions. The quarterback rating appears to capture this inconsistency. In odd games Favre posted a rating of 106.8. In even weeks his rating fell to 77.7.

Given this performance the Packers should have been very confident going into the playoffs. This game represented the Packers seventeenth game of the season. Unfortunately, the consistent inconsistency of Favre suddenly became inconsistent. In his one playoff game Favre threw one touchdown pass, four interceptions,

TABLE 9.1

Brett Favre in 2004: Game-by-Game Performance

GAME	Quarterback Rating	Passing Yards	Passing Attempts	Completions	Passing Touch-downs	Inter-ceptions
1	101.1	143	22	15	1	0
2	62.8	252	42	24	1	2
3	123.3	360	44	30	4	0
4	78.5	110	18	12	1	1
5	66.3	338	44	24	2	3
6	102.6	257	38	25	2	0
7	126.7	258	29	23	2	0
8	63.2	289	32	20	1	3
9	133.0	236	29	20	4	0
10	79.0	383	50	33	1	2
11	127.9	215	27	18	3	0
12	32.4	131	29	14	0	2
13	77.1	188	36	19	1	0
14	80.4	367	44	30	2	3
15	109.2	365	43	30	3	1
16	151.4	196	13	9	2	0
Odd Games	106.8	2,103	274	179	20	4
Even Games	77.7	1,985	266	167	10	13
Season	92.4	4,088	540	346	30	17
Playoff Game	55.4	216	33	22	1	4

and his quarterback rating of 55.4 indicates that his seventeenth performance was his worst of the season.

The Favre story suggests that NFL quarterbacks are not quite as consistent as NBA players. Like mutual funds, past performance is no guarantee of future returns. To further investigate the consistency and inconsistency of NFL quarterbacks, we need to spend a bit more time measuring the productivity of these athletes.

THE NFL'S QUARTERBACK RATING SYSTEM

Like baseball and football, the NFL tracks a number of statistics to measure productivity. In discussing Favre's performance we referenced passing yards, completion percentage, touchdowns, interceptions, and quarterback rating. This latter statistic is often cited by people inside and outside of professional football, but we suspect the calculation of this measure is not well understood.

With tongue firmly planted in cheek, we will begin by saying that the quarter-

back rating is very easy to compute. All you need to know is how many completions, yards, touchdown passes, and interceptions the quarterback has per pass attempt. Of course, once you have these four measures, you need to take a few additional steps.

If you read this next paragraph as fast as you can, you will truly appreciate the
genius that is the NFL quarterback rating.

> First one takes a quarterback's completion percentage, then subtracts 0.3 from this
> number and divides by 0.2. You then take yards per attempts, subtract 3 and divide by
> 4. After that, you divide touchdowns per attempt by .05. For interceptions per attempt,
> you start with .095, subtract from this number interceptions per attempt, and then di-
> vided this result by .04. To get the quarterback rating, you add the values created from
> your first four steps, multiply this sum by 100, and divide the result by 6. Oh, and by
> the way, the sum from each of your first four steps cannot exceed 2.375 or be less than
> zero.[3]

If we were not opposed to showing equations we could further explain with the actual mathematical formula. We are fairly certain, though, that seeing the actual
equation would not help clear up any confusion.[4]

Despite its lack of clarity, is this measure a reliable indicator of a quarterback's
contribution to team success? As noted, the rating only includes four aspects of
productivity. It is explicitly designed as a measure of passing efficiency, so the actions the quarterback takes with his legs are ignored. There is no consideration of
rushing yards, rushing attempts, or even fumbles. Clearly these actions impact the
outcome of a game. Can you design a single measure of performance that incorporates both a quarterback's actions with his arm and legs? Sure you can.

WINS AND NET POINTS PRODUCTION IN THE NFL

Once again we turn to the wonder that is regression analysis.[5] Basically we want to
define what a quarterback does on the field in terms of wins and points. Let's start
with wins.

Connecting Points to Wins

The data we use to measure productivity in the NFL begin with the 1995 season
and end with the 2004 campaign.[6] Our story begins where it began in our study of
the NBA; wins are determined by how many points a team scores and how many
points it allows. When we regress wins on points scored and allowed, we learn that
each additional point is worth 0.03 wins. Each point a team allows costs the team
0.03 wins.

If we think back to what we said about the relationship between scoring and wins in the NBA, our analysis of the NFL looks familiar. Just to review, from our study of the NBA we learned that each point scored in basketball is also worth about .03 wins. The similarity between the NBA and NFL stems from the observations that the NBA plays about five times the number of games and in each game, relative to football, scores about five times the number of points. Consequently, the value of each point in each sport is roughly the same.

Although the link between scoring and wins is similar in both the NFL and the NBA, our ability to explain wins with scoring in each league is not quite the same. When we looked at this relationship in the NBA we found that 95% of wins are determined by offense and defense. In the NFL, though, only 83% of wins are explained by these two factors. The difference between these two sports is the length of schedule. NBA teams play 82 games while an NFL team only plays 16. Consequently, any one game in the NFL has a much larger impact on the aggregate scoring totals.

The Atlanta Falcons in 2004 illustrate this point. Atlanta's record was 11–5. Only five teams won more regular season games. Yet for the season Atlanta only scored three more points than it allowed. Thirteen teams in the NFL bested Atlanta's point differential, including the Kansas City Chiefs, who only won seven games. The Falcons' relatively poor showing in point differential was primarily driven by their one meeting with the Chiefs in week seven. Atlanta entered the game with only one loss while Kansas City had only one victory. At the end of the day, though, Kansas City had 56 points while Atlanta only had 10. In the other fifteen games, the Falcons bested their opponents by 49 points while the Chiefs only outscored their opponents by 2. As this example illustrates, one game can dilute the relationship between points and wins in the NFL.

Still we go with what we have, and now that we have valued points in terms of wins, all we need to do is determine the impact quarterbacks have on a team's offensive and defensive performance. Why defense? Don't quarterbacks only play offense? Indeed they do, but we suspect that throwing interceptions doesn't just hurt a team's offense. So we need to look at both sides of the ball if we are going to fully assess a signal caller's value.

Modeling Team Offense

Let's start with a team's offense. What determines a team's yearly point production? Scoring is dictated by four broad actions: acquisition of the ball, moving the ball across the field of play, maintaining possession of the ball, and converting possessions into points. Let's talk about the details involved in each action.

Action 1: Acquiring the ball. A team can gain possession of the ball when the opponent kicks off,[7] punts, or misses a field goal. Additionally, the ball can be acquired when the opponent throws an interception or loses a fumble.[8] Once a team gains possession of the ball, the team must move the ball down the field.

Action 2: Advancing the ball. This effort begins with the progress the team makes on the play giving the team possession. So we need to note the average yardage a team gains on returned kicks, punts, and interceptions. With respect to punts, large returns are somewhat mitigated if the opponent has a powerful punter; therefore, we also need to take into account the average yardage of the opponent's punts.

After the play where the team acquires the ball, the team has to move across the field of play. Obviously the number of yards a team's offense gains is important. Specifically yardage can be gained via a team's rushing and passing attack.[9] Yardage can also be gained or lost via penalties by the offense and defense.[10]

Action 3: Maintaining Possession. Yards are not the only story. If a team moves too slowly, it will lose possession of the ball. When a team gains possession of the ball it has four plays to travel ten yards and earn a first down. Given the system of downs, the more plays the team runs, again holding all else constant including yards, the lower the team's ability to score. Plays include rushing attempts, passing attempts, and sacks. It is important to note that we expect a play with no yards gained will reduce a team's offensive point production.

Although a team technically has four downs to gain ten yards, the fourth down is rarely used to advance the ball.[11] If a team does try to move the ball on fourth down and fails, it loses possession. So on fourth down teams typically either punt or try a field goal. Given the realities of the fourth down, third down becomes very important. Specifically, the ability of a team to gain a first down on third down, measured via its third down conversion rate, is also important in determining offensive success.

If a team really wants to lose possession of the ball, there are other avenues open beyond just moving too slowly. Possession is lost when a team misses a field goal, throws an interception, or loses a fumble.

Action 4: Converting possessions into points. Of course teams are not trying to lose possession of the ball. If a team does not turn the ball back to its opponent it will ultimately score.[12] Of course, scoring via a touchdown is preferred to a field goal. To gauge the effectiveness of a team's offense we need to note how many points a team scored via each method. Specifically we want to know a team's touchdown rate, or the percentage of scores that are actually touchdowns.

In addition to touchdown rate, the final element we consider is a team's ability

TABLE 9.2

Factors Impacting a Team's Offensive Ability

General Actions	Specific Actions
Acquisition of the ball	Opponent's kick-offs
	Opponent's punts
	Opponent's missed field goals
	Opponent's interceptions
	Opponent's fumbles lost
Moving the ball	Average yards returned on kick-offs
	Average yards returned on punts
	Average yards returned on interceptions
	Average yardage of the opponent's punts
	Offensive yards gained, or rushing and passing yards
	Penalty yards lost
	Penalty yards lost by the opponent
Maintaining possession	Plays, or rushing attempts, passing attempts, and sacks
	Third down conversion rate
	Missed field goals
	Interceptions
	Fumbles lost
Scoring	Touchdown rate
	Extra points conversion rate

to earn points from its extra point attempts. A team's extra point conversion rate is calculated by dividing the number of points a team earns on its attempts by the number of attempts a team has earned.

So we see a team's ability to score is determined by its acquisition of the ball, its ability to move the ball, its ability to maintain possession of the ball, and finally its ability to turn possessions into points. All of this is summarized in Table 9.2.

How does knowing how a team scores allow us to evaluate quarterbacks? By regressing how many points a team's offense scored[13] on each of the factors listed in Table 9.2, we can learn the value of each action in terms of points scored.[14]

Much of what we estimated has nothing to do with the quarterback, yet the purpose behind modeling scoring was to talk about signal callers. There are four variables, though, that will help us measure a quarterback's productivity: offensive yards, plays, interceptions, and fumbles lost. Now offensive yards includes yardage gained rushing and passing. Furthermore, plays include passing and rushing attempts, as well as sacks. With the exception of touchdown passes thrown,[15] we have taken into account everything in the NFL's quarterback rating. Additionally we have added the actions a quarterback takes with his feet by including rushing yards, sacks, and fumbles lost.

Modeling Team Defense

Before we talk about the value of these actions, we need to talk briefly about defense. Quarterbacks seem to only play defense when they throw an interception.[16] Still, what the quarterback does impacts how a defense performs. Therefore, to understand how a quarterback contributes to team success we need to see how his actions impact the number of points a team's defense allows. Fortunately, a model of team defense is essentially the same as our model of team offense.

In essence all one needs to do is take what is listed in Table 9.2 and "reverse each factor." What does that mean? In modeling team defense we do not need to know about the *opponent's* kick-offs, punts, and missed field goals, but the *team's* kick-offs, punts, and missed field goals. We do not need to know the number of yards the *team* gained, but how many yards the *opponent* gained. Basically, if you see *opponent*, use the *team* factor. If you don't see the word "*opponent*" listed with a factor in Table 9.2, then you will need to use the *opponent's* accumulation of that factor to model team defense.[17]

A Simple Model of Quarterback Productivity

Now we have two regressions. One allows us to explain the number of points a team's offense scores. The second allows us to see the number of points a team's defense allows. We could tell many stories with these results, but let's maintain our focus on quarterbacks. Estimating our model of offensive scoring allowed us to see that each interception thrown by a quarterback costs a team approximately 1.4 points. Interceptions thrown also hurt a team's defense, allowing the opponent to score an estimated 2.3 additional points. If we put these two pieces of information together we see that an interception thrown reduces a team's point differential, or the difference between a team's scoring and its opponent, by about 3.7 points. A similar story can be told about fumbles. A fumble lost will cost a team approximately 1.4 points and increase, by about 2.6, the opponent's point production. Therefore, the net impact of losing a fumble is about 4.0 points.

Now let's contrast the impact of turnovers with the values associated with yards and plays. Each yard gained, either via a run or a pass, is worth approximately 0.08 points. A play, which can be a rushing attempt, passing attempt, or a sack, costs a team about 0.22 points. Let's consider a few scenarios to put this all in perspective.

Imagine Favre dropping back to pass. His lineman, though, fail to block effectively and Favre is sacked for a five-yard loss. Of course we don't want to assign blame to his lineman. Maybe Favre didn't get rid of the ball in a timely fashion.

TABLE 9.3

The Value of Various Quarterback Statistics

Variable	If each variable increased by one, and nothing else changed, Net Points would change by . . .	If each variable increased by one, and nothing else changed, Wins would change by . . .
Yards (rushing yards and passing yards)	+0.08	+0.002
Plays (rushing attempts, passing attempts, and sacks)	−0.22	−0.006
Interceptions	−3.7	−0.106
Fumbles lost	−4.0	−0.114

Maybe a running back failed to pick up a blitzing linebacker. Whoever is to blame, Favre has gone down. What is the impact of this event?

From our model, we learned that one yard was worth 0.08 points. So losing five yards costs the team 0.42 points. Each play costs the team 0.22 points, so the total loss from the sack is about 0.64 points. How can the Packers recoup this loss?

If Favre throws a fifteen-yard completion on the next play, the impact of the sack is more than offset. A fifteen-yard pass is worth 1.26 points. We still need to charge the cost of running a play (−0.22), so the total value of the twenty-yard pass is about a point. So a fifteen-yard pass completely erases the impact of a five-yard sack. Well, at least the impact on scoring. We are sure the feeling of having a large man drive you into the turf takes more than one play to erase.

Now what if Favre throws an interception on the next play? We said an interception costs a team about 3.7 points. To overcome this loss on the next possession, how many yards will Favre have to throw? After a bit of math we see that a quarterback can recoup the loss of one interception by throwing one pass of about 50 yards. A team can also recoup an interception on several plays. Given that each play imposes a cost, though, the more plays it takes to gain yards the more yardage the team will need to offset the cost of the pick. For example, if a team gained about 60 yards in five plays it would also equal the cost of the interception.

We now have some idea of the relative value of yards, plays, interceptions, and fumbles lost. We summarize what we have learned in Table 9.3. Given our earlier discussion connecting points to wins, we also can state the value each of these actions has on team wins.

Now there is one difficulty with Table 9.3. Once again, we have a bunch of little-bitty numbers. Let's make this simple. We have learned that each play costs a team, in absolute terms, about three yards. Interceptions and fumbles cost about, although not exactly, 50 yards. With these results in hand, we can create a very simple measure of a quarterback's productivity. We will call our simple measure QB Score, and its calculation is as follows:

$$\text{All Yards} - 3 \times \text{Plays} - 50 \times \text{All Turnovers}$$

It is important to note that the calculation of QB Score considers yards gained or lost from rushing, passing, and sacks. Our metric also considers all turnovers, so both interceptions thrown and fumbles lost are noted. In the end, once one has information on yards, plays, and turnovers, you can evaluate accurately any quarterback in the NFL. If we compare QB Score to the NFL's quarterback rating system it is pretty clear we have simplified the life of an NFL analyst quite a bit. QB Score also includes what a signal caller does with his legs as well as his arms. In other words, we not only have simple, we also have complete. When you add in the fact that this measure is based upon our models of offense and defense, we also have accurate. In sum, QB Score is simple, complete, and accurate, or just about everything one could want in a performance measure.

We would add that QB Score, Net Points, and Wins Produced are highly correlated. The correlation between these measures on a per play basis is 0.99. And each has their advantages. Net Points and Wins Produced are the easiest to understand. After all, sports fans understand points and wins. Still, each metric is a bit more difficult to compute. QB Score, like our Win Score measure for the NBA, is the easiest to compute, but perhaps not as easy to evaluate. In 2004 Brett Favre had a QB Score of 1,419, and given his participation in 568 plays, he had a per play QB Score of 2.5. What does that mean? Given that the average per play QB Score is about 1.1, Favre's performance in 2004 was very good. Of course you have to know the average QB Score to understand what Favre's rating means.

As we go forward in our discussion we will reference QB Score, Net Points, and Wins Produced. Hopefully one outcome of our book is that people move past the NFL's quarterback rating system—which is not simple, accurate, or complete—and begin noting each signal caller's QB Score, Net Points, or Wins Produced.[18]

THE QUARTERBACKS OF SUPER BOWL XXXIX

We now have a few accurate measures of an NFL quarterback's productivity. To illustrate how Net Points and Wins Produced can be used—we will get back to QB Score in a bit—let's assess the performance of the two starting quarterbacks in Super Bowl XXXIX, Tom Brady and Donovan McNabb. In the game Brady's New

England Patriots prevailed over McNabb's Philadelphia Eagles 24–21. Of course this three-point margin in the season's biggest game proves that Brady is the better quarterback.

Brady and McNabb in 2004

Of course we are joking. One game doesn't "prove" anything. We do want to discuss each player's performance in the Super Bowl. Before we get to that, though, let's evaluate what each player accomplished during the 2004 regular season. In Table 9.4 we report each player's performance with respect to passing yards, rushing yards, yards lost from sacks, passing attempts, rushing attempts, sacks, interceptions, and fumbles lost. Given what we have learned about the value of each action, we can now measure each quarterback's impact on net points and team wins.

A review of each player's statistics reveals that McNabb both passed and ran for more yards. Although Brady created nearly eight wins with his yards, McNabb's production of yards was worth closer to nine victories. Yards, though, are not the entire story. To gain yards one must spend plays. Each player participated in virtually the same number of plays; consequently, the cost of rushing attempts, passing attempts, and sacks were the about the same. In addition to plays, each quarterback also committed a few turnovers. Brady led in this category, committing nineteen turnovers while McNabb only lost the ball fourteen times.

TABLE 9.4

Tom Brady vs. Donovan McNabb, 2004 Regular Season

Variable	Tom Brady			Donovan McNabb		
	Totals	Net Points Produced	Wins Produced	Totals	Net Points Produced	Wins Produced
Games	16			15		
Passing yards	3,692			3,875		
Rushing yards	28			220		
Yards lost, sacks	162			192		
TOTAL YARDS	3,558	298.1	7.9	3,903	327.0	8.7
Pass attempts	474			469		
Rushing attempts	43			41		
Sacks	26			32		
PLAYS	543	−121.6	−3.2	542	−121.4	−3.2
Interceptions	14	−52.4	−1.5	8	−30.0	−0.9
Fumbles lost	5	−20.0	−0.6	6	−23.9	−0.7
SEASON TOTAL		104.1	2.6		151.7	3.9
Per game		6.5	0.163		10.1	0.261
Per play		0.192			0.280	

When we note the impact of yards, plays, and turnovers, we see that Brady produced about 104 net points and 2.6 wins in 2004. McNabb bested Brady's production, producing 151.7 net points and nearly four victories. Just like our analysis of NBA players, where we looked at per-minute and per-48-minute performance, it is useful to think about how quarterbacks perform per game and per play.[19] Brady's net points production per game was 6.5, while per play he produced 0.192. McNabb produced a bit more than ten net points per game, while per play he produced 0.256. To put these per play numbers in perspective we should note that from 1995 to 2005 the average quarterback produced 0.133 net points per play. So both Brady and McNabb were above average performers, although of the two, McNabb was the more productive.

From this analysis we can see that McNabb performed at a higher level than Brady over the course of the 2004 regular season. Although each player participated in virtually the same number of plays, McNabb accumulated 345 additional yards and threw six fewer interceptions. As a result, McNabb's greater efficiency resulted in his greater level of net points and wins production.

Another Myth—Assigning Wins and Losses to Quarterbacks

Our analysis of each player's wins production appears to contradict a myth frequently offered by commentators on professional football. Analysts often treat quarterbacks like pitchers in baseball by noting how often a team wins and loses when the quarterback starts. We already noted this practice when we stated Favre's ranking in career wins and career winning percentage. Our analysis of McNabb and Brady, two quarterbacks who are above average performers at their position, suggests that quarterbacks cannot drastically alter outcomes by themselves. We will show that McNabb's performance in 2004 was only eclipsed by Peyton Manning and Daunte Culpepper. In fact, as we will show below, McNabb's performance was one of the better showings by a quarterback in the NFL over the past decade. Yet McNabb's productivity only created an estimated 3.8 wins. The Eagles won thirteen games in 2004 and our analysis suggests that McNabb was responsible for about 30% of these victories. Brady's performance, which was also above the average, was worth less than 20% of the fourteen wins his team accumulated. So our analysis of productivity suggests that while quarterbacks are important to team success, they cannot be given full credit or blame when a team succeeds or fails on the field of play.

We also need to state quite clearly that our analysis has overestimated each quarterback's contribution. Let's think about basketball for a moment. Basketball players do not play by themselves, but a player like Michael Jordan can "take over the game." What does this mean? At times teams will rely heavily upon their star players, going to the same player over and over again when the game in on the line. At these times, it is almost like the star is playing without his teammates. Now this is a simplification, but certainly it was possible for Jordan to steal the ball at one end, dribble the length of the court, and then score. On a sequence like this, it is almost like Jordan was a one-man team.

Football, though, is never like this. A quarterback throws his passes to other players. Without an offensive line blocking, a quarterback would have no time to find these other players. In our analysis of McNabb and Brady, though, we credited the value of passing and rushing yards to the quarterbacks alone. We ignored the impact of the receivers catching these passes and the offensive line blocking. When we ignore the impact of the signal caller's teammates, we still cannot claim that the quarterback produces even 40% of his team's total wins production. Once we acknowledge that other players contribute significantly to a quarterback's statistical production, we have to conclude that the practice of assigning wins and losses to a team's quarterback is completely indefensible.

McNabb and Brady—Super Bowl XXXIX

With this statement in mind, let's look at Super Bowl XXXIX. As Table 9.5 reveals, in the Super Bowl McNabb again accumulated more yards than Brady. McNabb, though, threw three interceptions while Brady did not throw a pick and only turned the ball over once via a fumble. Consequently, on a per-play basis, Brady's

TABLE 9.5

Tom Brady vs. Donovan McNabb, Super Bowl XXXIX

Variable	Tom Brady			Donovan McNabb		
	Totals	Net Points Produced	Wins Produced	Totals	Net Points Produced	Wins Produced
Passing yards	236			357		
Rushing yards	−1			0		
Yards lost, sacks	17			33		
TOTAL YARDS	218	18.3	0.5	324	27.1	0.7
Pass attempts	33			51		
Rushing attempts	1			1		
Sacks	2			4		
PLAYS	36	−8.1	−0.2	56	−12.5	−0.3
Interceptions	0	0.0	0.0	3	−11.2	−0.3
Fumbles lost	1	−4.0	−0.1	0	0.0	0.0
Per game		6.2	0.156		3.4	0.068
Per play		0.173			0.060	

performance in the Super Bowl was very similar to what he offered in the regular season. McNabb's performance, primarily because of the increase in turnovers, was far worse. To put his decline in perspective, had McNabb's performance simply equaled his regular season effort, McNabb would have produced about seven additional net points. This change alone, which would have occurred had McNabb not thrown an interception, could have given the Eagles the victory in a game they lost by three points.

Of course as we said, quarterbacks don't win games themselves. In Super Bowl XL, the Pittsburgh Steelers won despite their quarterback, Ben Roethlisberger, who produced –2.3 net points. Matt Hasselbeck, quarterback of the losing Seattle Seahawks, produced 8.6 net points, besting Brady's efforts from a year earlier. Again, football is a team game and it is far too easy to overemphasize the contribution of the quarterback.

WHO IS THE BEST? THE QUARTERBACK'S STORY

So other players are important to a team's success. Still, we are focused on the quarterback. Now it is time to turn to the question we asked about NBA players: "Who is the best?"

We collected data on each NFL quarterback who registered at least 224 pass attempts—the minimum necessary to qualify for the NFL's quarterback rating leaders—from 1995 through the 2005 campaign. In all, 355 season performances met this criterion. We then evaluated each quarterback in terms of our measures of Net Points, Wins Produced, QB Score, as well as the NFL's quarterback rating system. We report in Table 9.6 the most productive quarterback, in terms of Net Points per play.

The Best Ever?

So for these eleven years who was the best? That honor falls to Peyton Manning. In 2004 Manning set the single season record for quarterback rating. For our sample of eleven seasons, Manning is the only quarterback who produced more than 200 net points. Per play, Manning was also the only player to crack the 0.400 level. In fact, in our sample, only three other quarterbacks produced more than 0.300 points per play. And one of these was Peyton Manning in 2005.

What about QB Score? When we look at our very simple measure, we see that Manning posted a QB Score of 2,339, which works out to 4.37 per play. Again, the average signal caller from 1995–2005 posted a per-play QB Score of about 1.1, so Manning was quite a bit better than the average player at his position. Although we did not look at NFL quarterbacks prior to 1995, we think Manning's performance in 2004 may be the best in NFL history.

TABLE 9.6

Eleven Years of the "Best" Quarterbacks in the NFL

Quarterback	Year	Rank Net Points per Play per season	Rank QB Rating per season	Net Points per Play	Net Points	Wins Produced	QB Score per Play	QB Score	QB Rating
Peyton Manning	2005	1	1	0.304	152.8	4.0	3.18	1,602	104.1
Peyton Manning	2004	1	1	0.402	215.3	5.6	4.37	2,339	121.1
Peyton Manning	2003	1	2	0.281	172.2	4.5	2.94	1,800	99.0
Trent Green	2002	1	4	0.284	149.5	3.9	2.93	1,543	92.6
Kurt Warner	2001	1	1	0.253	154.8	3.9	2.49	1,521	101.4
Kurt Warner	2000	1	3	0.316	121.5	3.1	3.18	1,226	98.3
Kurt Warner	1999	1	1	0.297	163.5	4.2	3.07	1,691	109.2
Randall Cunningham	1998	1	1	0.340	162.1	4.2	3.61	1,723	106.0
Steve Young	1997	1	1	0.297	130.8	3.4	3.14	1,385	104.7
Steve Young	1996	1	1	0.234	94.0	2.4	2.37	954	97.2
Troy Aikman	1995	1	3	0.285	133.3	3.5	2.99	1,396	93.6

NOTE: An average quarterback from 1995 to 2005 had a net points per play of 0.133 and a QB Score per play of 1.1.

What was this output worth in terms of wins? We estimate that Manning's output was worth 5.6 wins. In our sample, this was the most wins we estimate any one quarterback produced. Manning's team, the Colts, won twelve games in 2004. Our estimates indicate that a quarterback's performance that may be the best in NFL history was not worth half of the team's wins production. Again, although this result suggests the quarterback is an important part of any team's success or failure, the data make it clear that we shouldn't attribute a team's wins and losses solely to individual quarterbacks.

Quarterback Rating, Again

As with our analysis of productivity in the NBA, the story of the best player is not the only tale to be told. In our discussion of NBA players we noted the inconsistency between the measure of performance we offer and the measure suggested by the league. How does our measure of a quarterback's productivity compare to the quarterback rating system employed by the NFL?

If we look at Table 9.6 we see a great deal of consistency between the top players in each campaign. In seven seasons the best player according to net points per play was also the best in terms of quarterback rating. What if we move past the very best players? Do we still see consistency?

To answer this question we looked at our sample of 355 quarterback performances from 1995–2005. We ranked this sample in terms of net points per play and

TABLE 9.7

The Top 40 Quarterback Performances, 1995–2005

(*Minimum 224 Pass Attempts*)

Quarterback	Year	Rank Net Points per Play, 1995–2005	Rank QB Rating 1995–2005	Net Points per Play	Net Points	Wins Produced	QB Score per Play	QB Score	QB Rating
eyton Manning	2004	1	1	0.402	215.3	5.6	4.37	2,339	121.1
andall Cunningham	1998	2	4	0.340	162.1	4.2	3.61	1,723	106.0
urt Warner	2000	3	22	0.316	121.5	3.1	3.18	1,226	98.3
eyton Manning	2005	4	9	0.304	152.8	4.0	3.18	1,602	104.1
urt Warner	1999	5	3	0.297	163.5	4.2	3.07	1,691	109.2
eve Young	1997	6	7	0.297	130.8	3.4	3.14	1,385	104.7
aunte Culpepper	2004	7	2	0.292	199.4	5.2	3.06	2,089	110.9
ff Garcia	2000	8	26	0.292	191.6	5.0	3.07	2,016	97.6
rian Griese	2000	9	10	0.287	109.6	2.8	3.02	1,155	102.9
roy Aikman	1995	10	42	0.285	133.3	3.5	2.99	1,396	93.6
rent Green	2002	11	47	0.284	149.5	3.9	2.93	1,543	92.6
had Pennington	2002	12	8	0.282	127.0	3.3	2.96	1,334	104.2
eyton Manning	2003	13	20	0.281	172.2	4.5	2.94	1,800	99.0
onovan McNabb	2004	14	6	0.280	151.7	3.9	2.91	1,577	104.7
rent Green	2003	15	48	0.278	158.1	4.1	2.87	1,635	92.6
roy Aikman	1998	16	80	0.277	95.9	2.5	2.90	1,003	88.5
inny Testaverde	1998	17	12	0.275	127.7	3.3	2.86	1,328	101.6
rent Green	2000	18	11	0.268	76.2	2.0	2.76	785	101.8
en Roethlisberger	2005	19	21	0.264	85.0	2.2	2.67	859	98.6
eve McNair	2003	20	18	0.261	119.4	3.1	2.68	1,224	100.4
hris Chandler	1998	21	16	0.261	106.4	2.7	2.62	1,068	100.9
eyton Manning	2000	22	36	0.261	163.7	4.2	2.65	1,664	94.7
oug Flutie	1998	23	91	0.260	107.5	2.8	2.63	1,089	87.4
latt Hasselbeck	2005	24	23	0.259	131.6	3.4	2.66	1,352	98.2
rew Brees	2004	25	5	0.257	121.1	3.1	2.65	1,250	104.8
ich Gannon	2002	26	28	0.257	180.9	4.7	2.65	1,869	97.3
rent Green	2004	27	33	0.254	155.9	4.0	2.54	1,560	95.2
lark Brunell	1997	28	57	0.254	130.8	3.4	2.62	1,351	91.2
urt Warner	2001	29	13	0.253	154.8	3.9	2.49	1,521	101.4
ke Plummer	2005	30	64	0.252	131.8	3.4	2.60	1,360	90.2
rent Green	2005	31	66	0.251	144.1	3.7	2.56	1,470	90.1
eil O'Donnell	1995	32	88	0.250	113.9	3.0	2.58	1,174	87.7
rett Favre	2004	33	50	0.250	142.2	3.6	2.50	1,419	92.4
m Harbaugh	1995	34	17	0.250	100.3	2.6	2.57	1,035	100.7
oug Flutie	2000	35	98	0.249	69.0	1.8	2.57	712	86.5
cott Mitchell	1995	36	53	0.249	161.5	4.2	2.53	1,647	92.3
eyton Manning	1999	37	61	0.248	144.4	3.7	2.48	1,446	90.7
eve Young	1998	38	14	0.247	156.7	4.0	2.50	1,585	101.1
rett Favre	1995	39	19	0.247	158.3	4.1	2.49	1,601	99.5
arson Palmer	2005	40	15	0.244	137.3	3.5	2.47	1,386	101.1

NOTE: An average quarterback from 1995 to 2005 had a net points per play of 0.133 and a QB Score per play of 1.1.

then extracted those performances that ranked in the top 40. As we report in Table 9.7, of the performances we rank as top 40 in net points per play, 27 or 67.5% were also ranked in the top 40 by the NFL's quarterback rating. So there is certainly some consistency between our measure, which considers a player's ability with arm and legs, and the NFL's metric, which is strictly a measure of passing performance. Still, there are some noticeable differences.

Doug Flutie offered two top-40 performances, the first in 1998 and then again in 2000. According to the NFL's rating system, his 2000 effort was only the 98th best effort while his performance in 1998 ranked 91st. Troy Aikman also appeared undervalued by the quarterback rating system. His efforts in 1995 and 1998 rank, in terms of net points per play, tenth and sixteenth respectively. The NFL's metric ranked his 1995 effort as the 42nd best in our sample, while his 1998 performance was ranked 80th. The quarterback facing Aikman's Cowboys in Super Bowl XXX was Neil O'Donnell. O'Donnell in 1995 offered a performance ranked 32nd overall in net points per play, but was only ranked 88th overall via the quarterback rating.

Inconsistency in rankings goes beyond the participants in Super Bowl XXX. The aforementioned Brett Favre appears twice in our rankings. His 1995 effort ranks 39th in net points per play, although his quarterback rating from that season was ranked 19th. According to net points per play, his 2004 effort was the best of his career, ranking 33rd in our sample. The NFL's measure, though, ranked this performance as only the 50th best. So with respect to Brett Favre, not only is there inconsistency between our metric and the NFL's, the inconsistency is not consistent.

CONSISTENT INCONSISTENCY

The stories about Flutie, Aikman, and Favre are about more than consistency in performance metrics. Flutie had four seasons in his career where he threw at least 224 passes. In 1998 his net points per play was an outstanding 0.269. In 1999 his productivity dropped to 0.132. The next season it rose again to 0.235, only to fall to 0.138 in 2001. Inconsistency also plagued Aikman at the end of his career. Our sample begins in 1995. In 1995 and 1998 Aikman offered two of the best performances reviewed in our sample. In 1996, 1997, 1999, and 2000, though, Aikman's production per play was ranked 186th, 199th, 120th, and 327th respectively. Remember, our sample had 355 performances. So just like our story of Brett Favre at the start of this chapter, consistency seemed to elude Aikman in the last few years of his career.

The Brett Favre Story, Again

We have already examined Favre's game-by-game performance in 2004. Do we see consistency when we look at his season-to-season productivity? In Table 9.8 we consider eleven years of Brett Favre. For each season we looked at where Favre ranked among NFL signal callers. When we look at net points per play, we see that Favre was a top-ten quarterback in five seasons—1995, 1996, 1997, 2001, 2004—and not ranked in the top ten in six seasons—1998, 1999, 2000, 2002, 2003, and 2005. In fact, according to net points per play, Favre followed his best performance—offered in 2004—by his worst performance in 2005. Inconsistency is the story whether one considers net points per player, Wins Produced, QB Score, or the NFL's quarterback rating. In some years Favre is a top-ten signal caller. In other years, he is much closer to the average player at his position.

When we look at Favre's average performance across all eleven years, we see evidence that Favre has on average, been a very good quarterback. Whether we look at his production by any of our performance metrics, Favre's average performance is better than the average quarterback in the league. Although across his career he is well above average, this is not quite the story in each and every season. Let's go back briefly to our examination of NBA stars. Michael Jordan performed well above the average player in the NBA every year he played with the Chicago Bulls.

TABLE 9.8

Eleven Years of Brett Favre

| | Rank, per season | | | | | | | |
Year	Net Points per Play	QB Rating	Net Points per Play	Net Points	Wins Produced	QB Score per Play	QB Score	QB Rating
1995	5	2	0.247	158.3	4.1	2.49	1,601	99.5
1996	6	2	0.177	111.7	2.8	1.66	1,048	95.8
1997	4	3	0.194	115.6	2.9	1.83	1,090	92.6
1998	13	10	0.176	110.4	2.7	1.57	985	87.8
1999	18	25	0.132	86.5	2.1	1.04	686	74.7
2000	15	17	0.134	85.5	2.1	1.12	714	78.0
2001	3	4	0.198	112.8	2.8	1.87	1,066	94.1
2002	17	12	0.143	86.2	2.1	1.22	737	85.6
2003	14	6	0.140	71.0	1.7	1.11	565	90.4
2004	6	10	0.250	142.2	3.6	2.50	1,419	92.4
2005	28	31	0.053	34.3	0.6	0.04	26	70.9
AVERAGE	11.7	11.1	0.167	101.3	2.5	1.50	903	87.4

NOTE: An average quarterback from 1995 to 2005 had a net points per play of 0.133 and a QB Score per play of 1.1.

Only when Jordan was 38 years old and on his third tour of duty did his performance slip. Brett Favre, though, clearly has years in the prime of his career where his performance is not much different from an average quarterback. Just as we observed when we looked at his game-by-game performance in 2004, and much like Flutie and Aikman, Favre has also been inconsistent across his career.

The Simple Story of Inconsistency

Of course the story of Flutie, Aikman, and Favre does not an argument make. What if we looked at all quarterbacks from 1995 to 2004? Would we see consistent evidence of inconsistency?

To answer this question we constructed a sample of quarterbacks who attempted at least 100 passes in successive seasons. From 1995 to 2004 we gathered 277 observations, offered by 88 different signal callers. With this sample in hand, we then looked at how consistent these quarterbacks performed from season to season.

Let's start with something fairly basic. Previously we connected current productivity in the NBA to a collection of different factors, including what the player did last year. The measure we used in Chapter Seven did not incorporate assists. Let's repeat this analysis with our Win Score measure, which does include assists. Specifically we wish to know how much of an NBA player's Win Score per minute this season could we explain if all we knew was the player's per-minute Win Score per-minute for last year. When we run this simple regression we see that 67% of current production in the NBA is explained by last year's performance. If we look at NBA Efficiency, explanatory power is 66%.[20]

Now let's try this same exercise with our sample of NFL players. When we regress a quarterback's current net points per play on his net points per play last season, we find that our explanatory power is only 10%. In other words, only 10% of what a quarterback does this year is explained by what he did last year. What if we used a different metric? If we regress a player's current QB Score per play on last year's measure our explanatory power is 9.5%. Maybe our metrics are flawed in some way. What about the NFL's quarterback rating measure? Now our explanatory power rises, all the way to 11%. Hmmm . . . still not too good. Not to be discouraged, we also considered completion percentage, passing yards per passing attempt, passing touchdowns per passing attempt, rushing yards per rushing attempt, rushing touchdowns per rushing attempt, interceptions per passing attempt, fumbles per play, and fumbles lost per play. The explanatory power of each simple model is reported in Table 9.9.

TABLE 9.9

Percentage of Current Performance
We Can Explain with Past Performance

Variable	Explanatory Power (percent)
Net points per play	10.3
QB Score per play	9.5
Quarterback rating	11.0
Completion percentage	21.2
Passing yards per passing attempt	16.5
Passing touchdowns per passing attempt	6.5
Rushing yards per rushing attempt	26.7
Rushing touchdowns per rushing attempt	3.4
Interceptions per passing attempt	1.1
Fumbles per play	1.0
Fumbles lost per play	0.1

What do we learn from this simple exercise? It is beginning to look like Brett Favre is not an anomaly. If all we knew was a quarterback's past performance we would not seem to know very much at all about what he would do during the current campaign. This is especially true with respect to turnovers. We found turnovers to be very important in our efforts to explain how many points a team scores and allows. Yet if we looked at a quarterback's propensity to give the ball away in the past, we don't seem to be able to learn anything about his likelihood to commit such offenses in the future. With respect to both interceptions and fumbles, about 1% of current performance is explained by last year's production. For fumbles lost, the explanatory power is only 0.1%. So turnovers, a key facet of a quarterback's performance, seem to be entirely unpredictable.

Adding Just a Bit of Sophistication

Regressing one factor upon another is simple, but it lacks the sophistication we have grown to know and love in economics. What if we tried connecting current performance to a larger collection of explanatory variables? Would our explanatory power improve?

Before we get to explanatory power, let's examine what we found. As we note in Table 9.10, our slightly more sophisticated approach revealed that there was a positive and statistically significant relationship between the net points per play a quarterback posted in the current season and the following factors: net points per play last season, the productivity of a team's rushing attack, and games played. Be-

TABLE 9.10

What Explains Current Per-Play Productivity in the NFL?

Factors we found to be statistically related to current per-play productivity	How the factor is measured (more details in endnotes)
Quarterback's talent and ability	Net points per play last season
Being a young player	Having less than three years of experience
Productivity of team's rushing attack	Rushing yards accumulated by team
Player health	Games played
Factors we did not find to be statistically related to current per-play productivity	
Coaching ability	Years of head coaching experience and the head coach's lifetime winning percentage
Being an old player	Having more than ten years of experience
Team defense	Points allowed by team

ing a younger player was found to adversely impact performance in a statistical sense.[21] Coaching ability,[22] whether we measure the experience of the head coach or the lifetime won-loss record of the coach, was not found to be statistically important. The same could be said for being an older player and the quality of a team's defense.

When we include all these factors in our model of current net points per play, our explanatory power rises to 27%. Basically the same result was uncovered when we looked at quarterback rating. The same list of factors was significant statistically, and explanatory power is still 27%.

A more complete model does teach us some lessons about quarterback performance. The quality of a team's rushing attack impacts a quarterback's performance. Also we now see that the more games a quarterback plays, the better he performs. Finally, younger quarterbacks tend to perform worse than older signal callers.

Does any of this really help us forecast performance? We are definitely going to know which quarterbacks are young and which are old. Unfortunately, the other significant explanatory variables are not as predictable. Consider a team's ground attack. Only 14% of a team's rushing yards this season can be explained by a team's rushing yards last season. A team's rushing performance depends upon the quality and health of its running backs, offensive line, and probably its passing game. All of this can change from year to year; hence, like quarterbacks, a team's performance on the ground is unpredictable.

A similar story can be told with respect to how many games a quarterback will play. The number of games a quarterback played last year explains 7% of the variation in games played in the current campaign. The number of games a quarterback plays depends upon his health and the perception the head coach has of his performance. This latter point is important. Although we found more games lead to better performance, we are not sure the causality runs from games to performance. Certainly better performance likely leads to a quarterback playing more games.

Even if we knew the quality of a team's rushing attack and the number of games a quarterback would play, our ability to explain current performance is still less than 30%. Why are quarterbacks so inconsistent? As we stated earlier, the performance of a quarterback depends crucially upon the performance of his teammates. One can be the greatest quarterback ever, but if the line doesn't block and the receivers can't catch, the best quarterback will look very bad. In the past, quarterbacks had the ability to call the team's offensive plays. Today, though, coaches frequently make such calls, and so we have another factor beyond the control of the quarterback that can alter his performance. Finally, we need to make an observation frequently forgotten in sports. The other team is often trying to win, too. Quarterbacks are playing against a defense that is trying its best to make the quarterback look bad. Sometimes, no matter how good a player might be, the defense is successful.

Beyond all these issues there is the quarterback's level of experience. Consider the level of experience a football player can accumulate in his career relative to a typical professional basketball player. A basketball player can play a pick-up basketball game every day, a game that comes close to simulating an organized game. Furthermore, over the course of an NBA player's high school, college, and professional career he can play in well over a thousand organized contests.

In contrast, a quarterback cannot play a pick-up game that simulates an actual contest. Additionally, even over the course of a long career, a quarterback like Brett Favre only participates in a few hundred games. Given this relative lack of experience, we should not be surprised that quarterbacks appear to be relatively inconsistent.

CONSISTENCY IN SPORTS

For those with a passing familiarity with regression analysis, a flaw would be evident in our efforts thus far to compare consistency in football and basketball. We stated that about 70% of a basketball player's current performance can be explained by last year's production. In football, we find the explanatory power of last year's performance to be far less. Actually, though, one really can't compare the explanatory power of two models that are trying to explain different things. In essence, this is an apples and oranges issue. The NBA Efficiency measure, our Win Score metric, and a quarterback's net points produced per play are really different fruits.

To overcome the "fruit issue," let's take a different approach. We are three college professors and we have spent a fair amount of our careers grading the performance of students. What we wish to do is take advantage of this experience and assign grades to the players employed in the National Football League, Major League Baseball, and the National Basketball Association. After we assign the grades we will ask a simple question: How often do players maintain their grade from season to season?

Our grades will be assigned in the following fashion. The players will be ranked according to a specific performance measure. If a player ranks in the top 20%, then they will be given an A. The next 20% will get a B, the next 20% a C, with the final two groupings receiving a D and an F.[23]

Let's begin with the NFL. We began with the data set we used to examine the consistency of a quarterback's performance. As noted, we had 277 observations of signal callers who had significant playing time in two consecutive years. For each year we ranked the players by net points per play, assigning grades as we described. We then ranked these same players in terms of net points per play the previous season. Again, grades were assigned. With grades assigned, we then looked at how often these quarterbacks kept their grades from season to season, or conversely, how often these players changed their grades.

Before we get to the results for all players in our sample, let's discuss the grades we assigned to the only two players to receive significant playing time in every season we considered, Brett Favre and Kerry Collins. Let's start with Collins. As a rookie in 1995, Collins ranked in the lowest 20%, receiving an F. In 1996 his performance improved and he received a B. The next two seasons, though, Collins declined, earning an F in both campaigns. Then in 1999 he earned a C, followed by a B in 2000. After declining again, this time to a C, in 2001, Collins earned an A for his efforts in 2002. Unfortunately his success was short-lived, as his performance was worth a D in 2003. In 2004, the final year we examined, Collins earned a C.

Now back to Favre. We have already discussed Favre's inconsistency. We would note, though, that relative to Collins, Favre was solid as a rock. Favre received an A in five seasons, a B in two campaigns, and then a C in the remaining years. Despite never posting a D or an F, Favre only posted the same grade in consecutive seasons twice.

What do we see when we look at our entire sample of 277 performances? Of these, 68 quarterbacks, or 25%, kept their grades from season to season. From the other perspective, though, 209, or 76%, changed their grades in successive seasons. How many of these players who changed their grades changed more than two spots in our scale? For example, how many F players improved enough to receive a C, or B players declined enough to receive a D? When we look at our sample we see that 39% of quarterbacks saw their grades change more than two places. So if your quarterback earned an A last year, you would have a 39% chance he might decline to a C or worse this year. Such evidence suggests again that quarterbacks are inconsistent. Still, to put this in perspective we need a reference point.

Back to Baseball

When we began our story back at the beginning of the book, the sport we focused on was baseball. Since Chapter Five, though, we have been mostly spending time talking about basketball or in this chapter, the gridiron. Now it time to briefly talk about baseball again.

How consistent are baseball players? To answer this question, we need a measure of productivity. Back in 1974 Gerald Scully wrote the first major empirical study of economics and baseball. When this work was published in the *American Economic Review*, the top journal in our discipline, it revealed that economists could indeed spend their lives studying sports and still find an outlet for their work.

Scully wished to understand the relationship between pay and performance. To measure performance, Scully used slugging percentage, or total bases divided by at-bats. Since Scully wrote this work, research on measuring productivity in baseball has become increasingly sophisticated.

Actually, according to Alan Schwarz (2004), sophisticated measures for measuring productivity in baseball had been around long before Scully's work appeared. An example can be found in the story of Ferdinand Lane, a biologist Schwarz profiles who also had a love of baseball. Lane became extremely dissatisfied with the practice of measuring a baseball hitter's productivity with batting average, or the ratio of hits to at-bats. Batting average fails to differentiate between hits, treating an additional home run the same as an additional single. It also ignores stolen bases and walks. In essence, as Schwarz quotes Lane saying, batting average is "worse than worthless."

For followers of today's Sabermetric movement, Lane's critique seems quite familiar. Interestingly, Lane offered his attack on batting average toward the beginning of the 20th century. Without the aid of today's computers and our friend regression analysis, Lane was still able to deduce, through the extensive study of game-by-game data, the relative value of singles, doubles, triples, and home runs. According to Lane, a single was worth 0.46 runs, a double 0.79, a triple 1.15, and a home run was valued at 1.55 runs.

As Schwarz notes, Lane's work echoed the much later work of Pete Palmer, one of the early writers in the Sabermetric movement. Palmer developed a metric he called Linear Weights, which calculated the relative value of singles, doubles, triples, and home runs via regression analysis. The method and subsequent values are detailed in Thorn and Palmer (1984). Interestingly, the values that Palmer uncovered 60 years after Lane were actually quite similar to the much earlier work.

Using data from 1995 to 2004 we also employed regression analysis to find the relative value of these stats in terms of runs scored.[24] Our analysis indicates that a single is worth 0.55 runs, a double 0.65, a triple 0.89, and a home run is worth 1.40 runs scored.[25] Like Lane and Palmer, our regression analysis also indicates the value of a collection of other statistics tabulated for hitters, such as walks, stolen bases, etc. Such a regression explains 94% of runs scored, so it appears to be quite accurate.

Unlike our discussion of basketball and football, we are not covering any new ground with our measurement of a baseball player's performance. In basketball and football we demonstrated that the proper use of regression analysis could create metrics that improved upon the existing measures. As Lane noted almost a century ago, the traditional measure in baseball, batting average, is both a poor metric of performance and, with a bit of work, can be improved upon. The Sabermetric movement, led by Bill James, Pete Palmer, and many others, has made an incredible effort to provide measures with increasing accuracy. At the end of the day, we have little to add to this discussion and probably much more we ourselves could learn.

We do want to comment, briefly, on the relative merits of a few simple measures of performance. Schwarz notes that batting average was developed by H. A. Dobson in 1872. This is still the measure used by many to rank hitters today. If we regress runs scored on batting average, though, we learn that only 70% of a team's offense can be explained by how many hits it gets per at-bat. More recently people have trumpeted the value of on-base percentage[26] and slugging average. Each measure by itself improves on batting average. On-base percentage explains 83% of runs scored, while 81% of runs can be explained by a team's slugging average. When you combine the two metrics, though, explanatory power increases.

There is some question of how one should make this combination. One can add together on-base percentage and slugging percentage, creating a metric called OPS. Or one can multiply on-base percentage and slugging average, creating a measure which Dick Cramer and Pete Palmer call Batters Run Average[27] and Allen Barra calls SLOB. The evidence suggests that adding or multiplying doesn't make much difference. OPS explains 90% of runs scored, while SLOB explains 91%.

Wouldn't one just be better off using the Linear Weights method developed by Lane and Palmer? After all, we have already noted that the Linear Weights model explains 94% of runs scored and offers precise values for a host of actions a player takes on the field. To evaluate the merits of each method, we took the following steps. We began with each hitter who had at least 100 official at-bats in a season beginning in 1997 and ending in 2004. For these hitters we used the Linear Weight model to estimate the number of runs the player produced per plate appearance. We also calculated each hitter's OPS and SLOB. With measures in hand, the sample of players was ranked by runs produced per plate appearance, OPS, and SLOB.

We were specifically interested in the correlation between these various rankings. The simple correlation coefficient between runs produced per plate appearance and OPS was 0.97. For runs produced per plate appearance and SLOB we found a correlation of 0.96. Finally, there is a 0.99 correlation between OPS and SLOB. In essence, these correlation coefficients suggest that any of these metrics will give you a simple and accurate measure of a baseball hitter's contribution.[28]

Although we could have used any of these metrics, since we had gone to the trouble of calculating all three, we decided to employ all of these in our study of performance consistency. Like our study of football, we then examined each player's level of consistency from season to season. To do this, we constructed a data set of all players who had at least 100 at-bats in consecutive seasons. In all, from 1997 to 2004, we collected 2,689 observations of players with our minimum number of at-bats in successive seasons.

With data set in hand, we then began with the very simple questions: How much of a player's current production can be explained if all we knew was what the player did last year? If we use runs produced per plate appearance as our measure, we find that we can explain 29% of current performance with last year's production.[29] When we turn to OPS and SLOB, the results are similar. For OPS, 33% of current performance is explained by production last year, while for SLOB our explanatory power is 37%.

To compare the level of consistency we see in baseball to what we saw in football, we also put on our professor hats and graded each of the 2,689 baseball performances in our data set. We employed runs produced per plate appearance, although grades with OPS and SLOB were quite similar. How much did the player's grade change from year to year? Across our sample, 939 or 35% maintained their grades from season to season. Again, from the other side of the coin, 65% changed their grades in consecutive seasons. Consequently, compared to football, baseball players appear more consistent.

Of the players who saw their grades change, how many changed more than two spots in our scale? In football, 39% moved two places. Baseball players again exhibit greater consistency since only 28% saw their grades change two spots or more. Still, baseball players do demonstrate some inconsistency. Apparently, hitting a round ball with a round stick is not entirely predictable.

And Back to Basketball

So we have evidence that baseball players are more consistent than football players. What about basketball players? If we use our simple Win Score measure, 67% of current per-minute performance can be explained by last year's Win Score per minute.

What if we turn to our method of grading athletic performance? We looked at twelve years of player data and found that 48% maintained their grades from season to season.[30] So we have evidence that basketball players are more consistent, though the difference in the sports is not quite as great as the simple regression analysis suggests.

Again we looked at players who changed more than two spots in the grading scale. In our sample of basketball players 12% changed more than two spots, or from the other side, 88% of players either kept their grades or saw their grades change only one level.[31] It would appear that basketball players are more consistent than baseball players, and much more consistent than the quarterbacks we examined.

PAYROLL AND WINS

What does all this mean? We began our story with one piece of empirical evidence, that team payroll is a poor predictor of team performance in baseball, basketball, and football. Our examination of consistency gives us one reason why wages and wins are so poorly connected. Consider briefly the story of Brian Griese. A glance back at Table 9.7 reveals that Griese's production in 2000 ranked ninth best among the quarterbacks we examined from 1995 to 2005.

Griese only played ten games in 2000 for the Denver Broncos, but his performance was truly spectacular. His net points per play was 0.287 with a quarterback rating of 102.9. Nineteen of his passes were for touchdowns, while only four passes

were intercepted. We must remember that Griese inherited the job of Broncos signal caller from the legendary John Elway. When Elway led Denver to its Super
Bowl titles after the 1997 and 1998 regular seasons, his net points per play in each
campaign was 0.173 and 0.229, respectively. These were above average efforts, but
not nearly the level of production Griese offered in 2000.

Based on the ten games Griese played in 2000, the Broncos made him the highest paid player in the NFL. According to *USA Today*, the bonuses and base salary
paid to Griese in 2001 totaled $15,154,000. Clearly the Broncos interpreted
Griese's ten-game performance in 2000 as an indication that their quarterback was
one of the best, if not the best, quarterback in the game.

Unfortunately, as our analysis has indicated, quarterbacks are indeed like mutual funds. Again we note, past performance is no guarantee of future returns. In
2001, Griese's performance declined, specifically with respect to interceptions.
From our analysis of consistency, a quarterback's propensity to throw to the other
team is one of the most difficult facets of productivity to predict. In fifteen starts
in 2001, Griese had nineteen passes intercepted. As a result, his net points per play
declined to 0.066, a mark that is clearly below average.

The Griese story highlights the problem for decision makers in the NFL. Based
on his 2000 performance, Griese was the best quarterback in the league. Unfortunately, quarterbacks are consistently inconsistent. After paying Griese a salary justified by his productivity in 2000, his productivity in 2001 dropped considerably.
We would emphasize that we doubt this had anything to do with his effort level.
Griese probably tried just as hard in 2001 as he did in 2000. But the external factors that allow a quarterback to perform well—offensive line, receivers, running
game, coaching, opponent's defense—did not work as well for Griese in 2001 as
they appeared to work in 2000.

Of course members of the sports media might argue that the Broncos should
have known that 2000 was a fluke. Well, in 2002 Griese's net points per play rose to
a respectable 0.175. In 2004, playing for the Tampa Bay Buccaneers, his net points
per play was 0.161. Both efforts, although not equal to his 2000 effort, were above
average. With all that we have learned about a quarterback's performance from
season to season, it is not clear that the Broncos could have known that Griese's
performance would decline in 2001. In fact, it is not clear that anyone can accurately predict performance in the NFL.

Thus the basic premise behind the payroll and wins argument appears to fall
apart. People argue that teams can just buy wins. But for this to be true, one first
has to predict performance accurately. Given the inconsistency in performance in

sports, it is not clear that people can make these predictions consistently. At least, in the sports of football and baseball, this would seem quite difficult.

In basketball, though, we do observe some consistency in performance. Despite greater consistency, the link between payroll and wins in basketball is similar to what we observe in baseball. In the final chapter of our story we will explore a further problem with player evaluation on the court.

10 | SCORING TO SCORE

Once upon a time a high NBA draft choice could be expected to be paid like a star before he ever played an NBA game. What do we mean by star? Previously we discussed the legend of Michael Jordan, one of the all-time great stars in NBA history. In 1995–96 Michael Jordan produced 25 wins for perhaps the greatest team in NBA history. For his efforts he was paid like a star, earning $3.85 million. That same year Glenn Robinson, the first player chosen in the 1994 NBA draft, produced about five victories for the Milwaukee Bucks. Toiling under the contract Robinson received as a rookie, he was also paid like a star, earning $3.77 million.

For each win Jordan provided, the Bulls paid about $150,000. The Milwaukee Bucks paid Robinson close to $780,000 for each victory he created. Of course we are overstating the cost of Jordan's regular season wins, since we are leaving out the fact that he led his team to the NBA championship in 1996. That year Robinson's team won 25 games, a performance that earned Milwaukee another high draft choice.

When the 1995–96 season concluded the rules of the game had been changed with respect to high draft picks. After Robinson was chosen by the Bucks in 1994, Milwaukee and Robinson began a dance that had become quite common in the NBA. Essentially Robinson threatened to hold out, or in other words, not report to Milwaukee until he received a contract to his liking.

After missing training camp, Robinson finally signed a very lucrative contract right before the 1994–95 season began.[1] In his rookie season Milwaukee agreed to pay Robinson a bit less than $3 million. Obviously for most people the rookie salary alone would be a cause for celebration. This contract, though, called for so much more. For many workers pay only goes up when their boss decides he or she

TABLE 10.1

Ten Years of Glenn Robinson

Season	Salary	Wins Produced	Games	Minutes	Team	Cost per Win	Cost per Game	Cost per Minute	WP48
1994–95	$2,900,000	3.4	80	2,958	Milwaukee	$855,724	$36,250	$980	0.055
1995–96	$3,770,000	4.8	82	3,249	Milwaukee	$779,866	$45,976	$1,160	0.071
1996–97	$4,640,000	6.3	80	3,114	Milwaukee	$736,436	$58,000	$1,490	0.097
1997–98	$5,510,000	1.2	56	2,294	Milwaukee	$4,483,452	$98,393	$2,402	0.026
1998–99	$6,380,000	3.4	47	1,579	Milwaukee	$1,151,245	$82,771	$2,464	0.103
1999–00	$7,250,000	4.7	81	2,909	Milwaukee	$1,535,232	$89,506	$2,492	0.078
2000–01	$8,120,000	8.9	76	2,813	Milwaukee	$913,362	$106,842	$2,887	0.152
2001–02	$8,990,000	6.1	66	2,346	Milwaukee	$1,462,019	$136,212	$3,832	0.126
2002–03	$9,860,000	2.3	69	2,591	Atlanta	$4,300,987	$142,899	$3,805	0.042
2003–04	$10,372,000	−0.7	42	1,336	Philadelphia	NA	$246,952	$7,763	−0.024
TOTALS	$67,792,000	40.5	679	25,189	AVERAGES	$1,611,557	$96,174	$2,592	0.077

deserves a raise. Like Dagwood Bumstead, to get this raise the worker has to go to her or his boss and argue that an increase in pay is deserved. And for many workers, the boss is inclined to explain in painful terms why the worker should be happy to have a job and to stop asking for more money. Milwaukee saved Robinson this entire process. Before Robinson ever took the court his rookie season, Milwaukee already agreed to give him a raise when his first year ended. The Bucks also agreed to keep giving him raises, year after year after year. After all these raises Robinson's salary was scheduled to pass $10 million in 2004–05, and over the ten years Robinson signed, he would receive nearly $70 million.

Again, all of this was agreed to before Robinson played a single NBA game. Although Robinson had an exceptional college career at Purdue, the Bucks certainly did not have enough information to predict that Robinson would be worth $10 million ten years into his career.

As we tell this story, Robinson has completed this ten-year contract. Did Robinson prove to be worth $70 million? In Table 10.1 we report the first ten years of Robinson's career. As we stated, Jordan created nearly 25 wins in 1995–96. In Robinson's first ten years he produced 40.5 victories. So like virtually every player to ever play the game, Robinson has not been "like Mike." Has Robinson been at least a good player? Judging by his WP48, Robinson was above average, or good, in three seasons. Of course this means he was below average seven times.

What about his cost per win?[2] Again, Jordan produced each win in 1995–96 for about $150,000. In 1996–97 Robinson was the best bargain of his career, when he still charged more than $700,000 for each victory. In both the fourth and ninth year of his contract each win cost more than $4 million. Across his first ten seasons, Robinson charged nearly $1.7 million for each Win Produced.

After eight seasons Milwaukee dealt Robinson to Atlanta, who then traded him to Philadelphia. It was with the 76ers that Robinson spent his $10 million season, and primarily due to injuries, offered his worst performance of his career. Of course we have already shown the difficulty one has with predicting performance one season in advance. The Glenn Robinson story illustrates the difficulty anyone would have forecasting performance ten years in advance. Given these difficulties, we are not surprised to see some divergence between pay and productivity for players several years into a contract that was signed when they were rookies.

Contracts like Robinson's led to the introduction of the rookie salary scale we mentioned in Chapter Seven. Starting in 1996 each first round draft choice received a contract of a fixed number of years and for a salary determined entirely by his position in the draft.[3] Since this scale was put in place, there have been no more holdouts in the NBA. Once a player is drafted in the first round he signs the only offer he can take for the amount of money the scale determines.[4] After he completes his rookie contract, though, he becomes a free agent. At that point, NBA teams have a bit more information to determine a player's pay.

UNDERRATED AND OVERRATED IN 2004–05

Once players complete a rookie contract and enter a free market, we should expect the link between pay and performance to strengthen. Better players should command higher salaries. Worse players should be paid less. At least, that is what we expect.

To see this link we conducted a simple exercise. Specifically we collected performance and pay data for every player in the NBA who had at least four years of experience and played 2,000 minutes in 2004–05. In all, 72 players met these criteria.

These players were ranked in terms of Wins Produced and NBA Efficiency. We have already noted the difference in these two metrics. It is important to emphasize that although our measure differs from the NBA's, there are some similarities. To illustrate, we list twelve players in Table 10.2 where the evaluation by each measure was virtually the same.

We have already stated that both Wins Produced and NBA Efficiency indicated that Kevin Garnett was the best player in 2004–05. These two measures also place five other players in exactly the same spot in either ranking. For example, accord-

TABLE 10.2

Where Wins Produced and NBA Efficiency Agree

(Rankings of 72 Veterans in 2004–05 with 2,000 Minutes Played)

Player	Team	Difference in Rankings	Rank Wins Produced	Wins Produced	WP48	Rank NBA Efficiency	NBA Efficiency
Kevin Garnett	Minnesota	0	1	30.0	0.462	1	2,621
Shawn Marion	Phoenix	0	3	18.6	0.284	3	2,073
Paul Pierce	Boston	0	7	16.7	0.270	7	1,812
Shaquille O'Neal	Miami	0	9	15.9	0.306	9	1,784
Cuttino Mobley	Orlando-Sacramento	0	61	2.2	0.045	61	961
David Wesley	New Orleans-Houston	0	62	2.2	0.038	62	900
Andre Miller	Denver	1	21	10.3	0.173	22	1,412
Peja Stojakovic	Sacramento	−1	46	4.4	0.084	45	1,154
Kenny Thomas	Philadelphia-Sacramento	−1	52	3.1	0.068	51	1,080
Chucky Atkins	LA Lakers	−1	58	2.7	0.045	57	1,032
Jamal Crawford	New York	−1	60	2.4	0.042	59	1,015
Jeff McInnis	Cleveland	−1	66	0.4	0.007	65	895

ing to Wins Produced and NBA Efficiency, Shawn Marion was the third-best player ranked. For six other players the rankings by either metric only differ by one spot. Cuttino Mobley is the 61st best player, or 12th worst player in our sample, according to Wins Produced. He is the 62nd best player according to NBA Efficiency. Again, both NBA Efficiency and Wins Produced would not lead to different conclusions for all players. Both measures indicate that Garnett, Marion, Pierce, and Shaq are top-ten players. Given that 72 players are ranked, both metrics also indicate that Mobley, Wesley, Crawford, and McInnis are in the bottom fifteen.

Of course, as we have stated, there are differences. In Table 10.3 we list the most "underrated" players in 2004–05. Previously we have shown that evaluations based on NBA Efficiency appear to be closer to popular perception. So we argue a person is "underrated" when the ranking by Wins Produced is higher than what we see from NBA Efficiency. For example, the most underrated player was Damon Jones. Wins Produced ranked D. Jones as the eighteenth best player in our sample. According to NBA Efficiency, though, he was only the 53rd best player, or the 20th worst player we examined.

Although the average NBA player in 2004–05 makes a wage similar to Michael Jordan in 1995–96, the average player in our sample of 72 does quite a bit better.[5] In our sample of veteran players who played more than 2,000 minutes in 2004–05

TABLE 10.3

Twelve Most "Underrated" Players in 2004–05

(Rankings of 72 Veteran Players in 2004–05 with 2,000 Minutes Played)

Player	Team	Difference in Rankings	Rank Wins Produced	Wins Produced	WP48	Rank NBA Efficiency	NBA Efficiency	Annual Salary	Points per Game
Damon Jones	Miami	35	18	10.6	0.197	53	1,074	$2,503,000	11.6
Antonio Daniels	Seattle	30	36	7.5	0.178	66	891	$2,200,000	11.2
Mike Miller	Memphis	26	28	8.7	0.183	54	1,071	$6,000,000	13.4
Gary Payton	Boston	22	27	8.8	0.165	49	1,096	$4,408,700	11.3
Jason Kidd	New Jersey	21	2	19.9	0.393	23	1,384	$14,796,000	14.4
Jason Terry	Dallas	21	20	10.4	0.208	41	1,189	$7,500,000	12.4
Reggie Miller	Indiana	21	47	4.4	0.101	68	831	$5,500,000	14.8
Marcus Camby	Denver	20	12	12.8	0.304	32	1,284	$8,500,000	10.3
Ben Wallace	Detroit	15	5	17.3	0.310	20	1,416	$7,000,000	9.7
Tyronn Lue	Atlanta-Houston	15	56	2.9	0.070	71	804	$1,600,000	11.2
Lorenzen Wright	Memphis	14	42	5.7	0.119	56	1,068	$7,150,000	9.6
Derek Fisher	Golden State	14	53	3.0	0.064	67	861	$4,930,000	11.9
AVERAGES		21.2	28.8	9.3	0.191	50.0	1,080.8	$6,007,308	11.8

the average salary was close to $8.9 million. Of the twelve underrated players listed, only Jason Kidd had an annual wage exceeding $8.9 million. Ben Wallace produced a team-leading 17.3 wins for the Detroit Pistons yet was only paid $7 million. Granted, this is an immense amount of money for virtually anyone else living on the planet. Still, relative to Wallace's veteran peers in the NBA, he appears to be underpaid.

Now let's look at a list of twelve overrated veterans from 2004–05, which we list in Table 10.4. An overrated player is ranked higher in NBA Efficiency than he is in Wins Produced. Most of these players would be well known to a fan of the NBA. The aforementioned Antoine Walker tops this list, ranking 25th by NBA Efficiency but only 65th, or in the bottom ten, in terms of Wins Produced. Richard Hamilton, the leading scorer on the defending champion Detroit Pistons, ranked 35th in NBA Efficiency but was 22 spots lower in the Wins Produced rankings. The often noted Allen Iverson was 5th in NBA Efficiency, and only 23rd in our ranking. We should point out that Iverson was above average in both rankings, just not ranked as high in Wins Produced.

Beyond the difference in rankings, we would draw attention to the average annual wage of these players, which approaches $11 million. So these players, on average, were paid quite a bit better than the average underrated player. The average

TABLE 10.4

Twelve Most "Overrated" Players in 2004–05

(Rankings of 72 Veteran Players in 2004–05 with 2,000 Minutes Played)

Player	Team	Difference in Rankings	Rank Wins Produced	Wins Produced	WP48	Rank NBA Efficiency	NBA Efficiency	Annual Salary	Points per Game
Antoine Walker	Atlanta-Boston	−40	65	0.6	0.010	25	1,359	$14,625,000	19.1
Chris Webber	Sacramento-Philadelphia	−31	50	4.0	0.080	19	1,426	$17,531,250	19.5
Antawn Jamison	Washington	−24	64	1.2	0.021	40	1,219	$12,585,000	19.6
Zydrunas Ilgauskas	Cleveland	−23	40	6.4	0.117	17	1,497	$14,625,000	16.9
Michael Redd	Milwaukee	−23	54	2.9	0.049	31	1,289	$3,000,000	23.0
Richard Hamilton	Detroit	−22	57	2.8	0.046	35	1,253	$7,812,500	18.7
Desmond Mason	Milwaukee	−20	68	−0.2	−0.004	48	1,122	$6,529,630	17.2
Allen Iverson	Philadelphia	−18	23	10.0	0.152	5	1,865	$14,625,000	30.7
Steve Francis	Orlando	−17	30	8.5	0.137	13	1,609	$12,330,000	21.3
Jalen Rose	Toronto	−17	59	2.4	0.042	42	1,184	$14,487,000	18.5
Ricky Davis	Boston	−17	67	0.1	0.002	50	1,090	$5,455,000	16.0
Al Harrington	Atlanta	−17	69	−0.3	−0.006	52	1,076	$6,325,000	17.5
	AVERAGES	−22.4	53.8	3.2	0.054	31.4	1,332.4	$10,827,532	19.8

salary paid to the overrated players was actually dragged down by Michael Redd, who only earned $3 million in 2004–05. In the summer of 2005 this discrepancy was corrected, as Redd signed a six-year contract for a reported $90 million. Let's review for a moment. Redd produced about three wins for a team that won only 30 games in 2004–05. For this effort, Redd received one of the highest salaries in the game.

Why would Redd receive such a contract? A possible answer lies in the last column of Table 10.4 where we list how many points these players scored per game. Redd was one of the NBA's scoring leaders, averaging 23 points per contest. Scoring was not just a skill Redd displayed. All of the overrated players we identified averaged at least sixteen points per game. In contrast, none of the underrated players listed in Table 10.3 averaged more than fifteen points per game.

Our examination of the underrated and overrated highlights an important difference in the NBA Efficiency and Wins Produced metrics. As we emphasized earlier, NBA Efficiency treats a made field goal or free throw attempt as a free resource. Consequently, as long as a player exceeds a fairly low shooting percentage, the more shots he takes the higher his NBA Efficiency value. We can see this when we look at the relationship between NBA Efficiency and scoring. When we look at all players in 2004–05 we find a 95% correlation between their NBA Efficiency total and the number of points the player scores. Although the NBA Efficiency measure employs a variety of statistics, it is scoring totals that tend to drive a player higher in the NBA Efficiency rankings.

The scorers also tend to be the NBA "stars." And star power is important, at least as we discussed in Chapter Five, to the star's opponents. Gate revenue, again as we stated in Chapter Five, is not driven by star appeal. In fact if we add team scoring to the gate revenue model we previously estimated, we do not find a positive correlation between additional scoring and a team's performance at the gate.[6] As stated earlier, performance at the gate is about winning. And winning is about more than just having stars or scoring points. We see this when we look at our list of overrated players. All of these players can score. But, with the exception of Allen Iverson and Steve Francis, none of the overrated players rank in the top-half of Wins Produced.

What do we learn from this exercise? Our story of the overrated and underrated indicates that the NBA may have a problem evaluating talent. The overrated players can all score, and most of these players have also scored major paydays. The underrated players tend to produce wins, yet many are not receiving wages consistent with their Wins Production.

All of this suggests that people making decisions in the NBA are not as "rational" as economists tend to expect. What do we mean when we say "rational"? Let's get a bit "academic" for a moment. We are specifically referring to the idea of instrumental rationality.[7] What do we mean by this term? Instrumental rationality has been defined as the idea that "people choose efficiently the means that advance their goals."[8] If people in the NBA are "rational," as the term has been defined, then the decisions they make will be consistent with what these people are trying to achieve. If people in the NBA wish to win more games, then they would not pay more money to scorers who produce fewer wins. These same people would also not pay players who create substantial wins less money than the aforementioned scorers. At least they wouldn't if they were "rational."

Of course, NBA teams could be all about maximizing profits and so may not care much for increasing wins. This is not the story teams tell the press, but let's stop for a moment and consider this possibility. After a bit of thinking, we can see that our story is still the same. Profit is revenue minus cost. As we have shown, and more evidence will be offered to support this contention, scorers are expensive. So scorers drive up a team's costs. Scoring, though, by itself, cannot create many wins. Consequently, scorers do not add much to team revenue. If an NBA team is trying to maximize profits, hiring expensive scorers who do not add much to team revenue is not going to help.

Having said all this, we need to be very clear about what we are and are not saying. When we say "rational" or "irrational," we are not saying smart or stupid. We are also not saying sane or insane. What we are contending, and we think the evidence supports this notion, is that people in the NBA are mistaken about the relative value of scoring and other aspects of player performance. We do not think this miscalculation occurs because anyone in the NBA is stupid or crazy. We do think, though, that because people in the NBA do not have the statistical tools and techniques we employ, the conclusions they have reached about specific players are incorrect. At least, it is incorrect if people in the NBA wish to win games and/or maximize profits.

THE RATIONAL COACH

We recognize that we are making a fairly strong statement about talent evaluation in the NBA. We have already offered an examination of overrated and underrated players, indicating that the NBA does have some problems evaluating veteran talent. Now we wish to offer even stronger evidence by looking at NBA rookies. Why do we want to do this? Well, that will be clear in a moment.

The "Best" Rookie

Let's begin with twelve years of the "best" NBA rookies, which we list in Table 10.5. Listed are the players who were named Rookie of the Year, the rookie leader in Wins Produced, and the freshman leader in NBA Efficiency. Like our study of the MVP award, we see consistency between the NBA Efficiency measure and the player chosen as Rookie of the Year. In eight of the twelve years examined, the award-winning rookie also led his fellow first-year players in NBA Efficiency. In contrast, on only four occasions was the leader in Wins Produced named the best freshman.

On average only about five first-year players receive any consideration for this award.[9] Given such a small sample, it would be difficult for us to study voting for this award statistically. Furthermore, since the media chooses this award, such a study would not help us understand how people in the NBA evaluate talent.

The All-Rookie Team

There is an award, though, that allows us to evaluate the NBA's talent evaluators. Each year the all-rookie team is chosen by the NBA's head coaches. The voting for

TABLE 10.5

Twelve Years of the "Best" Rookies in the NBA

Year	Rookie of the Year	Most Productive Rookie	NBA Efficiency Leader, Rookies
2004–05	Emeka Okafor	Andre Iguodala (4)	Dwight Howard (3)
2003–04	LeBron James	LeBron James (1)	LeBron James (1)
2002–03	Amare Stoudemire	Yao Ming (2)	Yao Ming (2)
2001–02	Pau Gasol	Pau Gasol (1)	Pau Gasol (1)
2000–01	Mike Miller	Darius Miles (4)	Kenyon Martin (2)
1999–00	Elton Brand and Steve Francis (tie)	Elton Brand (1)	Elton Brand (1)
1998–99	Vince Carter	Paul Pierce (3)	Vince Carter (1)
1997–98	Tim Duncan	Tim Duncan (1)	Tim Duncan (1)
1996–97	Allen Iverson	Dean Garrett	Allen Iverson (1)
1995–96	Damon Stoudamire	Arvydas Sabonis (2)	Joe Smith (3)
1994–95	Grant Hill and Jason Kidd (tie)	Grant Hill (1)	Grant Hill (1)
1993–94	Chris Webber	Anfernee Hardaway (2)	Chris Webber (1)

this award is an example of NBA decision makers assessing player performance.

At the end of each regular season each head coach is asked to vote for the first-team and second-team All-Rookie teams. If a player is named to the first team by a coach, he receives two voting points. Placing the player on the second team earns the rookie one point. The five players with the most points, regardless of position played, are named to the first team.[10]

Let's begin our examination of this award by looking at the players where there was no disagreement. From 1995 to 2005, nineteen players were unanimous selections by the coaches. We have listed these players in Table 10.6.

We ranked all rookies who received any votes by the coaches in terms of where the player was taken in the draft, Wins Produced, NBA Efficiency, and points scored per game.[11] The nineteen rookies who were unanimously selected by the coaches tended to be high draft choices. These players also ranked quite high among rookies in both NBA Efficiency and points per game.

A high ranking was also generally seen in Wins Produced, although there were some noticeable exceptions. Specifically Ben Gordon, Carmello Anthony, and Keith Van Horn were not ranked in the top ten among rookies in Wins Produced. Yet all NBA coaches thought these players deserved to be placed on the All-Rookie First Team. What do these three players have in common? All three could score, but as we detailed in our discussion of Gordon in Chapter Eight, these three offered little more to their respective team's quest to accumulate victories.

Of course a sample of three is not much of a story. A better story can be told if

TABLE 10.6

Unanimous Selections to the All-Rookie Team, 1995–2005

Rookie	Year	Draft Position	Rank: Wins Produced	Wins Produced	WP48	Rank: NBA Efficiency	Rank: Points per Game
Dwight Howard	2004–05	1	2	13.0	0.234	1	3
Emeka Okafor	2004–05	2	5	7.4	0.137	2	1
Ben Gordon	2004–05	3	20	−0.7	−0.016	7	2
LeBron James	2003–04	1	1	6.4	0.099	1	2
Dwyane Wade	2003–04	5	3	5.9	0.133	5	3
Carmelo Anthony	2003–04	3	11	2.0	0.032	2	1
Yao Ming	2002–03	1	1	10.8	0.218	1	3
Amare Stoudemire	2002–03	9	3	7.1	0.133	2	2
Pau Gasol	2001–02	3	1	14.1	0.224	1	1
Mike Miller	2000–01	5	2	5.2	0.104	3	3
Elton Brand	1999–00	1	1	10.1	0.162	1	1
Steve Francis	1999–00	2	4	8.5	0.148	2	2
Paul Pierce	1998–99	10	1	12.0	0.216	2	2
Vince Carter	1998–99	5	2	9.2	0.153	1	1
Tim Duncan	1997–98	1	1	20.3	0.304	1	1
Keith Van Horn	1997–98	2	15	−1.5	−0.031	5	2
Shareef Abdur-Rahim	1996–97	3	9	2.0	0.034	3	2
Damon Stoudamire	1995–96	7	5	4.8	0.080	2	2
Jason Kidd	1994–95	2	2	8.7	0.157	3	8
AVERAGES		3.5	4.7	7.2	0.135	2.4	2.2

we look at the voting for all rookies from 1995 to 2005. For these rookies we looked at the relationship between the number of voting points the coaches gave the player, and two evaluations of the player's talent. The first evaluation is where the player was taken in the draft. This can be thought of as what the NBA thought of the player before he took the court.

We then considered how well the player played his rookie season. In evaluating the best rookies, it is this second measure that should matter. If a player is drafted high and can't perform, we would expect the coaches to know this and not vote the player to the All-Rookie teams. Likewise, if a player is not drafted high but plays well, then he should receive some consideration.

The key to this story is how one knows whether a player played well. To see how well a player plays we need to consult a measure of player performance. Which metric, though, should we choose? So far in every ranking of NBA players that we have presented, the NBA Efficiency measure is most consistent with perception. Is the same story seen when we look at the coaches' evaluations?

Again we turn to the wonderful world of regression analysis. When we regress voting points[12] on a rookie's draft position[13] and NBA Efficiency,[14] we see that 73% of the voting record can be explained by our two player evaluations.[15] Interestingly, both draft position and NBA Efficiency are statistically significant,[16] indicating that coaches do consider where a player was taken in the draft when voting for this award. The significance of draft position by itself is evidence that coaches are not evaluating players correctly.[17]

What happens when we consider a different measure of performance? When we look at the relationship between the voting record, draft position, and a player's Wins Produced,[18] our explanatory power drops to 43%. Clearly the NBA Efficiency measure is more consistent with the coaches' evaluation of playing talent.

What if we take an even simpler approach and just consider a player's scoring ability? When we consider both draft position and the number of points a player scored,[19] instead of NBA Efficiency or Wins Produced, our explanatory power is 74%. In other words, scoring alone trumps our two performance indices.

This led us to ask, what if we considered all the elements of NBA Efficiency and Wins Produced? So we regressed voting points on draft position, points scored, as well as rebounds, steals, blocked shots, assists, turnovers, personal fouls, and shooting efficiency.[20] When we add all these factors we are able to explain 76% of the voting record. So draft position and points scored explain 74%. Draft position, points scored, and eight additional measures of performance increase explanatory power by exactly two percentage points. Not much of a gain. Of even greater interest is what statistically matters. When we add the other statistics we see that voting points are statistically related to draft position, points scored, rebounds, and a player's shooting efficiency on field goal attempts.

Of these, which matters the most? Our estimation tells us that scoring has the largest impact on the votes a player receives. If a player increases his scoring by 10%, our estimation tells us that he can expect his voting points to rise by 23%. In contrast, a 10% increase in rebounds only leads to a 6% increase in voting points. Shooting efficiency is a bit more important, with a 10% improvement leading to a 15% percent increase in voting points received.[21] Again, all other factors, including turnovers, steals, assists, blocked shots, and personal fouls, were not found to be related to the coaches' voting for this award.[22]

So what have we learned? If a rookie can score, he will likely score consideration for the All-Rookie team. Although scoring efficiently is important, scoring totals appear to be more important. All other facets of a player's performance are either less important or appear to be completely irrelevant.

THE RATIONAL GENERAL MANAGER

The All-Rookie voting record indicates that coaches value scoring over all other aspects of player performance. We have already shown that scoring alone cannot create wins. So coaches are not evaluating talent in a fashion consistent with winning basketball games. Perhaps we are overstating our case? Have we really presented evidence that coaches do not evaluate talent correctly? After all, does anyone really believe that the coaches take this award that seriously? We can't imagine that coaches spend hours thinking about this vote. We are not even sure the head coach actually votes. It is entirely possible that the head coach delegates this job to someone on his staff. All we may have shown is that people working for the head coach have trouble evaluating talent.

Playing the "Right Way"

We also know from what the coaches say that there is more to the game than scoring. Let's turn to the well-traveled Larry Brown, famed coach of almost every team in the NBA, ABA, and college basketball—okay we exaggerate—but Brown has coached eight different professional franchises and two college teams. Brown is fond of saying that players must play "the right way." What is the right way? If we look at Larry Brown's 2004 NBA champion Detroit Pistons, we can glean some insights into Brown's basic message.

The Pistons won 54 regular season games in 2003–04, ranking sixth in the league in victories. Their winning record was not a product of scoring totals, where they only ranked 24th in the NBA. Their leading scorer, Richard Hamilton, averaged only 17.4 points per game, which was not even one of the 25 best scoring marks that season. Rasheed Wallace, a power forward known for his ability to score, came to the team in mid-season. In Portland, Rasheed averaged 17 points per contest. With the Pistons, where scoring was not emphasized, his average declined to 13.7 per game. Although we are not sure what exactly Brown means by the "right way," the structure of the 2004 Pistons suggests that scoring as many points as possible is not what he has in mind.

Although Brown might de-emphasize the importance of scoring, the paychecks given to the players seemed to indicate that even on the Pistons scoring was important. The leading scorer in the backcourt, Richard Hamilton, also led all Piston guards in salary. The same was true in the frontcourt where Rasheed Wallace both scored the most and was paid the most. To put this in perspective, the most productive Piston was Big Ben Wallace, who had a WP48 of 0.351 in 2003–04 while playing under a six-year contract worth $30 million. R. Wallace was also working with a six-year contract, worth $80 million and set to expire at the end of the 2003–04 campaign. Although the average salary of Rasheed more than doubled what Big Ben was paid, Rasheed's WP48 with the Pistons was only 0.152. We would add that if we consider Rasheed's year-by-year performance prior to 2003–04, the 22 games he spent in Detroit in 2003–04 were the most productive of his career. In contrast, Ben Wallace's 2003–04 performance, although outstanding by league standards, was actually a bit below what he did the previous four seasons.

Detroit did not negotiate Rasheed's $80 million contract. The Pistons did agree to his next contract signed in the summer of 2004. Although Rasheed's new contract paid him slightly less, the $60 million he was scheduled to receive over five seasons easily topped the wages of Ben Wallace. Let's clarify our point. Big Ben produced more wins. From 1997–98 to 2003–04, Ben Wallace produced 123 victories in the regular season while averaging less than seven points per game. Rasheed produced more points. From 1997–98 to 2003–04, Rasheed averaged nearly 17 points per contest but only produced 39 wins.

So what are the "Wages of Wins"? The story of Rasheed and Big Ben suggests that if you score, wages can be quite high, even if your Wins Production is not among the best in the league. If you do not score, even if you consistently produce wins, the relative wages of wins are quite low. Of course, a sample of two does not a study make. Still, what we have seen so far suggests that while Brown was preaching "the right way" on the court, off the court it still looks like scoring was the primary determinant of what the Pistons chose to pay their players.

Now we should note that unless the coach is running the entire basketball operation, he is not negotiating salaries. Salaries are negotiated by a team's general manager. When the Pistons appear to overpay scorers and underpay players like Ben Wallace, this is not a statement about Larry Brown's talent evaluation, but the decision making of those higher in Detroit's organization.

Playing to Score

Is the story we tell about Detroit's salary determination process the same if we look at a much larger sample of players? To answer this question we turn to the salary database kept by USA Today.com. This database reports four years of NBA salary and contract information, beginning with the 2001–02 campaign. We used this information to create a data set that would allow us to better understand the link between pay and performance.

Let's begin by noting that many players sign multi-year contracts, and as we saw in the Glenn Robinson story, it is difficult to forecast player performance many

TABLE 10.7

What Explains an NBA Player's Salary?

Factors we found consistently to be statistically related to a player's salary	How the factor is measured (more details in endnotes)
Performance last year	Various performance measures
Performance two years ago	Again, various performance measures
Star power	All-Star votes received
Position played	Whether a player was a center, power forward, shooting guard, or point guard
Experience of the player	Whether a player had more than twelve years of experience or less than four
Factors we did not consistently find to be statistically related to a player's salary	
Market size of city hosting team that signed player	Population of host city
Race of the player	Whether a player was black or not

years in advance. With this in mind, we wished to confine our inquiry to players who recently signed a new contract.[23] For such players the link between performance and pay should be the strongest. Consequently, we extracted from the *USA Today* database players whose contracts began in 2001, 2002, 2003, and 2004. We then looked at the relationship between the average pay the player received over the length of the signed contract and a collection of factors we thought would impact his wages.[24] We list these factors in Table 10.7.

Like our study of the All-Rookie voting, we considered various performance measures. Before we get to those, let's just comment briefly on what else we found. We begin with star power, which we found to be statistically important. The more All-Star votes a player received the higher his wage. The age of the player also matters. Specifically, being an older player has a statistically significant and negative impact on pay. Again, holding all else constant, being old in the NBA means you are paid less for your performance. Younger players, who can only enter our data set if they are a former second-round draft choice, tend to receive higher levels of compensation. Independent of productivity, being young leads to more money.

In addition to paying for youth, NBA teams also pay for size.[25] Independent of performance, being a center leads to more money, while shooting guards are paid less. Being a power forward or point guard, though, does not impact compensation. Similarly, the location of the team does not appear to matter. So player size impacts wages, but market size doesn't matter.[26]

What about race? We generally found that whether or not a player was black did not impact his wages. One should note, though, that if we do not consider position played in our model, then race is statistically significant when we measure performance with points scored. If we employ one specific measure of performance and a specific collection of additional variables, then we find that blacks in the NBA receive lower wages independent of productivity.

What does this mean? Well, there has been an abundance of studies into the relationship between race and compensation. The findings have been quite mixed. Some studies find that blacks in the NBA receive lower wages once you control for performance, other studies, though, find no evidence of discrimination.[27] Our findings suggest that how you measure productivity and construct your model dictates your findings with respect to race. For our study of salaries in the NBA we think it would be incorrect to ignore position played, and when this factor is included, race no longer statistically impacts how salaries are set.

Although prior studies into race in the NBA have found mixed evidence of discrimination, there was one area where one sees almost universal agreement. Player salary is primarily determined by how many points a player scores. Almost every study finds that points scored is statistically related to player compensation. These same studies, though, do not agree on any other aspect of performance. Specifically, rebounding, blocked shots, steals, assists, and shooting efficiency were not consistently found to be significant in these studies of race, pay, and performance in the NBA.[28]

Is this the same story we tell when we look at salaries? Like our study of All-Rookie voting, we began with the NBA Efficiency measure.[29] Specifically we linked salaries to two years of player performance. For example, if a player signed his contract in 2004, we considered the player's performance in 2003–04 as well as 2002–03. We found that both performances were statistically significant, with the more recent being the more important. We also found that we could explain 63% of player salary when we employed the NBA's performance metric in our model.[30]

What if we employ Wins Produced? Now our model only explains 47% of player salary, and performance from two seasons ago is not even statistically significant. Such results suggest, like our study of coaches, that Wins Produced is not perfectly consistent with how teams evaluate performance.[31]

Again we have evidence that NBA Efficiency trumps our measure of wins. What about points scored? If you only consider how many points a player scored over the past two seasons, our explanatory power is also 63%. Actually it is 63.5%, while our explanatory power with NBA Efficiency is precisely 62.9%. So by a very small, and probably insignificant margin, points scored alone appears to trump both NBA Efficiency and Wins Produced.

What if we include the other statistics? If we add a player's accumulation in the past season[32] of rebounds, steals, blocked shots, assists, turnovers, personal fouls, and shooting efficiency, our explanatory power rises to 64%. Of all these statistics, only blocked shots were found to significantly impact compensation. And like our study of the All-Rookie team, the number of points scored has the largest impact on player salary. Furthermore, increases in rebounds, steals, assists, turnovers, personal fouls, and shooting efficiency on both field goal and free throw attempts were not found to have a significant impact on player salary.

Our evidence suggests that coaches just might take the voting for the All-Rookie team more seriously then we might suspect. Certainly the story we tell of the general managers mimics what we said about the coaches. We found that the more a player scored the more likely he would be placed in the first or second All-Rookie team. Now we find, the more the player scores the more he will be paid. Given that shooting efficiency was not found to be significant, we have learned something important about the incentives a player faces. If he wishes to be paid like a star, he must score. If it turns out he really can't shoot well, he must ignore the harm he does to his team's chances of winning and keep hoisting shots.

Before moving on, there is one other possible explanation for the results we uncovered that we have yet to mention. We have found that scoring is the primary factor explaining player salary. Perhaps this is because NBA decision makers do not see the game of basketball as a game of five-on-five, but five games of one-on-one. In the latter scenario, all that might matter is how many points a player scores and allows. If this were the case, one would only consider offense and defense in explaining salary, and we would expect every other performance measure to be irrelevant. This is essentially what we found. Scoring was found to be significant, although the insignificance of shooting efficiency is troubling. We do not have data on defensive ability, so this measure could not be tested. Most other performance metrics, though, were found to be unimportant. Hence, maybe players are evaluated strictly in terms of offense and defense. Therefore, if the NBA game is five games of one-on-one, and we can convince ourselves that shooting efficiency is not relevant when a player's offensive ability is evaluated, then players in the NBA may be evaluated correctly by people in the league.

The only problem with this explanation is that basketball is not five games of one-on-one, but one game of five-on-five. Consequently, factors besides scoring matter. What does this mean for coaches? Well, if coaches wish to be like Larry

Brown they will want players to play "the right way." We think this means players have to do more than just focus on their own scoring. Players have to also rebound, create assists and steals, avoid turnovers, and shoot efficiently. Our results indicate, though, that a player needs to score if he wants to score a major payday. Therefore, players have an incentive to ignore most facets of the game and focus solely on chucking up as many shots as their coaches will allow. Players who do this will be defying coaches like Larry Brown. Furthermore, such players will not create many wins. Still, our analysis suggests that they will create additional dollars on their paychecks. And if that is the game they are ultimately playing, scoring will lead to victory.

Reviewing Our Pay and Productivity Lessons

Let's summarize what we have learned about pay and productivity.

1. Player productivity on the court determines team wins. We have already demonstrated that Wins Produced by the players sums quite closely to team wins.

2. Wins are not just about scoring. To win a team must rebound, create and avoid turnovers, and hit a high percentage of its shots.

3. Team wins are a driving force behind team revenue, not scoring or star power.

4. Player pay, though, is not determined by contributions to team wins, but by scoring and star power.

Given these lessons, we now have some idea why payroll and wins are not highly correlated in the NBA. Just to review, although NBA players are more consistent than those found in the NFL and Major League Baseball, the relationship between payroll and wins remains just as weak. Our study of salaries allows us to now see why NBA teams that pay the most don't often win the most. What we have found is that teams focus too much attention on scoring and not enough on the many other facets of the game that lead to victory. Consequently, teams often discover that their collection of scorers just can't win. When this happens, teams often mention the problem of team chemistry. Our analysis suggests that the issue of chemistry is probably overstated. When a collection of scorers can't win, the problem is likely to be found with how talent is evaluated. Scoring alone can't win basketball games. When scoring is the primary focus of talent evaluation, though, mistakes will be made in the construction of a team's roster that ultimately limit the number of wins a team should expect.

PREDICTING THE FUTURE

Now, decision makers in the NBA are not the only people who make mistakes. Economists are also known to have a few missteps along the way. Consider our propensity to make predictions. Economists often make predictions, and, unfortunately, many of these don't work out too well. Perhaps the most famous bad forecast of the future was uttered by Irving Fisher, one of the great economists from the first half of the 20th century. Five days before the stock market collapsed in 1929, Fisher stated that the nation had reached a permanent "high plateau of prosperity." The subsequent Great Depression suggested that Fisher's evaluation was more than a bit off the mark. Although Fisher had built a marvelous reputation prior to 1929, his stature declined step by step with the nation's economic decline in the 1930s.

Fisher's experience has been used as a lesson for all young economists about the need to make careful statements and avoid bold predictions. Consequently we have tried to refrain from making many statements about the future. Still, our study of NBA salaries presents a tempting test of our ideas. Specifically, we decided to re-estimate our salary model, only using the factors we consistently found to determine player salary. The list of factors includes the past two seasons of points scored, blocked shots in the last season, All-Star votes received, and measures of experience and position played.[33]

With model in hand we then turned to the NBA's sophomores in 2004–05. Specifically we looked at all second-year players who appeared in at least 41 games each of their first two seasons and averaged, again in both seasons, twelve minutes per contest. In all, 21 players met these criteria. We list in Table 10.8 these players, along with their predicted and current annual salary, points scored per game during their first two seasons, Wins Produced per season, and WP48.

The best player, in terms of Wins Produced, WP48, points scored per game, and general star appeal, was LeBron James. Not surprisingly, our salary model predicts that James would be the highest paid player in this grouping if he were not bound by his rookie contract. Specifically our model indicates that James would be paid more than $19 million. Unfortunately, the NBA's individual salary cap would limit James' annual wage to "only" about $16 million.[34] The only other player who comes close to a predicted salary equal to the NBA's maximum annual wage is Shaq's primary sidekick in Miami, Dwayne Wade. The model predicts Wade's wage to be $15.9 million, just a shade lower than the NBA maximum. So of these 21 sophomores, based upon what these players have produced thus far, only James

TABLE 10.8

Predicting the Annual Wage of the 2004–05 NBA Sophomores

Player	Rank: Predicted Salary	Rank: Wins Produced	Predicted Annual Salary	Current Annual Salary	Points Scored per Game	Wins Produced per Season	WP48
LeBron James	1	1	$19,587,085	$4,996,667	24.1	14.1	0.207
Dwyane Wade	2	2	$15,940,630	$3,085,000	20.6	9.1	0.171
Carmelo Anthony	3	12	$13,483,435	$3,777,500	20.9	1.1	0.019
Chris Bosh	4	6	$13,334,715	$3,405,000	14.2	5.9	0.102
Kirk Hinrich	5	5	$5,317,173	$2,560,000	13.9	6.7	0.117
Josh Howard	6	3	$4,184,334	$4,885,250	10.7	7.3	0.174
Chris Kaman	7	16	$3,646,149	$2,802,500	7.4	0.8	0.021
Luke Ridnour	8	7	$3,556,842	$1,755,000	8.0	3.8	0.100
Udonis Haslem	9	4	$3,116,302	$456,569	9.2	7.1	0.153
Maurice Williams	10	10	$2,803,619	$2,833,333	8.0	1.7	0.053
Keith Bogans	11	14	$2,393,743	$493,489	8.2	0.8	0.022
Jarvis Hayes	12	19	$2,098,536	$2,050,000	9.9	−0.4	−0.011
Marquis Daniels	13	8	$2,066,642	$2,200,000	8.8	3.5	0.135
Leandro Barbosa	14	13	$2,058,085	$1,072,500	7.5	1.1	0.042
Marcus Banks	15	15	$1,903,590	$1,825,000	5.3	0.8	0.031
Mickael Pietrus	16	11	$1,794,511	$1,972,500	7.6	1.1	0.052
Willie Green	17	21	$1,372,145	$493,500	7.3	−1.8	−0.093
Francisco Elson	18	17	$1,354,963	$560,000	3.6	0.3	0.018
Boris Diaw	19	9	$1,205,220	$1,290,000	4.6	1.8	0.055
Sasha Pavlovic	20	20	$1,024,222	$1,394,000	4.8	−1.3	−0.063
Steve Blake	21	18	$858,125	$493,489	5.3	0.3	0.016

and Wade are currently expected to receive a contract close to the NBA's individual salary cap.

Other players, though, can expect to do quite well. Carmelo Anthony's expected annual salary exceeds $13 million. When we look at Anthony's points scored per game, we see why his salary in the future should be so high. If we look at Wins Produced and WP48, though, we again see evidence that the wages of wins in the NBA are not entirely consistent. Although Anthony in his first two seasons has only produced about one victory per year, his future salary is predicted to easily pass $10 million per season.

In contrast, Josh Howard, who ranks third in our sample in Wins Produced, can only expect his annual salary in the future, according to our salary model, to be about $4 million. Udonis Haslem, who ranks fourth in Wins Produced, can expect an annual salary of about $3 million. Granted, both salaries are immense for virtually everyone else in the world. Still, relative to Anthony, these players are more effective performers. Unfortunately, the lack of scoring from Howard and Haslem reduces their future wages.

Again we come back to our title. What are the "Wages of Wins"? For a player who produces wins via scoring, wages tend to be quite high. In fact, if a player just scores and does not generate many wins, our research says wages will still be quite high. Players who produce wins without scoring, though, do not receive relatively high levels of compensation. Let's clarify that statement. Compared to professors of economics, Howard, Haslem, and Big Ben Wallace are still being paid really, really well. Relative to scorers, though, these players appear to be underpaid.

THE RATIONAL ECONOMIST

Our model predicts that the sophomore scorers, if they keep scoring, should score major paydays in the future. Non-scorers, yet productive performers like Josh Howard and Udonis Haslem, may help their respective teams win an NBA title in the future, but will not see wages like those paid to Carmelo Anthony.

Of course now that we have presented our evidence and made these statements, we should expect our predictions to be incorrect. With the publication of our book and subsequent publicity and fame that will obviously follow—yes, we are approximating humor again—we can expect people in the NBA to recognize the error of their ways. By the time the rookie contracts of these players expire the NBA will understand that points production does not necessarily equal wins production. So players like Carmelo Anthony will be paid less—sorry Carmelo—and Udonis Haslem and Josh Howard can expect much bigger paychecks.

This is actually the story economics teaches. When people are exposed to new and better information, this information is adopted and decisions are changed accordingly. We actually are not sure this story will play itself out in the NBA, even if millions and millions of people read our book. Still there is always hope.

We wish to note that economists do not argue that people learn about the workings of the world from the writings of academics. No, economists actually argue that people should understand their economic environment on their own. Given this proposition, why do people in the NBA overvalue scoring? The NBA has existed for more than 50 years. All of the data we used to measure Wins Produced have been tracked for players for almost 30 years. Given this time span, why would NBA decision makers still focus so much attention on scoring and so little attention on every other aspect of performance?

The Instruments of Rationality

Let's return to the topic of instrumental rationality. The process by which people adopt new information was summarized nicely by Nobel Laureate Douglass North (1994, p. 360) in the speech he gave accepting the Nobel Prize in Economics.

Players must not only have objectives, but know the correct way to achieve them. But how do the players know the correct way to achieve their objectives? The instrumental rationality answer is that, even though the actors may initially have diverse and erroneous models, the informational feedback process and arbitraging actors will correct initially incorrect models, punish deviant behavior, and lead surviving players to correct models.

Let's translate what North is saying. When he says players and actors he is referring to people making decisions. As North states, if people are rational they might start with a view of the world that is incorrect, but as new information becomes available, people change their perspective. If people do not change their ways, then they will lose to other people who adopt the new information. So either people change, or they lose. Whether people change their ways or simply lose out to those that do, the survivors in the game must know what they are doing.

Now North does not believe the instrumental rationality story applied to much of the world he observed. In his view, the conditions necessary for rationality to be achieved do not often exist.[35] Should we expect this story to work in the NBA? Although NBA teams compete on the court, the league is not actually competitive in an economic sense. There are significant barriers to anyone who wishes to become a person who makes decisions in the league. Specifically, to become an owner one must have a great deal of money and pass through an extensive review process. Becoming a coach is also difficult. An examination of the work history of the NBA coaches reveals, not surprisingly, that each had prior experience as an NBA assistant, player, or college head coach. Basically without prior connections, one does not work as a head coach in the NBA. Because it is not easy to get into the league, there is a barrier to the flow of new ideas and therefore one of the conditions necessary for the rationality assumption to hold may not exist.

Of course, it is still the case that when decision makers in the league make mistakes there are clear consequences. If you build a team poorly, the team will frequently lose, and those that put the team together will likely lose their jobs. Making bad decisions can lead to a loss of employment in all industries, so this is a consequence most people understand. There is an even bigger consequence for bad decision making in sports. Millions of people watch and pay attention to sports. When coaches and general managers make mistakes in sports, not only do they lose their jobs, but they are also open to ridicule from a very large group of people. So people who make mistakes in the NBA suffer fairly severe consequences.

Suffering consequences for your mistakes, though, does not necessarily mean the people know why the mistakes were made. Let's go back to the story of the Pistons in 2004. We are told that the Pistons played "the right way" and were rewarded with a championship. When we look at the team's payroll, though, they put their money with their scorers. Even on a team playing the "right way," scoring is still what brings the most money to the players.

The Pistons' experience illustrates the problem with seeing mistakes in professional sports. Sports are a zero-sum game, which means the number of winners equal the number of losers. Regardless of what methods teams use to evaluate talent, half the teams will win, half will lose. At the end of the season, one team will still be crowned champion. Every year the champions confirm that the basic approach used in the NBA is correct.

Let's put it this way. Imagine that every team believed it needed to play its mascot to win basketball games. If this were each team's approach, half the teams would win with their mascots, the other half would lose. At the end of the season, one team with its mascot would be crowned champion, confirming the need to play your mascot.

Following this analogy, scorers are the mascots of the NBA. We have shown that scoring by itself does not create wins. Yet many scorers, despite not offering many wins, are paid the most by their respective teams and are considered the key to whatever wins the team actually achieves. Sometimes this is not a problem. When the Spurs think their leading scorer, Tim Duncan, is their best player, they are right. When the Lakers thought that their two leading scorers, Shaq and Kobe, were their best players, they were right. When the 76ers, though, think their leading scorer, Allen Iverson, is their best player, the data tell a different story. Unfortunately, every year a team wins a title thinking their leading scorer is their best player; therefore, this particular mistake, without some statistical analysis, is quite difficult to see.

We would note that the focus on scoring may just be a way of simplifying the complex information talent evaluators face. The same abilities that allow a person to score in the NBA would also allow a player to rebound, generate steals, and create assists. Players like Jordan, Garnett, and Kobe are not just great scorers, but have athletic abilities that allow these players to accumulate rebounds and assists. So when people see an athlete who can score, a leap of faith might be made. If the player can score, he probably can do all the other things a team needs to win, and consequently significant scoring ability is seen as evidence that the player helps a team accumulate many wins.

Unfortunately there are clear exceptions to this simplification. When scorers do not actually contribute significantly to wins, teams often end up losing. Consequently, teams have turned to other explanations for why losses accumulate. Teams talk about the importance of coaching and team chemistry. And they add and subtract players, hoping to find the combination that works. Every year, one team hits the jackpot, while others keep searching. Unfortunately, without the proper statistical tools, many teams are left in the dark.

And this is a point we wish to emphasize. Without statistical analysis, one cannot see how the actions the players take on the court translate into wins. One can play basketball. One can watch basketball. One can both play and watch basketball for a thousand years. If you do not systematically track what the players do, and then uncover the statistical relationship between these actions and wins, you will never know why teams win and why they lose. Staring at these players play is not a method that will ever yield the answers that the proper analysis of statistics will yield. And this is true if you stare for one day, or as we said, if you stare for a thousand years.

The Economist's Fable

Like many of our stories, the importance of scoring is yet one more myth in sport. Telling this story, though, reveals another myth. And this one is all about economics. People in the NBA do not appear to process information as efficiently as some economists might suspect. Consequently, a treasured belief held by some is inconsistent with the data.

We would note that what we find is not a fable for all economists. In addition to Douglass North, other economists, including various Nobel Laureates, have noted that the rationality argument in economics may have been overstated. A leading voice in this group[36] is Herbert Simon, who was awarded the Nobel Prize in 1978. Simon (1992, p. 3) introduced the concept of "bounded rationality" in an effort to

> focus attention upon the discrepancy between the perfect human rationality that is assumed in classical and neoclassical economic theory and the reality of human behavior as it is observed in economic life. The point was not that people are consciously and deliberately irrational . . . but that neither their knowledge nor their powers of calculation allow them to achieve the high level of optimal adaptation of means to ends that is posited in economics.

This is the point we are making about decision making in the NBA. It is not that people in the NBA are lazy or stupid. It is just that the tools at their disposal do not allow them to see the value of the various actions players take on the court. We suspect that people in the NBA rely heavily on watching players play, not statistical analysis of their actions. When your method is visual observation, you will be drawn to the dramatic. Scoring is dramatic and memorable. Turnovers, missed shots, and rebounds do not tend to garner the same attention.

Despite the work of these Nobel Laureates, as well as the extensive research by an entire branch of our discipline, behavioral economics, strict adherents to the rationality assumption persist. This persistence is highlighted by Colin Camerer and Roberto Weber, who concluded their study of systematic mistakes in the NBA by stating: "Behavioral economists have learned that the best way to win an argument about the existence of systematic mistakes is to take the complicated rationalizations offered by critics seriously—no matter how cockamamie they are—and collect more data to test them" (Camerer and Weber, 1999, p. 81).

As we conclude this story we anticipate a few "cockamamie" responses and following the advice of Camerer and Weber, will continue to collect data and test what we can.

THE FINAL WORD?

So we have reached the end of our story. It has been a winding road and now that we have reached the finish line, let's take a moment to look back over where we have been. Although it may not have been apparent that our collection of myths and fables had any connection, indeed these disparate ideas were related. So let's review quickly the stories we have told and highlight the links between each story.

1. Teams cannot easily buy the fans' love. Payroll and wins are not highly correlated. It is this story that carries through the entire book and inspires the title to our tale.

2. Labor disputes do not threaten the future of professional sports. Attendance in baseball, football, basketball, and hockey has not been significantly impacted by player strikes or owner lockouts.

3. Labor disputes in baseball arise because owners demand player salary controls in the name of competitive balance. The data, though, tell us that relative to baseball's history, competitive balance has never been better.

4. More on competitive balance—competitive balance does not appear to be primarily about the policies leagues adopt, but rather about the underlying population of playing talent. Hence, basketball may have a competitive balance problem because of a "short supply of tall people." Yeah, we had to say that one more time.

5. Even more on competitive balance—contrary to the arguments of people in sports, and us poor economists who have spent much time looking at this subject, we do not have much evidence that fans really care about the level of competitive balance. Hopefully this finding will not hurt our book sales.

6. The lack of competitive balance in basketball led us to ask what causes fans

to come to NBA games. We found that it is not "star power" but team wins that primarily attract the fans.

7. Our study of the NBA stars also revealed that "star power" matters most to the teams the star plays against, not the team that pays the star's salary.

8. Once we saw the link between wins and revenue in the NBA, we then investigated the link between team wins and player action. This study revealed that the players who scored the most were not necessarily the players who produced the most wins.

9. Given our ability to measure productivity, we then turned to a couple of basketball-specific myths. First, both economic theory and the data tell us that the more productive a player's teammates, the less productive the player. So better players do not necessarily make their teammates better.

10. Better players do not tend to play even better in the playoffs. We found little evidence that any player could consistently raise his game when the games mattered most. In fact, many of the all-time greats in basketball often played a bit worse in the playoffs. Overall, though, players are just about as consistent moving from regular season to the playoffs as they are moving from season to season.

11. The consistency of NBA players was highlighted by a brief examination of football. We found that quarterbacks are quite inconsistent, which means predicting performance on the gridiron is extremely difficult.

12. Our study of performance in football also uncovered another myth. Wins and losses cannot be solely assigned to the play of the quarterback. Football teams win or lose games. Quarterbacks are important, but not the sole determinant of wins.

13. The relative inconsistency of football and baseball players allowed us to see why teams in those sports can't buy a championship. Although people may say they "know" who will be good tomorrow, the inconsistency we see in player performance suggests otherwise. Furthermore, because players are inconsistent, it is not easy to know which players a team should buy today if it wants to win more tomorrow.

14. Inconsistency does not appear to be the primary issue in the NBA. In the NBA player evaluation was shown to overemphasize scoring. Therefore, we think an important reason for the weak link between payroll and wins in basketball is that player evaluation is imperfect.[37]

15. Finally, the last myth we reported was about economics itself. Contrary to the belief of some, the evidence we present suggests decision makers in the NBA do not understand perfectly the data collected on player performance.

In Chapter One we presented a list of ten myths. In the end, we counted fifteen for the price of ten. So we also learn at the end that this book was a bargain.

We want to emphasize a point we made at the very beginning. All of this work has been driven by the data we collected and analyzed. As we noted, data offer many surprises. We believed that strikes and lockouts drove away significant numbers of fans. The data told us otherwise. We believed that star power must be what attracts fans to watch NBA games. The data told us otherwise. We believed that competitive balance was a key factor attracting fans in all professional sports. After writing many articles on the subject we are beginning to suspect that the data are telling us otherwise. When we first started looking at player productivity in the NBA we thought that scorers were generally the most productive players.[38] Again, the data told us otherwise. As you can see, despite what we believed, the data keep telling us that we are wrong.

Now that we have analyzed all these data, do we now have all the "right" answers? Well, let's close by quoting just one more famous economist. Yes, as we told our stories we did mention a few of the bright stars in our discipline. Well, maybe star is not the right word. MJ is a star. Brett Favre is a star. Somehow the word "star" can't work when talking about an economist.

Still, let's look briefly at the words of John Stuart Mill, another great economist from the 19th century who also died before basketball was invented. Back in Chapter Six we talked about the Labor Theory of Value, which we stated has since been dismissed by most economists. One of the first steps in moving past the Labor Theory of Value was taken by Mill, whose value theory shed much light on the workings of competitive markets. Mill seemed quite pleased with his work, stating: "Happily, there is nothing in the laws of value which remains for the present or any future writer to clear up; the theory of the subject is complete" (Mill, 1848, p. 436).

As time passed it became painfully clear that Mill was way off the mark when he made this statement. Economists are still making contributions to the study of prices and markets, and there appears no end in sight. So although we might be tempted to say after this work that nothing remains for any present or future writers to discuss, we suspect this is not true.

In fact, we know it is not true. As we conclude this book, our thoughts turn to the inevitable sequel. Already we can envision possible titles: "The Wages of Wins Strikes Back," or "Return to the Wages of Wins." How about, "The Wages of Wins, Part Deux"? The sequel to our work could address a few questions that remain unanswered. For example, what is the value of a head coach? Is Phil Jackson worth $10 million? Is Larry Brown worth the same wage? Or what about the link between college performance and NBA productivity. How much can NBA teams know about the future prospects of a drafted player the night he is selected? Finally, we noted that the wages of wins depend upon how wins are produced. Is there any relationship, though, between wages and wins? Does a player perform worse after he collects a big payday? Or does a player perform better in the last year of a contract? All of these questions can be investigated via the methods we have already employed and discussed.

At this point, we are not sure about the answer to most of these questions—although, to be honest, we already have some ideas. We do intend to keep working, to keep writing, and when the data give us a few more definitive answers, well, we will get right to work on that sequel.

REFERENCE MATTER

NOTES

CHAPTER 1

1. Not even out of the first paragraph and we already have an endnote. As you can see, we have many, many, many endnotes. These notes are offered to provide further information, clarify different points we make, and occasionally offer additional humorous insights. With this first note we wish to expand upon the statement that sports are just about having fun. It is possible for sports to profoundly impact society. One commonly cited example is Jackie Robinson taking the field for the Brooklyn Dodgers in 1947. Thomas Oliphant (2005) details the impact Robinson had on race relations in the United States. Certainly one can find other examples where what happens on the playing field transcends sports. Still, in general, sports are primarily just entertainment. Although fans may look at what happens as "life and death," so often this is not the case.

2. Alan Schwarz (2004), who provided a wonderful history of numbers in baseball, reports that the person who first started calculating batting average was H. A. Dobson in 1872.

3. Levitt and Dubner, 2005, pp. x–xi, italics added. Steve Levitt is quite an accomplished economist. Not only does he have a Ph.D. from MIT and works as a full professor at the University of Chicago, he was also recipient of the John Bates Clark award, which goes to the top economist under the age of 40. We would note that the three of us have much in common with Levitt. We are also not very good at math and are not interested in theory. Of course, the three of us also have a great deal in common with basketball legend Bill Walton, in the sense none of us jumps particularly well. Given these similarities, one could argue that this book is written by people who have much in common with both a top economist and a top basketball player.

4. Harry Landreth and David C. Colander, 2002, p. 278.

5. Michael Leeds and Peter Von Allmen (2004) define competitive balance as the degree of parity in a league.

6. We recognize the possibility that Bill James is not known by everyone. James is one of the founders of the modern-day Sabermetric movement, or what James calls "the search for objective knowledge about baseball." (David Grabiner, "The Sabermetric Manifesto" [www.baseball1.com/bb-data/grabiner/manifesto.html]).

7. To be fair, and we always wish to be fair, Oliver does state later in his book in a discussion of various methods to measure a player's contribution to team wins: "It is not scientifically appropriate to criticize any of the above methods by saying, 'Michael Jordan isn't ranked the best in their system, so it can't be right'" (2004, p. 256).

8. McCloskey should be standard reading for all people interested in economics. For a discussion of the difference between statistical and economic significance, we would recommend several works by Deirdre McCloskey (1998, 2000, 2002).

9. The story of how team wins is impacted by adding payroll and raising pay was originally told by David Berri and Todd Jewell (2004).

10. We would add that the impact adding payroll has on wins is also quite small. As Berri and Jewell (2004) note: "Surprisingly, though, the economic impact of PAYADD appears quite small. Specifically, the reported results suggest that a team would need to add $3.42 million in new salary to generate one additional win. To illustrate the economic significance of this result, in the time period examined, 75 teams managed to add at least $1 million more pay than the team lost. Of these 75 teams, though, only 39 actually saw an increase in wins. In other words, 48% of teams who added substantial pay to its payroll did not see a corresponding increase in wins" (pp. 135–136).

11. Berri and Jewell (2004) specifically connected changes in wins to adding or subtracting payroll, giving existing players a pay raise, the stability of a team's roster, lifetime winning percentage of a head coach, years of experience of a head coach, and the level of pay equality and inequality on a team's roster. Of all these factors, only adding and subtracting payroll and the winning percentage of the head coach were found to be statistically related to changes in team wins.

12. Because payroll has increased over the past three decades in professional sports, a relative payroll measure has to be employed. Relative payroll is team payroll in a season divided by the average payroll in the league that year.

13. When we refer to "percentage explained" we are referencing the R^2 that Szymanski reports. Throughout this book when we state "percentage explained" we will specifically be referring to adjusted R^2, or R^2 that has been adjusted for the number of variables included in the model.

14. Oddly, Szymanski (2003) finds that the relationship between pay and wins in soccer is quite a bit higher. For the Premier League in England, payroll explains 34% of wins. For the Bundesliga and Primera Liga, the explanatory power of payroll is 28% and 32% respectively. Finally, for Serie A in Italy, player pay was found to explain 56% of the variation in team wins. Unlike baseball, basketball, football, and hockey, soccer does not have an abundance of player statistics, yet pay is better connected to wins. Maybe player statistics just confuse decision makers in professional sports.

15. Some might look at these regressions of wins on relative payroll and say "well, the coefficient on relative payroll is statistically significant, so there is a relationship. Who cares about explanatory power?" When it comes to explanatory power, there is no definition of "high" or "low." What is "high" to one person may be though of as "low" to another. That being said, as we go forward in our discussion we will review the argument that payroll is the primary determinant of team wins. We would argue, though, that if pay only explains 18% of wins in baseball, or 12% in basketball, the argument that player pay is what matters most seems difficult to believe.

CHAPTER 2

1. Cannon's quote is taken from the Professional Sports Antitrust Bill of 1964. The quote was reprinted in Quirk and Fort (1992, p. 193).

2. What's the difference between a strike and a lockout? A strike occurs when workers leave the job. A lockout occurs when management prevents workers from coming to the job. Why would management lock out the players? Primarily this is done to avoid a strike at a later date. Management makes a substantial sum of money from the playoffs. Players, though, have already earned most of their money when the playoffs come about. So players have an incentive to strike toward the end of the season. To prevent this, owners may lock out players at the beginning of the season in the hope the dispute can be settled in time for the post-season to be played.

3. The following analysis replicates the work of James Quirk and Rodney Fort (1999, p. 68). Their comparison of labor disputes in sports to disputes in other American industries looked at only ten years (1987–1996). Over this time period, sports were 50 times more likely to have a work stoppage.

4. The analysis of Roger Noll appears in James Quirk and Rodney Fort (1999, pp. 70–71).

5. These quotes appeared in Steve Wine (2002).

6. The Johnny Damon quote came from Tony Massarotti (2002). The quote from Steve Kline was reported by Drew Olson (2002).

7. Jim Barrero (2002).

8. Paul Daugherty (2002).

9. Greg Couch (2002).

10. David Whitley (2002).

11. Barry Witt (2002).

12. The specific papers on this subject are Schmidt and Berri (2002a, 2004).

13. For our published academic articles, the attendance data were taken from a number of sources. For MLB, the attendance data were obtained for the years 1901–2000 from *The Sporting News Complete Baseball Record Book* (2001). The NFL data began in 1936 and concluded in 1999 and were obtained from *The Sporting News Pro Football Guide* (2000). Finally, attendance data for the NHL were obtained for the period 1960–2000 from *Total Hockey* (2001). Updates for these series, as well as the NBA attendance data employed, were

taken from the web site of noted sports economist Rodney Fort. www.rodneyfort.com/
SportsData/BizFrame.htm.

14. To read more on this, we would suggest one examine the sports economics text authored by Leeds and Von Allmen (2005).

15. Our specific methodology follows from the work of Enders, Sandler, and Cauley (1990). These authors wondered how anti-terrorism policies, such as the United States bombing of Libya in 1986, impacted terrorist activity.

16. The story of the 1981 strike was taken from the aforementioned work of Quirk and Fort (1992).

17. When the Colorado Rockies moved into Coors Field in 1995, seating capacity was reduced by over 40%.

18. The story is basically the same in the other sports. In the NBA regular season attendance has increased by 73%. In hockey team attendance rose by 33%. The lone exception is in the sport many now consider the national sport. Since 1980 NFL attendance has only increased by 13%.

19. See Paul Daugherty (2002).

20. ESPN is in 80 million homes in the United States, while ESPN Classic is only in 25 million houses. Even though ESPN Classic is the only channel devoted to re-runs in sports, its popularity is relatively low. Apparently people would rather watch a live game between two lesser contestants on ESPN than watch a classic game without uncertainty of outcome on ESPN Classic. We would like to thank Darren Rovell at ESPN.com for information on the market penetration of the various ESPN channels.

CHAPTER 3

1. "Of the Balance of Trade" is a chapter in a work entitled *Political Discourses*. This work was published in 1752. Much of this, including the chapter we cite, is posted at the web site [cepa.newschool.edu/het/].

2. The team payroll data we employ come from USATODAY.com, which reports payroll data for Major League Baseball from 1988 to the present. The payroll data are based upon each team's opening day roster.

3. This point was made in Levin et al. (2000, p. 3).

4. The irrelevance of motives in assessing an argument was made eloquently by Jamie Whyte (2005, p. 11). "It is perfectly possible to have some interest in holding or expressing an opinion and for that opinion to be true."

5. The Anaheim Angels are now called the Los Angeles Angels. For those not versed in Spanish, this literally means "The Angels Angels."

6. This quote appeared in the foreword of Zimbalist (2003, p. x).

7. Data on each United States city's population came from the 2000 U.S. Census Bureau. We specifically employed the size of each city's Metropolitan Statistical Area (MSA). For the Canadian cities we consulted Statistics Canada [www.statcan.ca/]. For cities with

more than one team we divided the city's MSA by two. We ran the regression without this adjustment and the results were unchanged.

8. For this model, population was significant at the 10% level. Typically a variable is thought to be significant at the 1% or 5% level.

9. The lack of a relationship between market size and wins was also made by John Fizel (1997). Specifically Fizel looked at the literature examining how often large market teams won after the institution of free agency in 1976. Fizel could find no evidence that after free agency began in 1976 large market teams began winning more often, suggesting that free agency does not allow large market teams to simply buy the best talent. In Fizel's words: "There is no apparent association between winning and large-market teams" (p. 67).

10. A representative sample of McCloskey's discussion of this topic would include: McCloskey and Ziliak (1996), McCloskey (1998, 2002).

11. To illustrate this point, McCloskey and Ziliak (1996) examined 182 papers published in the *American Economic Review* (AER) in the 1980s. The AER is the top journal in economics, and hence should represent the best work in the field. Of the 182 papers these authors reviewed, 70% failed to "distinguish statistical significance from economic, policy, or scientific significance" (p. 106).

12. Specifically, a team could expect 1.8 additional victories to be added to its season total. This conclusion was based on our regression of wins on relative payroll for the 2000 to 2005 time period.

13. This point was made in Hall, Szymanski, and Zimbalist (2002). Zimbalist (2003, pp. 45–46) also quoted this result.

CHAPTER 4

1. Here is but a sample of the alternative measures of competitive balance in the sports economics literature. We will begin with our work. In Schmidt (2001) and Schmidt and Berri (2001), we employed the Gini Coefficient to measure the level of competitive balance in baseball. Craig Depken (1999) and P. Downward and A. Dawson (2000) measured balance with the Herfindahl-Hirschman index. Brad Humphreys (2002) gave us the Competitive Balance Ratio. The aforementioned Quirk and Fort (1992) and Young Hoon Lee and Fort (2005) examined the Excess Tail Frequency. Not content with using the Gini Coefficient, Schmidt and Berri (2004)—that's us again—as well as Lawrence Hadley, James Ciecka, and Anthony C. Krautmann (2005) employed variations of a Markov model to measure competitive balance.

2. Although we have used the Gini Coefficient and Markov modeling, in Berri, Brook, Fenn, Frick, and Vicente-Mayoral (2005), Berri (2004a), and Schmidt and Berri (2003), we employed the Noll-Scully. This measure has also been used by John Vrooman (1995), as well as the aforementioned work of Quirk and Fort (1992) and Humphreys (2002).

3. We are committed to avoiding mathematical equations. How can one explain standard deviation, though, without the math? Well, Quirk and Fort (1997, p. 245) made a gal-

lant effort: "for each team, calculate the difference between the team's (winning) percentage for the season and the league average (.500). Square the difference for each team. Add these figures for all teams in the league, and then divide the total by the number of teams in the league. Take the square root, and you have the standard deviation of the league (winning) percentages for the season." All in all, pretty simple—we think.

4. To describe this measurement, we turn once again to the words of Quirk and Fort (1992, p. 245): "The idealized measure applies to a league in which, for each team, the probability of winning any game is one-half. The value of the idealized standard deviation depends on the number of games in a team's league schedule. If a team plays N league games in a season, then the idealized value of the standard deviation for the season-long (winning) percentage is (simply the mean value of winning percentage divided by the square root of schedule length)." Again, this seems pretty simple—to us.

5. Major League Baseball plays 162 games. The square root of 162 is 12.7. If we take the average winning percentage and divide by 12.7, we see that the idealized standard deviation in baseball would be 0.039. We need to note that the average winning percentage in baseball is not always 0.500. Two exceptions to this general condition are possible. First, the introduction of inter-league play in 1997 allowed for each league's average to differ from (0.500). A divergence from a mean of (0.500) also was possible prior to inter-league play. Major League Baseball has traditionally not played games between non-contenders toward the end of the season postponed due to inclement weather. When this happens, the number of games played for each team can differ. Given these possibilities, we used the actual mean winning percentage in the calculation of the Idealized Standard Deviation rather than the assumed value of (0.500).

6. For the NFL, if we take the mean winning percentage (0.500) and divide by the square root of schedule length (4), we get 0.125. In the NBA, where the schedule is 82 games, the idealized standard deviation is 0.055. In the NHL, and for soccer leagues, teams are not ranked by winning percentage but by points. Consequently, to calculate the Noll-Scully one first determines the standard deviation of standing points. One then takes the average of standing points and divides by the square root of schedule length to calculate the idealized standard deviation.

7. Not to beat this point to death, but we could not say at this point that this is the best book we have ever written. Well, we could, but since this the first book we have ever written, saying it is the best doesn't carry any meaning. Again, you need a reference point for terms like "the best" to tell us anything.

8. Technically soccer is called football. In America, though, football is played by very large people in pads chasing a pigskin. Because we do not wish to confuse our friends in Europe, though, we have to use the term "American football" for the game played in the National Football League. At least for now we will take this step. When we discuss "American football" in detail in Chapter Nine, we are just calling this "football."

9. We are following the lead of James Quirk and Rod Fort (1992), who also looked at competitive balance decade by decade. Their data ended with the 1990 season.

10. The trend in competitive balance was examined more formally in Schmidt and Berri (2003). By regressing the Noll-Scully for each league on time, we presented evidence that the trend in competitive balance in both the American and the National League was both negative and statistically significant. Statistically, across time, competitive balance improved in both leagues.

11. Although these authors did not originate the term, "Yankee tax" was noted in the aforementioned work of Leeds and Von Allmen (2005, p. 329).

12. This quote came on the August 30, 2002, PBS broadcast of the *NewsHour* with Jim Lehrer. The transcript with this quote can be found at [http://www.pbs.org/newshour/bb/sports/july-dec02/baseball_8-30.html].

13. We would like to thank Michael Leeds for reminding us that this challenge to the reserve clause was mostly about Andy Messersmith. Dave McNally was at the end of his career. As detailed by Marvin Miller (1991, pp. 243–245), Founding Executive Director of the Major League Baseball Players Association, McNally was only included in this challenge to the reserve clause by the players' union in case Messersmith backed out and signed his one-year contract.

14. Quirk and Fort (1992) report that the clause we quote appeared in player contracts from the 1920s to the 1950s.

15. In *Federal Baseball Club of Baltimore, Inc. vs. National League of Professional Baseball Clubs*, 259 U.S. 200 [1922], the Supreme Court handed down one of its oddest rulings. The Baltimore Terrapins of the defunct Federal League (1914–1915) had brought suit against the American and National League on the grounds that Major League Baseball had violated the Sherman Anti-Trust Act. The case went to the Supreme Court, where the Court unanimously ruled organized baseball was not subject to anti-trust laws because baseball was not interstate commerce. The ruling exempted baseball from anti-trust laws, a point the Court noted in *Toolson vs. New York Yankees*, 346 U.S. 356 [1953] and *Flood vs. Kuhn*, 407 U.S. 258 [1971]. Each of these latter cases involved a player challenging the reserve clause on the grounds that it violated anti-trust laws. Although the Court changed its view on the issue that baseball was interstate commerce, the 1922 decision was upheld in both the *Toolson* and *Flood* cases. In essence, although the Court ruled that the 1922 decision was incorrect, Congress had the power to remove baseball's anti-trust exemption. Because Congress did not, the Court saw no reason for it to take such action. In 1998 Congress did pass the "Curt Flood Act" which removed baseball's exemption with respect to its labor relations. For more details on these cases, one is referred to Quirk and Fort (1992, pp. 184–194) and Leeds and Von Allmen (2005, pp. 128–133).

16. Quirk and Fort (1992) note that the system of arbitration was instituted in the 1973 collective bargaining agreement. It was the institution of arbitration that allowed Messersmith and McNally to challenge baseball's reserve system. These authors also note that in the 1985 collective bargaining agreement the eligibility requirement for arbitration was changed from two years to three years of service.

17. Other policies leagues adopt in the name of competitive balance include caps on

payrolls and revenue sharing. Major League Baseball does not have a cap on payrolls, commonly called a salary cap, and revenue sharing is still limited.

18. This quote appears in "Ronald H. Coase—Autobiography" which can be found at the web site of the Nobel Prize [nobelprize.org/economics/laureates/1991/coase-autobio.html].

19. This point appears in "Ronald H. Coase—Prize Lecture" which can be found at the web site of the Nobel Prize [nobelprize.org/economics/laureates/1991/coase-lecture.html].

20. This quote from Stigler appears in Samuelson (1995, p. 2). Samuelson notes that the original quote is from George Stigler (1988).

21. Transaction costs are expenses or outlays, not including the price, associated with buying and selling a product. Coase is saying that if these costs are zero, then where a resource is employed will not depend upon who initially owns the resource. It is important to emphasize that Coase was not emphasizing the unimportance of legal rights, but the importance of transaction costs. Because transaction costs are not zero, legal rights do actually matter.

22. The Ruane (1998) study was cited by Rod Fort (2003, p. 247).

23. Details of the record in the men's 100 meter dash were taken from an ESPN.com news service article "Jamaican Breaks Montgomery's Record" posted June 14, 2005, at ESPN.com.

24. We thank Andrew Hanssen for providing the data on racial integration. The latter data have previously been utilized in Hanssen's (1998) study of discrimination in Major League Baseball.

25. We thank Sean Lahmen, author of the *Baseball Archive* [www.baseball1.com], for the data on the number of foreign-born players in Major League Baseball.

26. This statistical technique was developed by Clive Granger and Robert Engle, two economists who received the Nobel Prize in 2003. In the lecture he delivered when he received the Nobel prize, Granger (2004, p. 422) offered an intuitive explanation of what it means for two variables to be cointegrated: "Suppose that we had two similar chains of pearls and we threw each on the table separately, but for ease of visualization, they do not cross one another. Each would represent a smooth series but would follow different shapes and have no relationship. The distance between the two sets of pearls would also give a smooth series if you plotted it. However, if the pearls were set in small but strong magnets, it is possible that there would be an attraction between the two chains, and that they would have similar, but not identical, smooth shapes. In that case, the distance between the two sets of pearls would give a stationary series and this would give an example of cointegration. For cointegration, a pair of integrated, or smooth, series must have the property that a linear combination of them is stationary. Most pairs of integrated series will not have the property, so that cointegration should be considered as a surprise when it occurs."

27. We would note that we are not the only economists to employ the wisdom of Gould. Both the work of Sangit Chatterjee and Mustafa R. Yilmaz (1991) and Mustafa R. Yilmaz, Sangit Chatterjee and Mohamed Habibullah (2001) provided empirical tests of

Gould's work. The arguments offered by Gould were also echoed in the work of Andrew Zimbalist. In Zimbalist's 1992 classic, *Baseball and Billions* he argues: "It seems, however, that a more objective and powerful leveling force is at work, and that is the compression of baseball talent. . . . Today's major league ballplayers . . . are a smaller fraction of an increasingly prepared population. The difference between today's best, average, and worst players is much smaller than it was twenty or forty years ago. This results in greater difficulty in selecting dominating players and in greater competitive balance among the teams" (p. 97). We would note that while Zimbalist does not acknowledge the earlier work of Gould or Chatterjee and Yilmaz (1991), the sentiment is essentially the same. The increasing population of baseball talent has led to the improvement we observe in competitive balance. It is interesting that although Zimbalist notes the importance of talent compression in his 2003 book *May the Best Team Win*, he moves directly to a reiteration of the Blue Ribbon Panel's argument that competitive balance worsened in the years following the 1994–95 strike. In his discussion of this supposed decline in competitive balance, the importance of talent compression is ignored.

28. To be fair, and we always try to be fair, the Blue Ribbon Panel did note that it was important that baseball take steps to ensure the future of its talent pool.

29. The following story about Cal Ripken was from an article by David Ginsburg (2005).

30. Obviously it takes three economists to replace Schmidt.

31. We should note that when Vicente-Mayoral's results were first examined, it was not clear why these results were observed. It was his measurement of competitive balance across many leagues that led Berri to the work of Gould, and this led to the story we are telling in this chapter.

32. Schmidt and Berri (2003), building upon an earlier version of the "Short Supply of Tall People" authored by Berri and Vicente-Mayoral, offer further evidence in support of the idea that underlying population dictates competitive balance. These authors looked at average competitive balance in the NBA and ABA from 1967–68 to 1975–76; the NHL and WHA from 1972–73 to 1978–79; the NFL and AFL from 1960 to 1969; and the NL and AL from 1900 to 2000. They then noted that except for the NHL and WHA, every league pair was found to have a statistically equivalent average level of competitive balance. So we see the same sport at the same time, but different leagues. Despite differences in leagues, competitive balance was statistically the same.

33. One might argue that American football also faces a problem with a short supply of big people. Certainly the size of an athlete is a significant resource in both basketball and American football. What is meant by size and the nature of the restriction, though, differs across the two sports. In football, substantial weight may help to play certain positions. Such weight, though, may be manufactured via diet, exercise, and pharmaceuticals. For professional basketball, where height is the predominant physical characteristics, diet and exercise are not of much assistance. As people often state, you can't teach height. In other words, no amount of diet or exercise will make an athlete who is six feet tall into a seven-footer.

Hence, professional basketball faces a much more rigid restriction relative to professional football. Consequently, we would argue that only in basketball does the size requirement substantially limit the pool of available talent.

34. The exceptions were Tyrone (Muggsy) Bogues (5'3"), Earl Boykins (5'5"), Spud Webb (5'7") and Keith Jennings (5'7"). Three additional (5'10") players appeared in this time period (Damon Stoudamire, Brevin Knight, Tyus Edney). To be considered in this calculation players had to have played at least twelve minutes per contest and in 60 regular season games.

35. In essence we are arguing that the NBA cannot easily find substitutes for its major stars. This is true in other sports, but as we would argue, to a lesser extent. The aforementioned Walter Neale (1964) referred to the idea that certain players could not be easily replaced as "Bobby Layne Rigidity" (p. 12).

36. This point has been made, by us and others, in many places in the sports economics literature. It has also been made by Allen Barra (2002, pp. 183–192).

CHAPTER 5

1. If we go back fifty years, NBA champions have repeated seventeen times. So across five decades champions have defended 34% of the time.

2. We would add that the inequity in championship distribution we observe recently in the NBA is not a recent phenomenon. James Quirk and Rodney Fort (1992) examined the distribution of league championships in the NBA, NFL, NHL, AL, and NL for each season played between 1901 and 1990. Like our study of the past twenty years, these authors found that distribution of championships in the NBA was the most unequal, or least equal, or just not fair.

3. "The Best-Paid Athletes" at Forbes.com [www.forbes.com/2004/06/23/04athletes-land.html].

4. Details on the NBA television contracts can be found at InsideHoops.com. [www.insidehoops.com/nba-tv-contracts.shtml].

5. Hausman and Leonard (1997) used regression analysis to estimate Jordan's impact on television ratings. A simple example offered by these authors illustrates the lesson this study teaches. These authors report that the 1993 NBA Finals, which featured Michael Jordan's Bulls defeating the Phoenix Suns, averaged a Nielsen rating of 17.9. Before the start of the 1993–94 season, though, Jordan retired. The 1994 NBA Finals, between the New York Knicks and the Houston Rockets, had a Nielsen rating of only 12.2. In 1995, with Shaquille O'Neal leading the Orlando Magic against the Houston Rockets, the ratings rose to 13.9. Such anecdotal evidence seems to suggest that ratings depend upon the players and teams being televised.

6. As we stated, Hausman and Leonard's (1997) study of television ratings involved estimating several regressions. Their study of home and road attendance, though, was, in the words of these authors, "less formal" (p. 609). Essentially all these authors did was take a before and after snapshot. Specifically they looked at attendance when Jordan and the Bulls

played and compared this to attendance without Jordan. Unfortunately such an approach fails to account for all the factors that might impact a team's ability to attract fans. We will look at the same issue, but our analysis of gate revenue and road attendance will rely upon the wonder that is regression analysis.

7. Hausman and Leonard (1997) report that nearly 50% of the sale of NBA paraphernalia was connected to the Bulls and MJ in 1991–92.

8. The NBA salary data we employ came from Patricia's Various Basketball Stuff, a wonderful web site maintained by Patricia Bender [www.dfw.net/~patricia/]. Patricia Bender takes her data from various news sources. According to Bender's data, Larry Bird, Hot Rod Williams, Kevin McHale, and Reggie Lewis were all paid more than Jordan in 1991–92.

9. These teams, with wins listed in parentheses, were the Indiana Pacers (61), Minnesota Timberwolves (58), San Antonio Spurs (57), LA Lakers (56), and Sacramento Kings (55).

10. Data on ticket prices were taken from the web site of noted sports economist Rod Fort [www.rodneyfort.com]. Rod Fort cites the Team Marketing Report Fan Cost Index as his source for this information.

11. The economics of a business or a firm is based upon both the Law of Demand and the Law of Diminishing Returns. We will discuss the latter in a bit more detail in Chapter Seven.

12. Regular season home and road attendance can be found in each annual issue of *The Sporting News NBA Guide*. To determine gate revenue we multiplied the average ticket prices, taken from the web site of Rod Fort, by the aggregate home attendance for each team, reported in the *NBA Guide*.

13. The media select the Rookie of the Year. The NBA's head coaches, though, select the All-Rookie team. One coach, and voting is anonymous so we do not know who, placed Iverson on the All-Rookie second team in 1997.

14. Interestingly, Iverson only led the league in this category once when legendary Larry Brown was his head coach, but he has captured this dubious crown every year when Brown was not in Philadelphia.

15. To put Iverson's shooting skills in perspective, the average NBA player in 2004–05 converted 36% of his three-point shots and 47% of his attempts from two-point range.

16. Dan Gelston. The untitled story was posted on November 4, 2004, at [sports.yahoo.com/nba/recap?gid=2004110520].

17. For Berri, Schmidt, and Brook (2004) we analyzed gate revenue data from various issues of *Financial World*. The last season this periodical reported such information was for the 1995–96 campaign. To the best of our knowledge such information was not reported for the 1996–97 campaign. Data on revenue are reported for more recent years by *Forbes*, although *Forbes* does not report data specifically on gate revenue for each season. Consequently, we took a different route for the book and simply used average ticket prices and season attendance data to construct gate revenue for each team.

18. We employed the consumer price index reported by the U.S. Bureau of Labor statistics to calculate 2004 values of both gate revenue and the NBA's TV contract.

19. This note is for people who are interested in the econometric methodology we employed. For those who want even more detail, we have placed the estimated model on our web site. For here, though, we simply will list a few issues that might be of interest. First of all, our data set begins with the 1992–93 season and ends with the 2003–04 season. Due to the lockout, there was no All-Star game for the 1998–99 campaign so this season was excluded from our study. Here are some additional issues one might find interesting.

In "Stars at the Gate" (Berri, Schmidt, and Brook, 2004) we went into some detail about the correct functional form of the estimated model. In the literature, revenue functions have been estimated as linear models, which implies that the value of a win is the same for all markets. This is the approach taken in the seminal work of Gerald Scully (1974) and Andrew Zimbalist's (1992) book *Baseball and Billions*, among others. Economic theory, as we noted, says that the value of a win should vary from team to team. Consequently, a multiplicative or double-logged functional form would be preferred. As we note in our paper (Berri, Schmidt, and Brook, 2004), our statistical analysis indicated that the double-logged model should be employed, confirming the economic theory on this topic.

In addition to estimating a double-logged model, we also employed year-specific dummy variables. A dummy variable equals one when a condition holds, and zero otherwise. Given that average gate revenue varied somewhat from year to year in our data set, we employed dummy variables for each year. With the exception of the 1993–94 dummy, all of these were statistically significant and positive in our model.

In "Stars at the Gate" we did not employ dummy variables for each team. For the model we estimated here we employed both a common constant term and a model with team-specific fixed effects. The results we report here have a common constant term. When you employ the fixed effects model your explanatory power increases, but because population and the team-specific fixed effects are highly correlated, our population measure becomes insignificant. Furthermore, our measure of past championships won also becomes insignificant in a fixed-effects model. Finally, in the fixed-effects model the average value of a win declines—relative to the model with a common constant term—from close to $238,000 to about $124,000. This does not alter our conclusion that wins are more important than star appeal for a team's gate performance.

In our paper "Stars at the Gate" we also went to some lengths to address the potential correlation between wins and star votes. This is our comment on this issue from the paper: "To test for this possibility we calculated the Variance Inflation Factor (VIF). We would note that the VIF for (team wins) and (all star votes received) was 3.04 and 1.60 respectively. Although there is no statistical test for significance of the VIF, a general rule of thumb is if the VIF exceeds 10, multicollinearity is at such a level that the interpretation of results may prove difficult. Consequently, we do not believe multicollinearity is an issue with respect to (team wins) or (all-star votes received)" (p. 48). What does all this mean? We think star votes and wins are not the same. Our test for multicollinearity indicates that this is a reasonable conclusion. If you do not understand the issue of multicollinearity, do not despair.

Understanding the issue of multicollinearity has never been shown to make a person happier.

20. The very first paper published by Berri and Brook appeared in 1999. In this work we estimated a revenue model and employed as an explanatory variable a measure of past championships won. The variable was calculated by assigning a value to a team for each championship won in the past twenty years. This value was twenty if the team captured a championship during the prior season, nineteen if the championship was won two seasons past, etc. Data on regular season wins, playoff wins and championships can be found in *The Sporting News 2004–05 Official NBA Guide.*

21. Data on All-Star voting can be found at Patricia's Various Basketball Stuff, the web site of Patricia Bender. The top players at each position are chosen as starters for the mid-season classic. Additionally, the guard and forward receiving the second most votes at these positions are also named as starters. Because only one center is chosen, our analysis only considered the top five recipients of votes at this position. One should note that this measure is not without its flaws, as the anonymous referee of our forthcoming examination of NBA road attendance noted in his/her review. All-Star votes are dominated by the preferences of the home team. Although fans in major markets like New York or Los Angeles may regard a player a star, this assessment may not be shared by fans in other cities. For example, A. C. Green of the Los Angeles Lakers was chosen by the fans to start the 1990 All-Star game. We are fairly certain that outside of LA, Green would not be thought of as a star. The anonymous referee also noted that it is possible that higher attendance leads to more star votes, hence the direction of the relationship between votes received and attendance is unclear. We agree that this measure is not perfect. We would argue, though, that All-Star votes, which come directly from the consumer, are an improvement over the employment of All-NBA teams, the measure often employed in the sports economics literature. Such teams are chosen by the media and may not reflect accurately the preferences of fans.

22. For population we employed the Metropolitan Statistical Area (MSA) for each team's city. For the 1992–93 through 1994–95 campaigns we took the MSA value for 1990. After these seasons we used the value from 2000. These data were taken from the U.S. Census Bureau [www.census.gov/population/www/cen2000/phc-t29.html].

23. Data on stadium capacity and the age of the stadium were obtained from various annual issues of *The Sporting News NBA Guide.* The specific measure we employed for stadium age was a dummy variable, which took the value of one if a team played in a stadium that was less than three years old, and zero otherwise. It should be noted that in our data set about 23% of observations came from teams that sold out every home game. Stephan Shmanske (1998) in a study of golf courses noted that an increase in demand would elicit different responses from courses at capacity relative to those that still were capable of serving additional customers. Specifically, a course with excess capacity could increase both quantity and price in response to an increase in demand. Courses at capacity, though, could only increase price. Therefore, as Shmanske argues, the estimated parameters in the demand

function may differ depending on whether an organization is at capacity. To account for these differences, Shmanske incorporated a dummy variable equal to one if a course was at capacity. Given the similarity between Shmanske's subject and our own, we have incorporated a similar dummy variable, equal to one if a team is at capacity, zero otherwise.

24. Roster stability was measured by examining the minutes played by returning players over both the current and prior seasons. We then averaged the percentage of minutes played by these players for both of these campaigns. In our papers we use the following example to illustrate this calculation. During the 1994–95 season George McCloud's NBA career was resurrected by the Dallas Mavericks, who employed him for 802 minutes. The following year, McCloud's minutes increased more than threefold to 2,846. If we only consider McCloud's minutes during the 1995–96 season, we would be overstating the level of roster stability, since McCloud was not an integral part of the Mavericks in 1994–95. Consequently, in measuring roster stability we consider more than just how many minutes a player played during the current season, but also the number of minutes the team allocated to the player during the prior campaign. As we did in our published work, we wish to acknowledge the assistance of Dean Oliver, who argued that a better label for this measure is roster stability, as opposed to roster turnover. Data on minutes played, utilized to construct the roster stability variable, were obtained from various annual issues of *The Sporting News NBA Guide.*

25. Following the lead of Ha Hoang and Dan Rascher (1999) we employed the ratio of the percentage of minutes on the team allocated to white players to the percentage of white persons in the population of the city. If this variable increases in size, the racial match between the team and the city improves. Consequently, we would expect this ratio to have a positive sign if people within the market prefer a team that represents the racial mix of the city. For the percentage of white persons in each city we employed data from the U.S. Census Bureau [censtats.census.gov/pub/Profiles.shtml]. For the race of each player we utilized the pictures published in the various annual issues of *The Sporting News NBA Register.* We would like to thank Richard Campbell who helped us assemble these data.

26. A rudimentary illustration can support this contention. We regressed regular season wins on all-star votes received for each team, excluding those from the lockout year of 1998–99, from the 1992–93 season to the 2003–04 campaign. The data tell us that only 31% of wins can be explained by All-Star votes received. In Chapter Ten we will show that many players who are thought to be stars do not actually contribute many wins.

27. Let's add one last comment on our model of gate revenue. Scoring attracts attention in the NBA. As we will note in Chapter Ten, scoring is what primarily determines player salary. We considered scoring in our model of gate revenue and found no evidence that teams that score more are able to earn higher revenues. Specifically, we found that increases in scoring were negatively related to revenue, although the statistical significance of this finding was not robust to alternative specifications of our model. In other words, if we considered wins last season, scoring was statistically significant. When we considered playoff performance last season instead of regular season wins in the last campaign, the rest of our

model was virtually unchanged but scoring became insignificant. The key point we are making, though, remains. More scoring does not, by itself, lead to more revenue.

28. As with our discussion of our gate revenue model, we also have a few comments to make about the econometrics we employed in our examination of road attendance. Again, if you are not interested, this is an endnote to skip. If this note leaves you unsatisfied, you are referred to our web site for even more detail.

In the paper "On the Road with the National Basketball Association's Superstar Externality" (Berri and Schmidt, forthcoming) we looked at only four seasons (1992–93 to 1995–96). Like our study of gate revenue, we employed data from eleven season, including every year from 1992–93 to 2003–04, with the exception of the 1998–99 lockout season.

We also employed year specific dummies. Again, these were significant and positive in every season. The lone exception was the 1993–94 season.

In our paper we employed team-specific fixed effects. As we noted above, these fixed effects and our population measure are related. So we estimated the model we employed in this chapter with both a common constant term and fixed effects. Our discussion is based on the common constant term estimation. Like our estimation of gate revenue, if fixed effects are utilized our measures of championships won and population become insignificant. The value of a win, in terms of road attendance, increases for the fixed effects model. Our general conclusion, though, regarding the relative value of wins and star power remains unchanged.

Unlike our gate revenue model, the road attendance model employed a linear functional form. So the impact of an additional win on road attendance was the same for all teams.

29. As we note, to capture the impact time has on gate revenue and road attendance, we employed dummy variables for each year in our data set. Given these year-specific dummy variables, using a league competitive balance measure would not allow us to estimate the model. In statistical terms, our model would not be identified, which is fairly important when you are estimating a regression. Hence, we turn to the level of competitive balance at the conference level.

30. Mike Leeds is Von Allmen's co-author. We are friends with him also. To be fair, there are only two textbooks in this field. The other is written by Rod Fort—another friend—and Fort's book can also be thought of as one of the very best books on sports economics.

31. In "Stars at the Gate" (Berri, Schmidt, and Brook, 2004) we found that competitive balance did not statistically impact gate revenue. At the time we argued that the sample we used, which only covered four seasons, may not have been sufficient to uncover the true relationship. Of course, in this chapter we looked at gate revenue across a longer time period and came to the same conclusion. Gate revenue and competitive balance are not statistically related in the NBA. In the study of road attendance we report in this chapter we did find that competitive balance and drawing power on the road were related. In our academic article, where we again examined a smaller sample, we did not find a relationship. Interestingly, we spent little time discussing the lack of a statistical relationship between road attendance and competitive balance. This is what we said to introduce our measure of

competitive balance: "As noted by Schmidt and Berri (2001), the level of competitive balance, as measured by the Gini coefficient, was found to significantly impact demand in Major League Baseball (MLB). To test whether the balance of league competition affects road attendance, we introduced GINIC, or the measure of competitive balance in each conference. The larger the Gini coefficient, the greater the level of competitive imbalance." Later in the paper, we stated: "The estimation of this model reveals that only four variables can be considered statistically significant." That is all we had to say. We went on to note the four variables that were found to be significant, and since competitive balance was not on the list, the reader was to infer that it was not found to be statistically significant. So we are presenting a result that indicates that an article of faith for sports economists is incorrect, and we can't even say "competitive balance was found to be statistically insignificant."

32. The Gini Coefficient is a common measure of income inequality. It ranges from zero to one, with a value of zero indicating a society has perfect income equality. A value of one indicates a society has perfect inequality, or one person has all the income. Joshua Utt and Rodney Fort (2002) argue that the Gini Coefficient is inappropriate to measure competitive balance in sports because a value of one is not possible. One team cannot win all the games played, only all the games the team plays. We would argue that we would also not likely see a Gini Coefficient equal to one in any study of income inequality in a society. Although it is perhaps physically possible for a society to give all of its income to one person, such a society is not likely to be observed. Consequently, in a study of income distribution we would never know the most unequal distribution of income that could be observed in a society. This is not really a problem. Any value one estimates for the Gini Coefficient only has meaning when it is compared to other values of the Gini Coefficient. So from 1990 to 1999 the average Gini Coefficient in the American League was 0.071 while in the National League it was 0.075. What does this mean? Well, when we look at decades before 1980, we consistently see values of the Gini Coefficient in excess of what we observe in the last decade of the 20th century. Therefore, we can now say that wins in baseball, according to the Gini Coefficient, were more equally distributed in the 1990s, relative to what we observe in the decades before this point. This is the same result you see when you look at standard deviation or the Noll-Scully, and probably any measure of the distribution of wins in baseball.

33. For the larger data set we considered—running from 1901 to 1998—this is what we found. If the American League in 1998 went from the lowest level of competitive balance to the highest level we observe in the 20th century, how much would attendance change? We found that such a change in league balance would only increase each team's attendance by about 1,000 fans per game. This is only a 4% change in home attendance. A similar result would be observed for the National League.

34. In this study we examined attendance in the American League and National League from 1901 to 1998, as well as a smaller sample which went from 1975 to 1988. The smaller data set was necessary because across the entire 20th century we do not have data on various factors that might impact a fan's willingness to attend a game. A list of such factors would begin with ticket prices. We were able to obtain ticket prices from Rod Fort for the

years 1975 to 1988. We then used these prices to formulate a model that could further illuminate the relationship between attendance and competitive balance. In looking at balance, we measured the level in a single season, as well as how balanced the league was across three and five seasons. To calculate competitive balance across three years we computed each team's three-year average winning percentage. We then used this average performance to compute the Gini Coefficient. The same step was followed for the five-year measure, where we began with each team's five-year average performance. For example, if we were looking at the five-year measure for 1980, we would compute each team's average winning percentage from 1976 to 1980. If we wished to look at 1979, the average would be computed based upon the years 1975 to 1979.

35. The aforementioned Andrew Zimbalist (2003) noted a problem with using standard deviation or the Noll-Scully competitive balance measure. In his 2003 book he notes: "It follows that the most relevant measures of competitive balance are the ones to which the consumers show greatest sensitivity" (p. 36). He then continues this point in an endnote (p. 167): "Many sports economists have used the concept of an idealized standard deviation of win percentages. Statistically, it makes sense to compare this number with the actual standard deviation of win percentages because it standardizes for the length of the season. The problem with this index of competitive balance, however, is that fans do not experience it directly. . . . One meaningful way to distinguish among balance measures is to test how effective they are as predictors of attendance, controlling for relevant factors." Zimbalist then proceeded to discuss the findings offered by Humphreys (2002). We are not sure we agree with Zimbalist's characterization of the Noll-Scully. Although we agree that fans do not spend time calculating the Noll-Scully, we are not sure this is relevant. Fans probably do not spend time estimating the Gini Coefficient in baseball, and we also found this to have a statistically significant impact on attendance. Of course, as noted, the economic impact appears somewhat small.

36. The Herfindahl-Hirschman Index is commonly used in the field of industrial organization, or the study of the interaction between firms and markets. It is simply the sum of the squared market shares of all firms in an industry. Such a measure tells us about the distribution of sales in an industry, or when applied to the study of competitive balance in baseball, the distribution of wins among teams. In essence, it tells us something similar to standard deviation, the Noll-Scully, and the Gini Coefficient. The proliferation of different measures of competitive balance illustrates a problem in academia. You cannot get published unless your work is different from work already published. Often, though, the quest to be different leads writers to make cosmetic changes that really don't change the story being told. We note this problem, fully acknowledging that we might be just as guilty.

37. Humphreys (2002) defines the Competitive Balance Ratio (CBR) as follows: "The CBR scales the average time variation in won-loss percentage for teams in the league by the average variation in won-loss percentages across seasons; it indicates the relative magnitude of each type of variation across a number of seasons" (p. 137).

38. This point is also made in a paper delivered in 2005 by Stefan Szymanski. As Szy-

manski notes (p. 29), " if the (league) planner's objective were to maximize attendance she would choose a substantially more uneven distribution of win percentage than is observed in reality. In the AL, the (league) planner's standard deviation is more than twice as large as the actual, in the NL it is around 50% larger. Recall that the theory also suggested that the reason the planner would demand less balance is that the relatively small teams, with low win percents impose a large externality on the large teams with larger win percents."

CHAPTER 6

1. As economist Lawrence Kahn (2000, p. 75) notes, "There is no research setting other than sports where we know the name, face, and life history of every production worker and supervisor in the industry."

2. We derived the concept of points-per-field-goal attempt from an article by Rob Neyer (1996). In Neyer's article this statistic was labeled Points-Per-Shot (PPS). As Neyer explained, this is the number of points a player or team accumulates from its field goal attempts. Its calculation involves subtracting free throws made from total points, and then dividing by field goals attempted. Employing points per shot, rather than field goal percentage, allowed for the impact of three-point shooting to be captured more efficiently.

3. There is a debate in sports economics that can be traced to the work of Rottenberg (1956). Do teams seek to maximize wins or maximize profits? Rottenberg (p. 252) states that owners may want to maximize wins subject to breaking even instead of only maximizing profits. Yet Rottenberg seems to question this by stating later "it seems unlikely that people will subject capital of this magnitude to large risk of loss for the pure joy of association with the game." As sports fans we observe players, coaches, and general managers in the media stating that their goal is to win. We are not sure this sentiment should be questioned. In fact, the prohibition against players betting on games stems from a need to remove the suspicion that players are more interested in money than they are in winning. But the owners are unlikely to survive financially if the team wins but suffers large economic losses. Thus, when we talk about players, coaches, and even general managers, win maximization is a plausible hypothesis. For owners, though, we are not so sure. We will note, though, that our analysis of gate revenue suggests that wins and revenue go together. As we will note in Chapter Ten, whether teams seek to maximize wins or profit, many of our conclusions remain the same.

4. We would note that the list of specific approaches we review is not complete. For a more complete review we would once again recommend the work of Dean Oliver (2004, pp. 81–85).

5. Heeren's TENDEX formula is as follows:

$$\text{TENDEX} = \text{Points} + \text{Rebounds} + \text{Assists} + \text{Blocked Shots} + \text{Steals}$$
$$- \text{Turnovers} - \text{All missed shots}$$

This value is then weighted by minutes played and game pace.

Bellotti's basic Points Created formula is as follows:

Points Created = Points + Rebounds + Assists + Blocked Shots
+ Steals − Turnovers − All missed shots − ½ personal fouls.

6. Dave Heeren (1994, p. vii).

7. Dan Rosenbaum has expanded on the work of Winston and Sagarin. Rosenbaum's work can be found at [www.82games.com/comm30.htm] and [www.uncg.edu/eco/rosenbaum/NBA/winval2.htm].

8. Roland Ratings can be found at [www.82games.com].

9. We simplify in our description of plus-minus in hockey. Technically, a player's plus-minus increases by one if his team scores at even strength or when shorthanded. A player's plus-minus declines by one if a goal is scored by his opponent when the teams are at even strength or when his team is on a power play.

10. We would add that the inability to compare players on different teams is not the only criticism one could offer of this system. Dean Oliver (2004, p. 182) also argued that although plus-minus might tell you how productive a player is, it does not tell you why. Without knowing why a player has a positive or negative net plus-minus, it becomes difficult for a coach and general manager to use this information. We would also add that net plus-minus is influenced by how many minutes you are on the court. Players who are not on the court for very long cannot accumulate a high positive or negative value of plus-minus. This is one reason that hockey players who accumulate large amounts of ice time on good teams tend to also have high plus-minus values.

11. Oliver (2004, pp. 8–28) has developed a method of scoring a game that records every pass, dribble, shot, etc. If this system were employed for every game the NBA plays, the data generated would certainly increase the accuracy of any measure of player productivity.

12. A difficulty in basketball is that teams can play at different speeds, or play at a different pace. Consequently, a team can increase scoring by simply taking less time on each possession. As a result, scoring per game is not a good measure of team offense or team defense. Oliver (2004, pp. 25–40) does discuss a few alternatives, including points per possession (points divided by possessions employed), which we will employ; offensive and defensive rating (points scored per 100 possessions employed); floor percentage (percentage of possessions where a team scores at least one point); and field percentage (percentage of a team's non-foul shot possessions in which the team scores a field goal).

13. Oliver (2004, pp. 69–76) discusses the likelihood that any team will win three games in a row at some point in a season. For example, a team that only wins 20% of its games has a 47% chance of a three-game winning streak at some point in the season. In other words, one should not get too excited if a bad team enjoys a modest winning streak.

14. We would like to thank Dean Oliver for providing us his measure of net points for each player in the 2003–04 season.

15. One can easily move from a correlation coefficient to a discussion of how much of one factor is explained by another. For example, the correlation coefficient between wins and points scored is 0.41. If we square 0.41 we get 0.17, which simply means that only 17% of wins can be explained with the number of points a team scores per game.

16. Bob Bellotti (1992, pp. 28–29).

17. Dean Oliver (2004, pp. 89–92).

18. To be fair—and we always strive for fairness—Oliver did expand upon his analysis by controlling for difference in shooting percentage. This analysis demonstrated that offensive rebounds were not the least important statistic. Such analysis is also a step toward regression analysis, which can control for many additional variables. Had Oliver employed regression analysis he might have concluded, as we do, that offensive rebounds are just as important as turnovers, defensive rebounds, etc.

19. The history of the model of productivity we develop in this chapter, and further simplify in Chapter Seven, begins with a paper published by Berri and Brook in 1999. The player productivity model detailed in the Berri and Brook work was further developed in a paper published by Berri, also in 1999. Berri's 1999 model was employed by Berri and Schmidt (2002) in a study of voting for the All-Rookie team in the NBA. The Berri and Schmidt (2002) work will be expanded upon in Chapter Ten. Not to give anything away, but the conclusion we reach in Chapter Ten will be the same as what we reported in our 2002 work. Berri's work from 1999 is not employed here, but should be thought of as an ancestor to the actual model we are detailing. The specific measure of productivity we are employing here was detailed in a working paper by Berri (2004b) titled: "A Simple Measure of Worker Productivity in the National Basketball Association." This working paper has been cited in a number of published and unpublished papers including: Berri and Eschker (2005), Berri and Schmidt (forthcoming in 2006), Berri, Brook, Fenn, Frick, and Vicente-Mayoral (2005), Berri and Fenn (2004), Berri and Krautmann (2006), Berri, Brook, and Schmidt (2004), Lee and Berri (2004). As this list illustrates, once one has a measure of worker productivity, there are many, many stories one can tell.

20. Dean Oliver (2004, pp. 25–26) notes that he thought he had invented the concept of possessions in 1987. Later Oliver learned that this concept was employed by Frank McGuire and one of his assistant coaches, Dean Smith. Smith went on to become a coaching legend at North Carolina. As Oliver notes, this concept does go back decades in coaching circles, but has yet to be noticed much by the average NBA fan.

21. According to Hollinger (2002, p. 2) here is the specific calculation for possessions employed:

$$\text{Possessions Employed} = \text{Field Goal Attempts} +$$
$$0.44 \times \text{Free Throw Attempts} + \text{Turnovers} - \text{Offensive Rebounds}.$$

Because more than one free throw can be taken on a given possession, free throw attempts, in terms of possessions, are only worth a fraction of the other three statistics. Our estimation of team rebounds allowed us to determine this specific fraction. As noted below, our estimates indicate it is equal to 0.45, or a value quite close to what Hollinger indicates. Dean Oliver (2004, p. 24), though, argued that the correct value is 0.4. We are not sure this difference matters. As we will note in Chapter Eight, you can use 0.5 and not dramatically alter your evaluation of player productivity.

22. There is a 24-second shot clock in the NBA. If a team does not take a field goal or free throw attempt in 24 seconds then the team commits a shot clock violation. The result of this violation is a turnover, since the other team is then awarded the ball. Hence, if a team does not turn the ball over, it must take a shot.

23. Team rebounds are basically an accounting device. The number of missed shots and rebounds should be equal at the end of a game. If a missed shot goes out of bounds, though, a rebound cannot be credited to an individual. Likewise, if a player misses the first of two free throws, no rebound can be recorded for an individual player. Hence, these events are also listed as team rebounds.

24. Here is the ultimate endnote. We are going to try and explain how we calculate the number of team rebounds that change possession. In the spirit of the book, the math will be minimized. For a complete description, please visit our web site. Let's begin by emphasizing that we are only interested in the number of team rebounds where a team acquired possession of the ball. This information is not reported by the NBA, but it can be estimated. To see this we begin by noting that the number of field goals a team attempts in a game must equal:

$$\text{Opponent's made field goals} + x^*\text{Opponent's free throws made}$$
$$+ \text{Opponent's Turnovers} + \text{Rebounds} - \text{Turnovers}$$
$$- z^*\text{Free throw attempts}$$

Rebounds include defensive rebounds, offensive rebounds, and team rebounds. We can estimate (x) and (z) by simply noting that each time a team gets the ball it has earned the right to take one field goal attempt. So we can construct a variable we will call Field Goal Attempt Differenced, which equals:

$$\text{Field goal attempts} - \text{Opponent's made field goals} - \text{Opponent's turnovers}$$
$$- \text{Rebounds} + \text{Turnovers}$$

Employing team data from the 1993–94 to 2004–05 seasons, we regressed Field Goal Attempt Differenced on the Opponent's free throws made and free throw attempts. From this regression we can estimate the value of (x), (z), and team rebounds. Basically our linear regression gives us the value of (x) and (z). Both were, in absolute terms, equals to 0.45. Such a value is quite close to Hollinger's estimate of 0.44. In addition to providing this value, our regression also gave us a constant term—the estimated value of Field Goal Attempt Differenced if Opponent's free throws made and Free throw attempts were zero—and an error term. The error term is the difference between the actual value of Field Goal Attempt Differenced and the value our model predicts. If you add together the constant term and the error term for each team, you now have an estimate for how many team rebounds a team accumulated that actually gave the team possession of the ball. We would add that this measure also captures the number of times a team gains possession of the ball from the opening tip-off and at the beginning of quarters. We would thank Dean Oliver for this last observation.

25. Here is the specific formula for possessions acquired:

> Opponent's field goals made + 0.45*Opponent's free throws made
> + Defensive rebounds + Team rebounds + Opponent's turnovers

26. For example, in Game Seven of the 2005 NBA Finals we estimate that the Pistons employed 81.28 possessions and acquired 81.14. The Spurs employed an estimated 81.53 possessions and acquired 81.44. Remember, we can only estimate team rebounds and the value of free throws, so our calculation of possessions is also only an estimate. Still our results indicate that each team had between 81and 82 possessions.

27. We hope our explanation appears quite simple and easy to follow. In Berri's paper (2004b) he goes through a number of equations, beginning with wins regressed on points scored and points surrendered, progressing to a discussion of what determines scoring and shot attempts, before arriving at this simple statement. As we stated, we are following the Marshallian method, so this math has been left out of our discussion here.

28. We used team regular season data from the 1993–94 season through the 2004–05 campaign. One should note that our explanatory power in the regression of wins on efficiency measures is the same as what one uncovers when you regress wins on points scored and allowed per game. This should not come as a surprise. Because possessions employed equal possessions acquired, statistically these two regressions are virtually the same models.

29. We would note that Oliver (2004), Hollinger (2002), and Bellotti (1992), among others, have attempted to derive the value of player statistics without using regression analysis. The advantage of regressions is that it allows you to estimate the value of each statistic in terms of wins. Attempting to deduce these values is not only more time consuming, it also does not give one the same accuracy a regression provides.

30. There are basically two methods one can employ to derive these values. The first method begins by regressing wins on points scored per possession employed and points allowed per possession acquired. Then one takes the derivative of wins with respect to points scored, possessions employed, points allowed, and possessions acquired. From this, one refers to the calculation of possessions employed and possessions acquired to determine the value of each of the statistics comprising these measures. If you do not like this approach, one could just regress wins on points scored and points surrendered. Then, because teams average about one point per possession—the exact number is 1.02 for the seasons stretching from 1993–94 to 2004–05—you could simply argue that one point is worth one possession. Either approach will basically result in the same values for the various statistics we list in Table 6.5.

31. Three times the value of a point scored is, after rounding, 0.100. When we subtract

the value of a field goal attempt, or 0.034, we arrive at the value of a three-point field goal that we report.

32. We do not need to consider the impact of an opponent missing a field goal or free throw. When the opponent misses a shot the team can collect the defensive rebound, which we include in our evaluation. If the opponent collects the rebound it will now have an opportunity to make a shot, miss a shot, thus creating another rebound opportunity, or turn the ball over. All of these actions are accounted for in our metric. So opponent's missed shots add nothing to our story.

33. Not all violations of the rules are personal fouls. If a player is called for traveling—or taking steps without dribbling the ball—he is not charged with a personal foul. He does commit a turnover, so traveling is actually a worse crime than hacking a player when he takes a shot.

34. The estimated value is actually 1.14. Our specific model was estimated with data from 1993–94 through the 2004–05 seasons. We included dummy variables for the years and teams examined. Our model explains about 88% of the variation in the opponent's free throws made.

35. The specific model we estimated regressed two-point field goals made by the opponent on both the opponent's two-point field goals attempted and a team's blocked shots. We estimated our blocked shot model across the same years as our model of personal fouls, and we also included dummy variables for the years and teams examined.

36. A blocked shot does not lead to a one-to-one reduction in the opponent's two-point field goals. This is likely due to the fact that only a percentage of blocked shots would have actually gone in had the shot not been deflected. We would also add that we could look at the impact blocked shots have on made three-point baskets by the opponent. Unfortunately, we do not have data on whether a player blocked a two-point or three-point attempt. We assume that most blocked shots are for two-point attempts, hence we simply restricted our examination of blocks to these shots.

37. As one can see, the value of possession statistics, in absolute terms, is basically the same. In the next chapter we will take this result and develop a simple model of player productivity. We wish to note that this result can be uncovered with a bit of adjustment to the model of productivity reported in Berri's 1999 publication. In this paper, which explicitly examined player productivity in the NBA, wins were regressed on points-per-shot, free throw percentage, free throw attempts, offensive rebounds, defensive rebounds, assist-to-turnover ratio, opponent's turnovers, and points allowed. Upon further reflection, assists do not belong in this model since once one knows shooting efficiency, knowing the passing that leads to that level of efficiency is irrelevant. In other words, as we show in Chapter Seven, assists do not directly lead to more wins by themselves, but indirectly cause teammates to produce more wins. So this is one deficiency in Berri's original work. Additionally, Berri's 1999 model ignores team rebounds. If we correct for the problem with respect to assists and team rebounds, and simply regress wins on points-per-shot, free throw percentage,

free throw attempts, offensive rebounds, defensive rebounds, team rebounds, turnovers, opponent's turnovers, and points allowed one learns the following: the impact of rebounding
and turnovers is statistically the same. At least, the Wald Test, which is a statistical test used
to determine if coefficients equal a specific value, is unable to reject the hypothesis that all
the coefficients for these variables, in a statistical sense, are the same. Consequently, Berri's
1999 work, when modified somewhat, confirms the argument we make here. Rebounds and
turnovers have the same impact on wins. Furthermore, the estimated impact of rebounds
and turnovers is 0.03, which is what we report here. We would also add that when we take
the modified Berri 1999 model and derive the value of points and field goal attempts, we
also see that these are worth 0.03 in absolute terms. Again, that is what we report here. So
whether one regresses wins on possessions and efficiency, or one regresses wins directly on
the individual statistics, the answer is essentially the same.

38. If you do not account for position one would have to argue that most wins are created in the front court. In our view, given the complementary nature of these positions, it
seems more reasonable to presume that each position on average creates the same number
of wins.

39. Our relative wins evaluation results in virtually half the players having positive productivity and the other half having negative scores. This is what happens when you evaluate people relative to an average. Actually, this statement depends on the symmetry of the
distribution. That issue, though, is not the point of this endnote—as if these endnotes have
to have a point. We wish to comment briefly on the approach Zimbalist took to measure a
baseball hitter's output. As we noted above, Zimbalist is one of the few sports economists to
use OPS, hence in this sense he moved ahead of the pack. Where we will quibble with Zimbalist is in his practice of measuring a player's value as the difference between the player's
productivity—in terms of wins and revenue—and the average player's output (1992, p.
190). By evaluating players relative to the average, the summation of player values would
simply be zero. In other words, if you argue that salary and economic value must be equal,
then the practice Zimbalist apparently employs suggests a team's aggregate payroll should
be zero. Player's who are below average should pay for the right to play—since predicted
salary is negative—and this money should just go to the players who are above average. We
follow Zimbalist when we calculate relative wins production, but we need another step to
get at the actual value of a player's productivity.

40. One could add to this list team turnovers. An example would be a 24-second clock
violation. The value of a team turnover is equal to the value of a turnover. We would also
note that in evaluating blocked shots we discussed the number of two-point field goals
made by the opponent that blocked shots erased. In evaluating team statistics, the made
two-point shots a team avoided need to be considered. Hence, in constructing our team statistic adjustment we employed both the made two-point shots an opponent accumulated,
as well as the made two-point shots by the opponent a team's blocked shots avoided.

41. Both Dan Rosenbaum and Dean Oliver have separately made an effort to assess

each player's defensive ability. So work is being completed in this area. We are not sure how to mesh their work with our calculations; still it is possible this can be done in the future.

42. We will follow a convention that we first saw in an article by Frank Scott, Jr., James Long, and Ken Sompii (1985) and later employed by Berri (1999).

43. In addition to adjusting productivity for team defense, the team statistical adjustment also accounts for the pace the team plays. Team pace is a factor many have noted to be important in evaluating a player. If a team plays at a faster pace, its players will have more statistics, and hence any statistical measure will inflate the value of these players. Our team statistical adjustment corrects for this bias.

44. We calculated the average difference, in absolute terms, between team wins and the summation of wins produced for ten seasons. From 1993–94 to 2004–05, this average difference was 2.4.

CHAPTER 7

1. The estimation of our model linking wins to offensive and defensive efficiency allows one to determine the impact of points, possessions employed, points allowed, and possessions acquired. To do this, we use a bit of calculus and take the derivative of wins with respect to these four factors. This step allows us to see why the value of these four factors is basically the same in terms of wins. The derivative of wins with respect to points scored is calculated as follows: Estimated impact offensive efficiency has on wins divided by the average number of possessions employed. The derivative of wins with respect to possessions employed is a bit more complicated. First, multiply the estimated impact offensive efficiency has on wins by the average number of points scored. Then divide the product of step one by the average number of possessions employed, squared. Finally, multiply everything by (−1). When you look at the derivative of wins with respect to points, and the derivative of wins with respect to possessions employed, there is actually only one difference mathematically. The only real difference between each calculation is that the derivative of wins with respect to possessions employed utilizes the ratio of points to possessions employed. This ratio tends to be close to one, hence the impact of points and possessions employed on wins is basically the same. The same argument can be used with respect to points allowed and possessions acquired.

2. We get ahead of ourselves with this estimation. We used our measure of wins produced that incorporated assists to estimate that Jordan produced nearly 25 wins. This choice was made because assisted wins production is ultimately the measure we will use in the stories we tell. Basically we did not want to go back and tell this particular Jordan story again once we had defined assisted wins production. We would note that his unassisted wins production is quite similar. Again, as we go along, we will explain how assists are employed in our Wins Produced metric.

3. Again, this is assisted wins production. The unassisted wins production for these players, since most were good passers, would be a bit lower. Specifically John Stockton pro-

duced 12.7 unassisted wins, Nick Anderson 12.9, Scottie Pippen 16.7, Dennis Rodman 29.9, and Shaquille O'Neal offered 26.7. The total unassisted wins produced of these five players was 98.9, which is still in excess of the 82 maximum wins possible.

4. A regression connecting current productivity to past productivity in the NBA was also presented in Berri and Krautmann (2006) and Berri (2001). Each work indicated that the Law of Diminishing Returns applies to the NBA.

5. Our sample is comprised of all players who played substantial minutes in successive seasons. By substantial, we looked at players who averaged at least twelve minutes per game and who appeared in at least twenty games. Over the time period we considered, we had 1,936 player observations. Finally, we only considered players who did not change teams in mid-season in either the current or lagged season.

6. As with our study of gate revenue, we included year-specific dummy variables. We also included dummy variables for position played, which were statistically significant for centers, power forwards, and small forwards.

7. The direction of this relationship likely goes in both directions. The better the player, the more games a coach will use the player.

8. The dummy variable for younger players was equal to one for any player with only one prior year of experience; it was zero for all other players. The dummy variable for older players was equal to one for all players with at least twelve years of experience, zero otherwise. The coefficient on our measure of older players was negative and statistically significant at the 5% level. The coefficient on our measure of younger players was positive, but only statistically significant at the 15% level.

9. We used the coaches' winning percentage before the current season began. If the team had more than one coach, we used a weighted average—weighted by the number of games coached in the current season—of the coaches' lifetime records. For rookie coaches, we employed the average lifetime rookie coaching records of all coaches used in our sample. We employed two rookie averages, one for coaches whose first season was a full schedule. Another average was constructed for coaches who began their head coaching careers in the middle of a season.

10. To calculate the productivity of a player's teammates we measured each player's unassisted wins production. For each player we subtracted the number of unassisted wins the player produced from the team's total unassisted wins produced. We also subtracted the number of minutes the player played from team minutes. In other words, we calculated the number of unassisted wins produced by a player's teammates and the number of minutes these players played. With these two calculations in hand, we then divided the teammate's unassisted wins production by the minutes these teammates played. This calculation yielded the per-minute productivity of a player's teammates.

11. To calculate the teammates' assists we followed the same steps we employed to measure teammate win production. Specifically we divided assists accumulated by a player's teammates by the minutes these teammates played.

12. Here are the specific steps we followed to determine the value of an assist. From our per-minute productivity model we learned that a one unit increase in team assists increased per-minute productivity by 0.64. We adjusted per-minute unassisted productivity for each player in 2004–05 for the quantity of assists accumulated by the player's teammates. Next we determined for each team in 2004–05 the quantity of a team's simple unassisted productivity that was determined and not determined by assists. We then allocated the quantity of production that was due to assists across the members of the team according to the number of assists each player accumulated. Once this allocation was complete, we had a simple measure of unassisted productivity that was adjusted for assists. We wondered then how much assists matter. So we regressed our adjusted per-minute productivity on both our simple unassisted per-minute measure and the number of assists the player had accumulated per minute. The coefficient on assists from this regression was 0.67. From this we concluded that each assist was worth 0.67 the value of a point, rebound, etc. or everything of equal value in our simple unassisted productivity model.

We would add that John Hollinger (2002) argued that a scoring play involving an assist involves three parts. A player must get open, a teammate must pass him the ball, and then the player must make the shot. The passer takes one of these three actions, so according to Hollinger the passer should receive a third of the credit of a made shot. So on a two-point basket, an assist is worth 0.67 points. Although Hollinger's logic echoes Oliver's difficulty theorem, his valuation of an assist is actually consistent with what we found.

13. We measured productivity with the precise values of each variable and with the simple Win Score model. Per-minute productivity and per-minute Win Score have a 99% correlation. In other words, using the exact values does not have any significant impact on the evaluation of players.

14. With the numerous performance indices developed in baseball and basketball, naming a new index is difficult. John Hollinger (2002) calls one of his indices Game Score. Hopefully no one has called an index previously developed any name closer to our choice of Win Score.

15. Our model has one point of similarity to the formula for the IBM award, which also considered field goal attempts rather than missed shots. The IBM model, though, stated that assists, blocked shots, and personal fouls were equal in value—in absolute terms—to points, rebounds, steals, and turnovers. The IBM model also weighted player statistics by team wins and a team's statistical production.

16. To measure each player's Wins Produced we followed the same steps we employed to measure unassisted wins production. Now, though, we incorporated the value of an assist in calculating the value of each player's statistical production. We also included a team's accumulation of assists in our team statistical adjustment. Basically every player's unassisted production was reduced by the number of assists on the team and augmented by the number of assists the player accumulated. If a player was a primary source for assists on his team, his value rises. If not, once assists are noted, a player's estimated value will fall.

17. The specific number is 0.00626. Per minute Shaq produced this many wins. Discussing numbers that are this small typically gives us a headache.

18. It is important to note that the league MVP is based solely on regular season performance. We would also add that the relationship between league MVP, NBA Efficiency, and wins production were discussed in a working paper by David Berri and Aju Fenn (2004).

19. First-place votes alone do not determine the league's MVP. The winner of this award is actually determined in the following fashion. Each member of the voting media lists five players on his or her ballot. The first person listed receives 10 voting points, second is worth 7 points, 5 points are awarded for third, with 3 and 1 point awarded for fourth and fifth places respectively. The player with the most points is given the award. In 2005 Nash had 1,066 voting points while O'Neal earned only 1,032. Data on the MVP voting award were taken from Basketball-Reference.com.

20. In Berri's 1999 attempt to measure player productivity his results indicated that Dennis Rodman was the most productive player in the NBA in 1997–98. Dean Oliver objected to this result, and after many, many, many emails, finally convinced Berri that he (Oliver) was right. Berri's original wins model had overvalued the contribution of rebounds and turnovers. At the end of the day, Berri was also right. Even with the model described here, where wins are connected to offensive and defensive efficiency, Rodman is still the most productive player in 1997–98. So this was one of those happy endings where everyone got to be right.

21. It is still possible to sign for more than $20 million. The maximum contract a player can sign, according to NBA.com, is 25% of the NBA's payroll cap or 105% of the player's salary in the last year of his last contract. So if a player's contract called for him to make $20 million before the maximum salary cap was enacted, he could sign for $20 million after the cap on individual salaries was enacted.

22. Such a conclusion is consistent with the Roland Ratings, which as we noted, look at how a team does on the floor with and without a specific player. Roland Beech's ratings only go back to the 2002–03 season, so the sample of Iverson's net plus-minus is only three seasons. Still, in these three seasons Iverson never placed better than fourth on the 76ers in net plus-minus.

CHAPTER 8

1. *Sinatra Live in Paris: Frank Sinatra and Sextet.* Reprise Records. 1994. Originally Recorded: June 6, 1962. A question readers might want to ponder: Which was the more obscure beginning to a chapter – the reference to David Hume in chapter three or the Sinatra reference at the onset of this chapter? Perhaps this would be a good question to pose on our web site.

2. Jordan averaged about 39 minutes per game in his career. In a 48-minute game there are 240 player minutes available, so with Jordan, a team has 201 minutes to allocate. If the players in those 201 minutes are average, or produce 0.100 WP48, then they will produce a

bit more than 34 wins. Jordan, if his WP48 is 0.406, would be worth nearly 27 wins. Hence, Jordan and a collection of average players are worth 61 wins.

3. Now we need to clarify that statement just a bit. Commentators often seem to be from Lake Wobegone where all the children are above average. When describing a player who plays poorly, commentators will say, "that player is just average." If a distribution of players is both normal and symmetrical, then the median and mean will be equal. In this instance, half the players will be above average and half will be below. So if a player is "just average," he is still better than half the players in the league.

4. In the 1980s people debated the relative merits of Magic, MJ, and Larry Bird. If Bird is thought of as a small forward, and in a frontcourt of Robert Parish and Kevin McHale Bird would play this position, then Bird's career wins production was quite close but not equal to what MJ achieved. Since Bird played fewer minutes in his career, his WP48 at small forward would be higher than Jordan, though still behind Magic's mark. If you place Bird at power forward, though, he is clearly the least productive of these three stars.

5. Like the NBA, the NHL also uses a lottery to assign draft choices.

6. Gordon did start three games in 2004–05.

7. Our examination of post-season performance in the NBA is based on an article by Berri and Eschker (2005). This paper used a model like Win Score, but it excluded personal fouls, blocked shots, and assists. It also only examined 1995 to 2003. The conclusions reached, though, were very much the same.

8. We stated back in Chapter Five that Jordan did increase his per-game scoring from the regular season to the playoffs. As we note in Chapter Ten, scoring tends to be the primary statistic people focus upon in evaluating players. We also note in Chapter Ten that when one only focuses on scoring, mistaken conclusions will be reached.

9. Ten games is not much of a sample. As we show, though, players who play at least ten playoff games are almost as consistent from regular season to post-season as we observe players perform from year to year.

10. We should note that Manu Ginobili may be a "prime-time" performer. We restricted our sample to players who had four extended post-seasons. As of 2005, Ginobili had played only three seasons. In all three seasons his playoff Win Score eclipsed his regular season performance. We suspect, given our analysis of all players from 1995 to 2005 and our study of the game's major stars, that as people recognize Ginobili's abilities defenses will begin focusing more attention on Manu during the post-season. As this happens, his performance will probably decline.

11. Sixteen teams make the playoffs each year. These teams are the eight teams with the best record in the Eastern and Western conferences. Prior to the 2004–05 season, each conference was divided into two divisions. A team was given a one seed if it had the best record in the conference. A two seed was given to the team leading the division not occupied by the best team in the conference. The remaining six teams were seeded in order of the team's winning percentage.

CHAPTER 9

1. It may not be obvious, but some thought is given to chapter titles and section headings. The title to this section is inspired by Brett Favre's appearance in the movie *There's Something about Mary*, where Favre convincingly played the role of an NFL quarterback named Brett Favre who happened to be the long-lost love interest of Mary—played by Cameron Diaz. We thank Rich Campbell for suggesting the title to this section.

2. The pattern we note in Favre's 2004 performance was first observed by Reuban Frank (2004) at SI.com. Favre's game-by-game data, which we report in Table 9.1, were taken from Yahoo.com.

3. ESPN.com, as well as other web sites, reports the steps necessary to calculate a quarterback's rating.

4. Although the quarterback rating system appears arbitrary, there is a certain logic behind the formula. Don Steinberg (2001) of GQ tracked down the creator of the system, Don Smith. From Steinberg's interview we learn that Smith was an executive with the Pro Football Hall of Fame in 1971. Given his reputation as someone who understood statistics and football, he was asked to create a standardized measure that would allow one to compare quarterbacks from different years. Smith took the four primary statistics tracked for quarterbacks (completion percentage, yards per pass attempt, touchdowns per pass attempt, and interceptions per pass attempt) and created a scale that would give a quarterback one point for an average performance, two points for a extraordinary effort, and zero points for very low productivity. The formula Smith developed is designed around this point system.

5. The model we describe is detailed in an unpublished paper by Berri (2005) entitled "Back to Back Evaluations on the Gridiron." This model was also employed by Berri and Simmons (2005).

6. Team and player data for the NFL from 1995 to 2004 can be found in various issues of the *National Football League Record and Fact Book* as well as various issues of the *Sporting News 2005 Pro Football Guide*. For the 2005 player data we consulted NFL Statistics—Yahoo! Sports. We also utilized the Yahoo! site for all data on fumbles and fumbles lost for individual quarterbacks.

7. We would note that our source of data for the 1995 to 2003 seasons did not record the number of opponent kick-offs. Given that kick-offs occur after a touchdown, a field goal, and once at either the start of the game or the start of the second half, we were able to estimate this variable. We compared our estimate to the number of kick-offs listed for 2004 at ESPN.com. The correlation between our predicated number of kick-offs and the actual number recorded was 0.98, suggesting our measure was a reasonable approximation.

8. A team also can gain possession of the ball when the opponent turns the ball over on downs. Our source of data (*NFL Record and Fact Book*) does not record this event.

9. One should note that passing yards and yards from receptions are not the same. Reception yards are yards gained from completed passes. Passing yards subtract from recep-

tion yards the yardage lost from being sacked. Hence, the impact of sacks is noted in the tabulation of passing yards.

10. Unfortunately, the *NFL Fact and Record Book* does not record penalties by a team that were committed by the team's offense, or penalties by the team's opponent that were only committed by the team's defense. We would suspect that a team losing yardage from offensive holding has a greater impact on offensive scoring than the same team giving the opponent yardage from defensive pass interference. The data source we employ, though, does not allow us to separate penalties committed by a team's offense and defense.

11. David Romer (forthcoming in 2006) has presented evidence that NFL coaches are far more conservative on fourth down relative to what the data suggest. Romer's work builds on a basic rule in economics: If the expected benefits of an action exceed the expected costs, then you should take the action. Romer finds that often coaches choose to punt even though the expected benefits of going for a first down on fourth down exceed the expected costs. In Chapter Ten we will examine decision making in the NBA. Romer's work suggests more study needs to be offered in the future into decision making in American football.

12. Teams can maintain possession and not score if the second or fourth quarter ends.

13. In looking over the data offered by the NFL, we uncovered a problem with the NFL's tracking of points scored. In baseball and basketball, points are only scored by a team's offense and only allowed by the team's defense. In football, scoring is a bit more complicated. Although most points are scored by a team's offense, some points are scored by a team's defense and special teams. If we wished to evaluate a team's offensive capabilities we want to focus solely on the points scored by a team's offense. To measure these points, we began by noting that a team's offense can score touchdowns via its rushing and passing attack. Each of these touchdowns also presents an opportunity for an extra point. Finally, if a team fails to score a touchdown, a team can also score points via field goals. A problem exists because the NFL does not record how many extra points are derived from offensive touchdowns and how many come from touchdowns generated by a team's special teams or defense. To overcome the problem of extra points, we looked at the percentage of touchdowns scored by the team's offense and assumed that this percentage represented the percentage of extra points scored after offensive touchdowns.

14. We should note that our model was estimated with team data taken from the 1995 to 2004 seasons. We employed both team fixed effects and dummy variables for each year in the estimation of our model. The estimation of our model across these data reveals that nearly all of our coefficients are of the expected sign and are statistically different from zero. The lone exceptions are the opponent's missed field goals and interception return average. Although these variables have the expected sign, the t-statistics suggest neither corresponding coefficient is different from zero. Our model explains 87% of the variation in points scored. Are there any missing variables that might enhance our explanatory power? One should note that although we have yardage gained, we do not know precisely where each

team began its drive. In other words, if a team's average starting position is at the 20, and the team averages 60 yards per drive, this is not quite as good as a team starting at its own 40 and averaging 50 yards per drive. Although factors like return yards give us an indication of starting position, these factors are only proxies for these missing variables.

15. We cannot include touchdown passes in our model since one cannot regress one variable (points) on another variable that is essentially the same (touchdowns). We would note that the omission of touchdown passes thrown is quite similar to measures of performance in baseball, like batting average, slugging percentage, and on-base percentage, that omit runs scored and runs batted in.

16. Technically a quarterback could also play defense on any turnover by the offense. It seems, though, the interest in tackling increases for a quarterback when he throws an interception.

17. We estimated our model of team defense for ten years of data, beginning in 1995. Our model explains 83% of the variation in the points a team's defense allows. Like our model of offensive scoring, our model of points allowed by a team's defense focused solely on points scored by an opponent's offense. We should note that we again employed both team fixed effects and dummy variables for each year in the estimation of our model. Once again, virtually every coefficient is statistically different from zero. The exception is kickoffs, which is close to being statistically significant at the 5% level, and the opponent's interception return average. As noted, interception return average was not significant in our model of offensive scoring, suggesting this variable does not substantially impact the number of points an offense scores or a defense allows.

18. Our QB Score measure is similar to the metric developed by Allen Barra (1986). Barra multiplies interceptions by 50 and subtracts this from gross passing yards. He then takes this result and divides by the number of passes thrown. We would like to note that these measures of a quarterback's productivity should not be considered the final word on this subject. The work offered by Aaron Schatz (2005) and the people at FootballOutsiders.com, published annually in the *Pro Football Prospectus*, goes beyond our measures of Net Points, Wins Produced, and Win Score. For those interested in measures with more complexity, their work is recommended.

19. We only look at net points per play. Per play Brady produced 0.00461 wins, while McNabb produced 0.00710 wins. As we said, thinking about tiny numbers can make your head hurt. So these are omitted from our evaluation of quarterbacks.

20. These results were based upon player data taken from twelve years, beginning in 1993–94 and ending with the 2004–05 campaign. To be included in the data set a player had to play at least twelve minutes per game in the current and past campaign and appear in twenty games each season. We should note that explanatory power drops when one considered WP48. Only 54% of current WP48 is explained by past performance. The primary difference lies in the adjustment WP48 makes to position played. Win Score and NBA Efficiency do not adjust for position played. Hence, these measures tend to be dominated by frontcourt players. When one adjusts for position this upward bias is corrected, and the

consistency in performance drops. As we will see, though, even with this adjustment NBA players are more consistent than what we observe in the NFL and Major League Baseball.

21. This result is odd, since we would expect younger players to actually show improvement. This result suggests that quarterbacks after their first season become systematically worse.

22. Like our discussion of the NBA, this was the coaches' record and experience level before the current season being examined.

23. Just to be clear to current and future students taking our classes, this is not how we grade in our classes.

24. We used the baseball data from Sean Lahman's Baseball Archive [www.baseball1.com].

25. We specifically follow the lead of Asher Blass, who presented a model of runs scored in an article published in 1992. Like Blass we regressed the number of runs a team scored in the regular season on each team's accumulation of singles, doubles, triples, non-intentional walks, hit batsmen, stolen bases, sacrifice flies, the summation of double plays and caught stealing, and outs. Blass's model used data from 1976 to 1986 and explained 95% of the variation in runs scored. His work indicated that a single was worth 0.52 runs, a double 0.63, a triple 0.85, and a home run was valued at 1.38 runs scored.

26. On-base percentage is a measure of how many times a player reaches base per plate appearance. To calculate this, add together the number of hits, walks, and hit by pitches a player accumulates and then divide by at-bats, walks, hit by pitches, and sacrifice flies.

27. Schwarz (2004, p. 124). Schwarz also notes that Bill James independently created the same measure (p. 124). Barra (2002, pp. 200–201) tells the story of how SLOB was created. Interestingly he credits George Ignatin, an economics professor at the University of Alabama-Birmingham where Barra was a student in the 1970s.

28. Interestingly, despite all these perfectly suitable measures, many of our fellow sports economists still follow the lead of Scully and measure a batter's productivity with slugging percentage. One of the key exceptions to this practice can be found in the work of Andrew Zimbalist, who used OPS in his 1992 study of baseball. Still, many others, and we will not name names here, followed the example of Scully. Well, we shall break with this odd tradition here.

29. We were actually a bit surprised that baseball players were this inconsistent. Our research on baseball has not focused on player productivity, so we thought we might have made a mistake working with a data set where we are not as experienced. To check our work, we asked John-Charles Bradbury and Jahn Hakes, two economists who have extensive experience working with baseball's productivity measures, to also look at how consistent baseball players were across time. Independently Bradbury and Hakes confirmed our general finding. We would like to thank both for their assistance.

30. If we grade players according to WP48 we find that 42% of players maintain their grade. Again, once you adjust for position, consistency is somewhat lessened. Again, though, NBA players are still more consistent than NFL or Major League Baseball players.

31. If we use WP48 to grade players we see that 19% of players changed more than two spots in their grade. Again, players are not quite as consistent when we adjust for position played, but more consistent than what we see in baseball or football.

CHAPTER 10

1. Robinson signed his contract after missing training camp in 1994. Five games into his NBA career Glenn Robinson made the following observation quoted in an Associated Press article written by Jim Litke (1994): "I expect to do what I'm supposed to do. But a lot of people that don't know the game, they think it's all about scoring. I look at it from a team perspective. We have to do well as a team. I don't need to go out there and score 30 points a game and have us lose. That won't do us any good. It would help me individually." Robinson added: "But I want to see all of us get something done." So a very young Robinson notes that scoring helps him individually but may not help the team. It is interesting that this quote captures the essence of the argument we make in this chapter. Scoring does help a player earn more money. Wins, though, are about more than scoring.

2. In 1998–99 the NBA's regular season was only 50 games due to the lockout. Consequently, in calculating Robinson's cost per win, per game, and per minute, we adjusted Robinson's averages for the shortened season. The salary reported for 1998–99 is the wage called for if the lockout had not occurred.

3. For example, Emeka Okafor was the first person taken in the 2004 draft. He received a four-year contract worth $17.5 million. His team, the Charlotte Bobcats, also has an option for a fifth year, which means Okafor may not face a completely free market until he has played five seasons in the NBA.

4. A player taken in the second round is not given the same guaranteed contract offered first round choices. If such a player is perceived to be good, his actual salary can increase dramatically after his rookie contract expires. The best recent example of this is Gilbert Arenas. Arenas was taken in the second round by the Golden State Warriors in 2001. After only two years with the Warriors he became a free agent and received a six-year contract worth $64 million from the Washington Wizards. Kwame Brown was taken with the first pick of the 2001 draft, again by the Washington Wizards. Brown's rookie contract called for him to be paid $17.29 million over four years.

5. According to USA Today, NBA teams paid $1.66 billion in salaries in 2004–05. According to our count, 463 players played that season, so the average salary was $3.6 million. If we look at the 419 players whose salary USA Today reports, the average wage paid is $3.9 million.

6. For those following along with the endnotes, this statement is a review from Chapter Five. For those who are just looking at the endnotes now, there are more details on the relationship between gate revenue and team scoring in the endnotes to the fifth chapter.

7. As noted by Amitai Etzioni (1988, p. 145), instrumental rationality has also been called calculative rationality, intentional rationality, or procedural rationality.

8. This definition comes from Etzioni (1988, p. 136).

9. According to the voting record reported by Basketball-Reference.com, 49 rookies received votes from 1996 to 2005.

10. A coach cannot vote for players on his team, so the maximum voting points a player could receive in the 30-team NBA in 2004–05 is 58. From 1995–96 to 2003–04 only 29 teams played in the NBA, so the maximum points was only 56. Prior to 1995–96 only 27 teams played, so maximum points was only 52. The voting data we used were taken from the web site of Patricia Bender.

11. As we have stated, in 1998–99 only 50 games were played. To allow us to compare rookies from this season to the other years we consider, the production of wins listed for Paul Pierce and Vince Carter is what these players would have produced had the season been 82 games. In other words, we simply multiplied these players' Wins Produced by 82/50.

12. As we noted, the number of maximum voting points a player could receive depends upon the number of teams in the league. Given that the number of teams increased from 27 to 30 in our sample, we adjusted the number of voting points a player received so we could make a comparison across the years we considered. Specifically, we adjusted upward, so that a player who received 52 voting points in 1995, the maximum possible in a league of 27 teams, was given 58 voting points or the maximum possible in 2005.

13. There are two rounds to the NBA draft across the time period we examined. In 2004, because Minnesota lost its first-round draft choice due to a violation of salary cap rules, 29 players were taken in the first round and 30 were taken in round two. From 1996 to 2003, with 29 teams selecting, 58 players were taken in the annual draft. Prior to 1996, the last player taken was the 54th player chosen. Some players in our data set, though, were not drafted. For those players we assigned a draft position of 60.

14. The NBA Efficiency measure varies depending upon position played. On a per-minute basis, power forwards and centers average between .49 and .50, while small forwards and guards range from 0.41 to 0.43. To overcome this position bias, we calculated a position adjusted NBA Efficiency measure. Specifically we determined each rookie's per-minute NBA Efficiency value. We then subtracted the average at each position, and then added back the average value for NBA Efficiency across all positions, or 0.45. Once we took these steps, we then multiplied what we had by the number of minutes a player played. For example, Tim Duncan's per-minute NBA Efficiency was 0.677 in his rookie season of 1997–98. The average power forward has a per-minute measure of 0.49. We subtracted this value from 0.677, then added back 0.45, or the average value across all players. This value of 0.638 was then multiplied by Duncan's minutes of 3,204 to give us Duncan's position adjusted NBA Efficiency measure; which was 2,044. All of this effort did not change the fit of our model. If we use NBA Efficiency our model explains 73% of the variation in voting, while when we adjust by position, explanatory power was exactly the same. In the end, not much of a return for a fair amount of effort. Still, our analysis suggests that coaches understand that productivity does vary by position played.

15. Here are a few more details regarding our voting points model. We included in our study all players who received votes, as well as all rookies who did not receive votes yet who

played at least twelve minutes per game and appeared in 41 contests. In other words, we considered rookies with zero votes who conceivably could have been considered for these teams. There is an interesting feature common to both ends of our sample. If a player received the maximum number of votes possible, improvements in performance would not lead to more votes. For those who received zero votes, further declines in performance would not have reduced the number of votes received. Consequently, we estimated a TOBIT or censored model, which one can learn about in any number of econometric textbooks. In all we had 294 observations, of which 200 were uncensored. We would also note that we estimated a double-logged model, rather than a linear model. Again, details on the difference would be in any good econometrics book.

16. We also consider position played in our model. Although we did adjust for position played in our measure of productivity, we still wondered whether position played in itself impacted the coaches' evaluations. Specifically we wondered if centers garnered more attention independent of productivity. Our results indicate that this was not the case. We included position played in each of our voting models, and this was not a significant factor for any specification.

17. This result is consistent with the work of B. M. Staw and Ha Hoang (1995) and Colin F. Camerer and Roberto A. Weber (1999). Each of these authors examined the escalation of commitment in the NBA, defined by Camerer and Weber (pp. 59–60) as follows: "when people or organizations who have committed resources to a project are inclined to 'throw good money after bad' and maintain or increase their commitment to a project, even when its marginal costs exceed marginal benefits." With respect to the NBA, Staw and Hoang (1995) and Camerer and Weber (1999) investigated the impact a player's draft position has on playing time. Both of these sets of authors offer evidence that, after controlling for the prior performance of the player, where a player was chosen in the draft still impacts the amount of playing time the player receives after the first two years of the player's career. Such a finding suggests that NBA decision makers are slow to adopt new information, maintaining an assessment of a player when the available evidence suggests that the initial perspective is incorrect.

18. A potential problem with Wins Produced is that it includes adjustments for team statistics that perhaps coaches would not consider in evaluating specific individuals. Consequently, we considered evaluating players with Win Score, adjusted for position played but not for team statistics. It is important to note that we followed the same steps adjusting Win Score for position that we followed with respect to NBA Efficiency. When our position-adjusted Win Score metric was employed, explanatory power rose to 60%. Hence even when we extract out the team statistics from Wins Produced, it is still the case that NBA Efficiency is the preferred measure.

19. We also adjusted points scored by position played to account for position differences. Once again, explanatory power was the same. We also considered both total points scored and points scored per game and found total points offered greater explanatory power.

20. We adjusted rebounds, steals, blocked shots, assists, turnovers, and personal fouls for position played. All of these are totals, not per-game or per-minute measures. Shooting efficiency for field goal attempts was measured via points-per-shot or points-per-field goal attempt. As we stated earlier, this is calculated by subtracting free throws made from total points scored and dividing by field goals attempted. Free throw percentage, or free throws made divided by free throws attempted, was used to measure shooting efficiency on free throws. Neither shooting efficiency measure was adjusted for position played.

21. We would note that draft position has the smallest impact of those factors that were statistically significant. A 10% change in draft position only changes voting points received by 2.5%.

22. We used a double-logged functional form in estimating this model. If we used a linear model then we find that in addition to draft position, points scored, rebounds, and shooting efficiency on field goal attempts, the linear model also indicates that assists, turnovers, and free throw efficiency were also statistically significant. Blocked shots, steals, and personal fouls were still insignificant. When we look at how responsive voting points were to each of the individual statistics, the linear model still tells us that points scored is the most important. A 10% increase in points scored leads to a 16% increase in voting points. With respect to shooting efficiency on field goal attempts, a 10% improvement is expected to lead to a 10% increase in voting points received. A 10% increase in any of the other statistically significant factors would lead to a less than 10% change in a player's votes. We did use the test for functional form developed by J. Mackinnon, H. White, and R. Davidson (1983) and the test was inconclusive.

23. By looking at players who recently signed contracts we are following the example of Jeffery Jenkins (1996).

24. Let's note a few econometric issues. Following convention, we employed a double-logged functional form rather than a linear model. In addition to the variables we list in Table 10.7 we also used year-specific dummy variables, which was only significant for the year 2004. Finally, our data set had 238 observations.

25. Dummy variables for center, power forward, shooting guard, and point guard were employed. We also estimated separate regressions for guards and big men. When we looked at guards—shooting guards and point guards—we found that salary was statistically related to scoring, blocked shots, assists, star power, and being old. Of these, scoring was the most important. All other productivity factors were not significant. For big men—power forwards and centers—only scoring and blocked shots were significant. Again, scoring was the most important. Nothing else, including star power and age, was found to matter for big men. The basic story from our examinations of positions was still what we report in the chapter. Scoring dominates the determination of pay in the NBA.

26. We used the same population measure we used in our study of gate revenue.

27. Various studies employing data from the 1980s found evidence that blacks were paid a lower wage for equivalent productivity. The aforementioned work of Jeffery Jenkins (1996) examined the 1980s and 1990s with a data set comprised entirely of free agents.

Jenkins reasoned that the link between productivity and pay would be strongest at the time the salary was determined. With this restricted data set Jenkins found no evidence of salary discrimination. Later studies using more recent data and a variety of more sophisticated statistical techniques also found little evidence of discrimination. The exceptions to this general statement can be found in the study offered by Barton Hughes Hamilton (1997), who reported a premium paid to white players in the upper end of the NBA's income distribution; and the work of Erick Eschker, Stephen J. Perez, and Mark V. Siegler (2004), who found evidence of discrimination for the 1998–99 season. One should note we believe Jenkins is still the only published writer to restrict the data to recently signed free agents.

28. A full comparison of these various racial discrimination studies was conducted by Berri (2006). We would note one specific study Berri reviewed. The importance of scoring was explicitly highlighted in the work of Ha Hoang and Dan Rascher (1999). In an examination of the determinants of employment in the NBA, which did present evidence of a racial bias against blacks, Hoang and Rascher found that points scored was the only player productivity factor to statistically impact the likelihood a player would lose his job.

29. Like our study of the voting for the All-Rookie team, all performance measures were adjusted for position played. Again, the impact on our results from this adjustment was quite small.

30. We should note that we do not think we could construct a model that could explain all of the salary a player is paid. Salary data tend to be "noisy." What do we mean by that? Well, no matter which performance measure we employed, there was always at least 30% of player salary that we could not explain. As any fan of sports has seen, the pay some players receive appears to defy explanation. Occasionally a general manager "falls in love" with a player and consequently the pay the player receives appears quite different from what one might expect just looking at the athlete and his performance. Further complicating matters, the NBA has a collection of rules teams must follow in structuring contracts, including payroll caps, salary caps, and various exemptions that also alter the pay any player receives. Finally, and this may be the most important issue, player salary is a statement of what the team expects the player to do in the future. We have seen that NBA players are, relative to baseball and football, more consistent. Still, like a mutual fund, past performance is no guarantee of future returns. Such uncertainty further complicates our study of salaries.

31. Again we considered Win Score, adjusted for position played. When this performance metric is considered explanatory power rises to 53%. Like our study of the All-Rookie team, Win Score is a better predictor of player salary than Wins Produced, but not quite as good as the NBA's Efficiency measure.

32. We also considered using the player's accumulation of all these statistics from two seasons ago. When we did this, the two-year values of everything were insignificant, except turnovers. Our model suggested that the more turnovers the player committed two years ago the higher his salary would be. Given the correlation between current and lagged performance, such a result is suspect.

33. We also used year-specific dummies. In predicting salary we used the estimated impact of the dummy variable for 2004 on salary.

34. According to NBA.com, the payroll cap for 2004–05 was $43.87 million. A player signing a maximum contract with six or fewer years of experience receives an initial salary of 25% of the salary cap. If the cap stayed the same when James became a free agent, his first-year salary with a maximum contract would pay him nearly $11 million. If he re-signed with his current team, the Cleveland Cavaliers, he would be eligible for a salary increase of 12.5% per season of the contract, which could be extended to seven seasons. Given these numbers, the total value of a maximum contract signed by James would be $112 million, or $16 million per season.

35. In North's words (1994, p. 360): "Individuals typically act on incomplete information with subjectively derived models that are frequently erroneous; the information feedback is typically insufficient to correct these subjective models."

36. The number of researchers in this group is actually quite large. In fact there is a field of behavioral economics, led by the likes of Richard Thaler and Colin Camerer, which is devoted to the study of how people actually make economic decisions. So we could discuss any number of additional researchers. We do want to comment briefly on the work of 2002 Nobel Laureate Daniel Kahneman (2003, p. 163), whose research with Amos Tversky provided "a direct challenge to the rationality assumption itself, based on experimental demonstrations in which preferences were affected predictably by the framing of decision problems, or by the procedure used to elicit preferences." In addition to his work on human rationality, Amos Tversky also furthered our understanding of basketball. In a 1985 article Tversky and two co-authors (Gilovich and Vallone) presented evidence that the "hot hand," or the ability of basketball players to temporarily reach a "zone" where hitting shots becomes easier, does not actually exist.

37. To further illustrate this point, Lee and Berri (2004) examined the relationship between the number of wins a team achieved and the productivity of its players in the previous season. This work indicates that between 65% and 75% of current wins can be explained by what a team's players did in the prior season. In other words, knowing past productivity allows one to predict better than one could if all you knew was the current salary players were scheduled to be paid.

38. To illustrate this point, when the Detroit Pistons traded Dennis Rodman to the San Antonio Spurs for Sean Elliott and David Wood in October 1993, Berri was convinced this move was going to allow the Pistons to contend for a title. Elliott was taken with the third pick in the 1989 draft and in his fourth season with the Spurs averaged 17.2 points per game in 1992–93. Rodman, who had some on-court and off-court problems, only averaged 7.5 points per contest that season. The trade, though, was a disaster for Detroit. The Pistons won 40 games in 1992–93 with Rodman only playing 60 games. The Spurs won 49 games with Elliott as the team's starting small forward. In 1993–94, the Spurs improved to 55 games while the Pistons only won 20 contests. Had Berri and the Pistons calculated each

player's Wins Produced from 1992–93, the enthusiasm for this trade would have been far less. In 1992–93 Rodman produced 24.5 wins, while Elliott and Wood only offered 5.9 wins to the Spurs. The next season Elliott and Wood produced 1.5 wins for the Pistons and the Spurs received 29.6 wins from Rodman. Looking at the data today we now can see that this trade worked out as one would expect given the difference in each player's productivity.

REFERENCES

Barra, Allen. 1986. *Football by the Numbers*. Upper Saddle River, N.J.: Prentice Hall.

———. 2002. *Clearing the Bases: The Greatest Baseball Debates of the Last Century*. New York: Thomas Dunne Books.

Barrero, Jim. 2002. "Fans Hate to Hear It, but They Do Come Back." *Los Angeles Times*, August 18, Sports, Part 4, p. 2.

Bellotti, Bob. 1992. *The Points Created Basketball Book 1991–92*. New Brunswick, N.J.: Night Work Publishing.

Berri, David J. 1999. "Who Is Most Valuable? Measuring the Player's Production of Wins in the National Basketball Association." *Managerial and Decision Economics,* 20, no. 8 (Fall), 411–427.

———. 2001. "Mixing the Princes and the Paupers: A Case Study of Worker Productivity and Pay Inequality." Presented at the Western Economic Association, San Francisco, California in July.

———. 2004a. "Is There a Short Supply of Tall People in the College Game?" In *Economics of Collegiate Sports*, eds. John Fizel and Rodney Fort (pp. 211–223). Westport, Conn.: Praeger.

———. 2004b. "A Simple Measure of Worker Productivity in the National Basketball Association." Working paper.

———. 2005. "Back to Back Evaluations on the Gridiron." Working paper.

———. 2006. "Economics and the National Basketball Association: Surveying the Literature at the Tip-off." In *The Handbook of Sports Economic Research*, ed. John Fizel (pp. 21-48). Armonk, NY.: M.E. Sharpe.

Berri, David J., and Stacey L. Brook. 1999. "Trading Players in the National Basketball Association: For Better or Worse?" In *Sports Economics: Current Research*, ed. John Fizel, Elizabeth Gustafson, and Larry Hadley (pp. 135–151). Westport, Conn.: Praeger.

Berri, David J., Stacey L. Brook, Aju Fenn, Bernd Frick, and Roberto Vicente-Mayoral. 2005. "The Short Supply of Tall People: Explaining Competitive Imbalance in the National Basketball Association." *Journal of Economic Issues*, 39, no. 4 (December), 1029–1041.

Berri, David J., Stacey L. Brook, and Martin B. Schmidt. 2004. "Does One Simply Need to Score to Score?" Presented at the Western Economic Association; Vancouver, British Columbia, in July.

Berri, David J., and Erick Eschker. 2005. "Performance When It Counts: Playoff Productivity and the Playoffs in the NBA." *Journal of Economic Issues*, 39, no. 3 (September), 798–807.

Berri, David, and Aju Fenn. 2004. "Is the Sports Media Color-Blind?" Presented at the Southern Economic Association, New Orleans, Louisiana, in November.

Berri, David J., and Todd Jewell. 2004. "Wage Inequality and Firm Performance: Examining a Natural Experiment from Professional Basketball." *Atlantic Economic Journal*, 32, no. 2 (June), 130–139.

Berri, David J., and Anthony Krautmann. 2006. "Shirking on the Court: Testing for the Dis-Incentive Effects of Guaranteed Pay." *Economic Inquiry*. (February 1): 10.1093/ei/cbj033.

Berri, David J., and Martin B. Schmidt. 2002. "Instrumental vs. Bounded Rationality: The Case of Major League Baseball and the National Basketball Association." *Journal of Socio-Economics* (formerly the *Journal of Behavioral Economics*), 31, no. 3, 191–214.

———. Forthcoming in November 2006. "On the Road with the National Basketball Association's Superstar Externality." *Journal of Sports Economics*.

Berri David J., Martin B. Schmidt, and Stacey L. Brook. 2004. "Stars at the Gate: The Impact of Star Power on NBA Gate Revenues." *Journal of Sports Economics*, 5, no. 1 (February), 33–50.

Berri, David J., and Rob Simmons. 2005. "Race and the Evaluation of Signal Callers in the National Football League." Presented at the Western Social Science Association, Albuquerque, New Mexico, in April.

Blass, Asher. 1992. "Does the Baseball Labor Market Contradict the Human Capital Model of Investment?" *Review of Economics and Statistics*, 74, no. 2, 261–268.

Burger, John D., and Stephen J. K. Walters. 2003. "Market Size, Pay, and Performance: A General Model and Application to Major League Baseball." *Journal of Sports Economics*, 4, no. 2 (May), 108–125.

Camerer, Colin F., and Roberto A. Weber. 1999. "The Econometrics and Behavioral Economics of Escalation of Commitment: A Re-Examination of Staw and Hoang's NBA Data." *Journal of Economic Behavior and Organization*, 39, 59–82.

Cavalaris, Chuck. 2002. "Fans Warn Against Baseball Stoppage." *Knoxville News-Sentinel (Tennessee)*, p. C2; August 18, Sunday Final Edition.

Chatterjee, Sangit, and Mustafa R. Yilmaz. 1991. "Parity in Baseball: Stability of Evolving Systems?" *Chance*, 4, 37–42.

Coase, Ronald. 1937. "The Nature of the Firm." *Economica*, 4 (November), 386–405.

————. 1960. "The Problem of Social Cost." *Journal of Law and Economics*, 3 (October), 1–44.

Costas, Bob. 2000. *Fair Ball: A Fan's Case for Baseball.* New York: Broadway Books.

Couch, Greg. 2002. "A Threat or a Bluff?" *Chicago Sun-Times*, August 20, p. 104.

Daugherty, Paul. 2002. "Baseball Knows Fans Will Return." *Cincinnati Inquirer*, August 19.

Depken, Craig. 1999. "Free Agency and the Competitiveness of Major League Baseball." *Review of Industrial Organization*, 14, 205–217.

Diamond, Dan, James Duplacey, Ralph Dinger, Igor Kuperman, Eric Zweig, and Ernie Fitzsimmons. 2000. *Total Hockey. The Official Encyclopedia of the National Hockey League.* 2nd ed. Kingston, N.Y.: Total Sports Publishing.

Downward, P., and A. Dawson. 2000. *The Economics of Professional Team Sports.* London: Routledge.

Eckard, E. Woodrow. 2001. "The Origin of the Reserve Clause: Owner Collusion Versus 'Public Interest.'" *Journal of Sports Economics*, 2, no. 2 (May), 113–130.

El-Hodiri, Mohamed, and James Quirk. 1971. "The Economic Theory of a Professional Sports League." *Journal of Political Economy*, 79 (November–December), 1302–1319.

Enders, Walter, Todd Sandler, and Jon Cauley. 1990. "Assessing the Impact of Terrorist-Thwarting Policies: An Intervention Time Series Analysis." *Defense Economics*, 2 (December), 1–18.

Eschker, Erick, Stephen J. Perez, and Mark V. Siegler. 2004. "The NBA and the Influx of International Basketball Players." *Applied Economics*, 36, 1009–1020.

Etzioni, Amitai. 1988. *The Moral Dimension: Toward a New Economics.* New York: Macmillan.

Fair, Ray. 2005. "Estimated Age Effects in Baseball." Working paper.

Fizel, John. 1997. "Free Agency and Competitive Balance." In *STEE-RIKE FOUR! What's Wrong with the Business of Baseball?*, ed. Dan R. Marburger (pp. 61–72). Westport, Conn.: Praeger.

Fleitz, David. "The Yankees and the A's, 1955–1960." Baseball Reference.com. David Fleitz's Baseball Page [www.wcnet.org/~dlfleitz/index.html].

Fort, Rodney. 2003. *Sports Economics.* Upper Saddle River, N.J.: Prentice Hall.

Frank, Reuban. 2004. "Billy Ball Titans: QB Volek Throws for Record Yardage in First Seven Starts." Posted December 22 [sportsillustrated.cnn.com].

Galbraith, John Kenneth. 1958. *The Affluent Society.* New York: Mentor Books (Reprinted 1984, New York and Scarborough, Ontario).

Garner, Trish, and John Gardella. 2004. The Sporting News. *2004–05 Official NBA Register.* Sporting News Publishing Company.

Gilovich, T., R. Vallone, and A. Tversky. 1985. "The Hot Hand in Basketball: On the Misperception of Random Sequences." *Cognitive Psychology*, 17, 295–314.

Ginsburg, David. 2005. "Having a Ball: Cal Ripken Jr. Is Living the High Life in Retirement." Associated Press, July 22, in the *Bakersfield Californian*.

Gould, Stephen Jay. 1983. "Losing the Edge: The Extinction of the .400 Hitter." *Vanity Fair*, 120 (March), 264–278.

———. 1986. "Entropic Homogeneity Isn't Why No One Hits .400 Any More." *Discover* (August), 60–66.

———. 1996. *Full House: The Spread of Excellence from Plato to Darwin*. New York: Three Rivers Press.

Grabiner, David. "The Sabermetric Manifesto" [www.baseball1.com/bb-data/grabiner/manifesto.html].

Granger, Clive. 2004. "Time Series Analysis, Cointegration, and Applications." *American Economic Review*, 94, no. 3 (June), 421–425.

Hadley, Lawrence, James Ciecka, and Anthony C. Krautmann. 2005. "Competitive Balance in the Aftermath of the 1994 Players' Strike." *Journal of Sports Economics* 6, no. 4 (November), 379–389.

Hall, Stephen, Stefan Szymanski, and Andrew Zimbalist. 2002. "Testing Causality between Team Performance and Payroll: The Cases of Major League Baseball and English Soccer." *Journal of Sports Economics*, 3 (May), 149–168.

Hamilton, Barton Hughes. 1997. "Racial Discrimination and Professional Basketball Salaries in the 1990s." *Applied Economics*, 29, 287–296.

Hanssen, Andrew. 1998. "The Cost of Discrimination: A Study of Major League Baseball." *Southern Economic Journal*, 64, no. 3, 603–627.

Hausman, Jerry A., and Gregory K. Leonard. 1997. "Superstars in the National Basketball Association: Economic Value and Policy." *Journal of Labor Economics*, 15, no. 4, 586–624.

Heeren, Dave. 1994. *Basketball Abstract 1994–95 Edition*. Indianapolis: Masters Press.

Henderson, Joe. 2002. "Baseball Pushing Its Luck in Dispute?" *Tampa Tribune (Florida)*. Sports, p. 1. August 18, Sunday Final Edition.

Hoang, Ha, and Dan Rascher. 1999. "The NBA, Exit Discrimination, and Career Earning." *Industrial Relations*, 38, no. 1 (January), 69–91.

Hollinger, John. 2002. *Pro Basketball Prospectus 2002*. Washington D.C.: Brassey's Sports.

———. 2005. "Hockey Stat, with a Twist, Useful in NBA, too." Posted at ESPN.com on March 29 [proxy.espn.go.com/nba/columns/story?id=2024296].

Hume, David. 1752. "Of the Balance of Trade." *Political Discourses*. Available at the History of Economic Thought web site [cepa.newschool.edu/het/].

Humphreys, Brad. 2002. "Alternative Measures of Competitive Balance in Sports League." *Journal of Sports Economics*, 3, no. 2 (May), 133–148.

Jenkins, Jeffery. 1996. "A Reexamination of Salary Discrimination in Professional Basketball." *Social Science Quarterly* 77, no. 3 (September), 594–608.

Kahn, Lawrence. 2000. "The Sports Business as a Labor Market Laboratory." *Journal of Economic Perspectives*, 15, no. 3 (Summer), 74–94.

Kahneman, Daniel. 2003. "A Psychological Perspective on Economics." *American Economic Review*, 93, no. 2 (May), 162–168.

Klapisch, Bob. 2002. "Selig, Fehr Are Destroying the Game." *The Record* (Bergen County, N.J.), p. S03, August 30.

Landreth, Harry, and David C. Colander. 2002. *History of Economic Thought,* 4th ed. New York: Houghton Mifflin.

Lee, Young Hoon, and David Berri. 2004. "A Re-Examination of Production Functions and Efficiency Estimates for the National Basketball Association." Presented at the Western Economic Association in Vancouver, British Columbia, in July.

Lee, Young Hoon, and Rodney Fort. 2005. "Structural Change in MLB Competitive Balance: The Depression, Team Location, and Integration." *Economic Inquiry,* 43, no. 1 (January), 158–169.

Leeds, Michael, and Peter Von Allmen. 2005. *The Economics of Sports,* 2nd ed. New York: Addison Wesley.

Levin, Richard C., George J. Mitchell, Paul A. Volcker, and George F. Will. 2000. *The Report of the Independent Members of the Commissioner's Blue Ribbon Panel on Baseball Economics.* (July). Available at [www.mlb.com/mlb/downloads/blue_ribbon.pdf].

Levitt, Steven D., and Stephen J. Dubner. 2005. *Freakonomics: A Rogue Economist Explores the Hidden Side of Everything.* New York: William Morrow.

Lewis, Michael. 2003. *Moneyball.* New York: W. W. Norton.

Litke, Jim. 1994. "Big Dog's Big Push to Get Out of the Big Doghouse." Associated Press, November 16.

Mackinnon, J., H. White, and R. Davidson. 1983. "Tests for Model Specification in the Presence of Alternative Hypothesis: Some Further Results." *Journal of Econometrics,* 21, 53–70.

Massarotti, Tony. 2002. "Baseball; Covering All Bases; Quarreling Clans at Last Agree with Fans." *Boston Herald,* p. B06, September 1.

McCloskey, Deirdre. 1998. *The Rhetoric of Economics,* 2nd ed. Madison: University of Wisconsin Press.

———. 2000. *How to Be Human: Though an Economist.* Ann Arbor: University of Michigan Press.

———. 2002. *The Secret Sins of Economics.* Chicago: Prickly Paradigm Press.

McCloskey, Deirdre N., and Stephen T. Ziliak. 1996. "The Standard Error of Regressions." *Journal of Economic Literature,* 34 (March), 97–114.

Mill, John Stuart. 1848. *The Principles of Political Economy: With Some of Their Applications to Social Philosophy.* Available at the History of Economic Thought web site [cepa.newschool.edu/het/].

Miller, Marvin. 1991. *A Whole Different Ball Game: The Inside Story of Baseball's New Deal.* New York: Fireside Book, published by Simon & Schuster.

Mosteller, Frederick. 1952. "The World Series Competition." *Journal of the American Statistical Association,* 47, no. 52 (September), 355–380.

NFL Record & Fact Book, The. Various editions.

Neale, Walter. 1964. "The Peculiar Economics of Professional Sports." *Quarterly Journal of Economics*, 78, no. 1, 1–14.

Neyer, Rob. 1996. "Who Are the 'True' Shooters?" In *STATS Pro Basketball Handbook, 1995–96* (pp. 322–323). New York: STATS Publishing.

Noll, Roger. 1988. "Professional Basketball." *Stanford University Studies in Industrial Economics,* no. 144. Working paper.

North, Douglass. 1994. "Economic Performance Through Time." *American Economic Review*, 84, no. 3, 359–368.

Oliphant, Thomas. 2005. *Praying for Gil Hodges: A Memoir of the 1955 World Series and One Family's Love of the Brooklyn Dodgers.* New York: Thomas Dunne Books.

Oliver, Dean. 2004. *Basketball on Paper*. Washington D.C.: Brassey's.

Olson, Drew. 2002. "The Healing Begins; Fans, Players Start the Process at Wrigley Field." *Milwaukee Journal Sentinel*, p. 1C, August 31.

Quirk, James, and Rodney Fort. 1992. *Pay Dirt: The Business of Professional Team Sports.* Princeton, N.J.: Princeton University Press.

———. 1999. *Hardball: The Abuse of Power in Pro Team Sports.* Princeton, N.J.: Princeton University Press.

Romer, David. Forthcoming in 2006. "It's Fourth Down and What Does the Bellman Equation Say? A Dynamic-Programming Analysis of Football Strategy." *Journal of Political Economy.*

Rottenberg, Simon. 1956. "The Baseball Players' Labor Market." *Journal of Political Economy*, 64, no. 3 (June), 242–258.

Ruane, Tom. 1998. "Player Movement." Baseball Think Factory. [www.baseballthinkfactory.org/btf/scholars/ruane/articles/player_movement.htm].

Samuelson, Paul. 1995. "Some Uneasiness with the Coase Theorem." *Japan and the World Economy*, 7, 1–7.

Schatz, Aaron et al. 2005. *Pro Football Prospectus.* New York: Workman Publishing.

Schmidt, Martin B. 2001. "Competition in Major League Baseball: The Impact of Expansion." *Applied Economics Letters*, 8, No. 1, 21–26.

———. 2006. "On the Evolution of Talent: An Application of Nonlinear Tests." *Applied Economics*, 38, No. 1, 1–12.

Schmidt, Martin B., and David J. Berri. 2001. "Competitive Balance and Attendance: The Case of Major League Baseball." *Journal of Sports Economics*, 2, no. 2 (May), 145–167.

———. 2002a. "The Impact of the 1981 and 1994–95 Strikes on Major League Baseball Attendance: A Time-Series Analysis." *Applied Economics*, 34, no. 4 (March), 471–478.

———. 2002b. "Competitive Balance and Market Size in Major League Baseball: A Response to Baseball's Blue Ribbon Panel." *Review of Industrial Organization*, 21, no. 1 (August), 41–54.

———. 2003. "On the Evolution of Competitive Balance: The Impact of an Increasing Global Search." *Economic Inquiry*, 41, no. 4 (October), 692–704.

———. 2004. "The Impact of Labor Strikes on Consumer Demand: An Application to Professional Sports." *American Economic Review*, 94, no. 1 (March), 344–357.

———. 2005. "Another Look at Competition: A Regime Switching Approach." *Applied Economics*, 36, no. 21 (December), 2453–2460.

———. 2005. "Concentration of Playing Talent: Evolution in Major League Baseball." *Journal of Sports Economics* 6, no. 4 (November), 412–419.

———. 2005. "Convergence and Clustering in Major League Baseball: The Haves and Haves Not?" *Applied Economics*, 36, no. 18 (October), 2007–2014.

Schwarz, Alan. 2004. *Numbers Game: Baseball's Lifelong Fascination with Statistics*. New York: Thomas Dunne Books, St. Martin's Press.

Scott, Frank Jr., James Long, and Ken Sompii. 1985. "Salary vs. Marginal Revenue Product Under Monopsony and Competition: The Case of Professional Basketball." *Atlantic Economic Journal*, 13, no. 3, 50–59.

Scully, Gerald. 1974. "Pay and Performance in Major League Baseball." *American Economic Review*, 64, 917–930.

Scully, Gerald W. 1989. *The Business of Major League Baseball*. Chicago: University of Chicago Press.

Seymour, Harold, and Dorothy Jane Mills. 1960. *Baseball: The Early Years*. New York: Oxford University Press.

Shmanske, Stephan. 1998. "Price Discrimination at the Links." *Contemporary Economic Policy*, 16 (July), 368–378.

Simon, Herbert. 1992. "Introductory Comment." In *Economics, Bounded Rationality and the Cognitive Revolution*, eds. Herbert Simon, Massimo Egidi, Robin Marris and Riccardo Viale (pp. 3–7). Brookfield, Vt.: Edward Elgar Publishing.

Sinatra, Frank. 1962. *Sinatra Live in Paris: Frank Sinatra and Sextet*. Reprise Records. 1994. Originally Recorded: June 6, 1962.

Spalding, Albert G. 1991. *America's National Game*. San Francisco: Halo Books.

Sporting News Complete Baseball Record Book, The. Various editions.

Sporting News NBA Guide, The. Various editions.

Sporting News NBA Register, The. Various editions.

Sporting News: Pro Football Guide, The. Various editions.

Staw, B. M., and Ha Hoang. 1995. "Sunk Costs in the NBA: Why Draft Order Affects Playing Time and Survival in Professional Basketball." *Administrative Science Quarterly*, 40, no. 3, 474–494.

Steinberg, Don. 2001. "How I Learned to Stop Worrying and Love the Bomb: A Survival Guide to the NFL's Quarterback Rating System." *GQ* (October), online edition.

Stigler, George. 1988. *Memoirs of an Unregulated Economist*. New York: Basic Books.

Sullivan, Dean A. (Ed.) 1995. *Early Innings: A Documentary History of Baseball, 1825–1908*. Lincoln: University of Nebraska Press.

Szymanski, Stefan. 2003. "The Economic Design of Sporting Contests." *Journal of Economic Literature*, 41, no. 4 (December), 1137–1187.

————. 2005. "Tilting the Playing Field: Why a Sports League Planner Would Choose *Less*, Not More, Competitive Balance." Presented at the Western Economic Association, July 7, in San Francisco.

Taylor, Beck A., and Justin B. Trogdon. 2002. "Losing to Win: Tournament Incentives and the Draft Lottery in the National Basketball Association." *Journal of Labor Economics*, 20, no. 1 (January), 23–41.

Thorn, John, and Pete Palmer. 1984. *The Hidden Game of Baseball: A Revolutionary Approach to Baseball and Its Statistics.* New York: Doubleday.

Utt, Joshua, and Rodney Fort. 2002. "Pitfalls to Measuring Competitive Balance with Gini Coefficients." *Journal of Sports Economics*, 3, no. 4 (November), 367–373.

Vrooman, John. 1995. "A General Theory of Professional Sports Leagues." *Southern Economic Journal*, 61, no. 4, 971–990.

Whitley, David. 2002. "Forget Tough Talk, Baseball Fans Never Walk." *Orlando Sentinel*, August 26, p. D1.

Whyte, Jamie. 2005. *Crimes Against Logic.* New York: McGraw-Hill.

Wine, Steve. 2002. "Marlins Concerned About Fan Reaction." Associated Press, August 16.

Witt, Barry. 2002. "History Shows Baseball Fans Forgive, Forget Work Stoppages." *San Jose Mercury News*, August 29, p. 1A.

Yilmaz, Mustafa R., Sangit Chatterjee, and Mohamed Habibullah. 2001. "Improvement by Spreading the Wealth: The Case of Home Runs in Major League Baseball." *Journal of Sports Economics* 2, no. 2, 181–193.

Zimbalist, Andrew. 1992. *Baseball and Billions.* New York: Basic Books.

————. 2003. *May the Best Team Win: Baseball Economics and Public Policy.* Washington D.C.: Brookings Institution Press.

WEB SITES

Basketball-Reference.com

Bender, Patricia. Patricia's Various Basketball Stuff [www.dfw.net/~patricia/].

"The Best-Paid Athletes." Forbes.com [www.forbes.com/2004/06/23/04athletesland.html].

ESPN.com

FootballOutsiders.com

Fort, Rod. [www.rodneyfort.com/SportsData/BizFrame.htm].

History of Economic Thought web site [cepa.newschool.edu/het/].

InsideHoops.com

Lahman, Sean. The Baseball Archive [www.baseball1.com].

National Basketball Association [nba.com].

National Hockey League [nhl.com].

NFL Statistics—Yahoo! Sports [sports.yahoo.com/nfl/stats].

Packers.com [www.packers.com].

Pro Football Hall of Fame [www.profootballhof.com].

Rosenbaum, Dan. [www.82games.com/comm30.htm].

———. [www.uncg.edu/eco/rosenbaum/NBA/winval2.htm].

Statistics Canada [www.statcan.ca/].

U.S. Census Bureau [www.census.gov].

USATODAY.com. Baseball Salaries Database [asp.usatoday.com/sports/baseball/salaries/default.aspx].

INDEX

In this index an "f" after a number indicates a separate reference on the next page, and an "ff" indicates separate references on the next two pages. A continuous discussion over two or more pages is indicated by a span of page numbers, e.g., "57–59."